The Limits to Certainty

# The Limits To Certainty

## Facing Risks in the New Service Economy

by

ORIO GIARINI
and
WALTER R. STAHEL

*PROGRES, Programme of Research on the Economics of Services, Geneva, Switzerland*

KLUWER ACADEMIC PUBLISHERS
DORDRECHT / BOSTON / LONDON

Library of Congress Cataloging in Publication Data

Giarini, Orio.
  The limits to certainty : facing risks in the new service economy
/ by Orio Giarini and Walter R. Stahel.
    p.   cm. -- (International studies in the services economy ; v.
1)
  ISBN 0-7923-0468-3 (U.S.)
  1. Service industries.  2. Uncertainty.  3. Risk.   I. Stahel,
Walter R.  II. Title.   III. Series.
HD9980.5.G52   1989
658.4--dc20                                           89-24513

ISBN 0-7923-0468-3

Published by Kluwer Academic Publishers,
P.O. Box 17, 3300 AA Dordrecht, The Netherlands.

Kluwer Academic Publishers incorporates
the publishing programmes of
D. Reidel, Martinus Nijhoff, Dr W. Junk and MTP Press.

Sold and distributed in the U.S.A. and Canada
by Kluwer Academic Publishers,
101 Philip Drive, Norwell, MA 02061, U.S.A.

In all other countries, sold and distributed
by Kluwer Academic Publishers Group,
P.O. Box 322, 3300 AH Dordrecht, The Netherlands.

*Printed on acid-free paper*

To Fabio Padoa, whose support and enthusiasm have been essential in preparing this report.

# Acknowledgements

This book is published under the auspices of the Club of Rome. It is in fact a follow-up to a report to the Club of Rome published in 1980, "Dialogue on Wealth and Welfare" (Giarini, Orio – Pergamon Press, Oxford) that proposed the idea that the "limits to growth" were essentially the limits of a specific type of economic growth that had been successfully developed by the Industrial Revolution over a period of 200 years. This earlier report went on to propose that a new economic growth needed to intergrate economic *and* ecological factors, in practice as well as in theory and therefore revise the notion of economic value.

This (economic) transition developed parallel to a growing movement at a more fundamental philosophical level favoring indeterminism against determinism: the notions of risks and uncertainty are increasingly considered as the realm of the new challenges, as compared to a perception – typical of the deterministic era – according to which risk and uncertainty reflect a level of "imperfect knowledge" which science would or should eliminate: a positive versus a negative connotation of risk and uncertainty.

The starting point for the new project leading to the present book was a meeting by the "*Risk Institute Project Group*" held in Paris in 1986; among the participants were Raymond Barre, André Danzin, Montague March, Fabio Padoa, Richard Piani, Edward Ploman, Ilya Prigogine, Jean-Pierre Ritter, Alvin Toffler and Orio Giarini.

The next step was the foundation of PROGRES (Programme of Research on the Economics of Services) in Geneva in 1987: the ideas proposed in the report to the Club of Rome had in the meantime matured and it had become clear that the present economic situation was not simply a "post-industrial" one, in the same sense that the Industrial Revolution was not only a "post-agricultural" economic phenomenon. Bearing in mind that the key to economic progress has always been a matter of a better allocation of resources, and that the majority of resources are available today in the form of service activities, the next intellectual step was to admit that for measuring and exploiting such resources, one needed a theoretical framework of reference based on the notions of risk and uncertainty, rather than on the deterministic values based on a traditional economic system assumed to be in a "perfect (certain) equilibrium". Services mean performances, in real periods of time, and thus require, for the identification of values, to rely on probabilities. This can be compared to fixing the "price" of an insurance policy, i.e. assessing the probability and cost of a distribution of events in the future. A situation of equilibrium is only *one* possibility among others, depending on "bifurcations", as Ilya Prigogine would say. This is the reason why "The Limits to Certainty" are also about the economic foundations of the "Service Economy". The teaching and research activity of PROGRES at the Graduate Institute of European Studies of the University of Geneva, has enabled the authors to constantly verify and discuss the themes of this book.

We wish to thank here all those who, over the years, have contributed to and stimulated our research in this field. But we are of course the only ones responsible for the imperfections of this essay and look forward to its pitiless "falsification".

Geneva, August 1989
The authors

# Preface

I consider it as a privilege to have been invited to write a preface for "The Limits to Certainty". It is however paradoxical that a theoretical physicist be asked to write about a monograph dealing mainly with service economics. Notwithstanding, I am delighted to do so. Indeed, it is strinking that two fields so widely different as physics and social science, including economics, may interact in a most constructive way. There is no question of reductionism. Nobody claims to be able to reduce social sciences to physics, nor to use social interactions in order to formulate new laws for atoms. What is at stake here is more important than reduction; the long-standing separation between so-called "hard sciences" and "soft sciences" is breaking down.

This separation has a long history. First, one should recall the influence of the Newtonian accomplishment for the formulation of scientific goals. This influence has induced the formulation of equilibrium models for the meeting of offer and demand, as was noticed by Walter Weisskopf: "the Newtonian paradigm underlying classical and non-classical economics interpreted the economy according to the patterns developed in classical physics and mechanics, in analogy to the planetary system, to a machine and to a clockwork: a closed autonomous system ruled by endogenous factors of a highly selective nature, self-regulating and moving to a determinate, predictable point of equilibrium" (The Geneva Papers on Risk and Insurance (1984) vol. 9, no. 33, pp. 335–360). Giarini and Stahel write "There can no longer be any "scientific" justification for considering a state of equilibrium in economics (as referred to the Newtonian model) as the premise of economic analysis" (section 1.2.).

Indeed, to try to combine classical mechanics with human sciences was trying an unnatural marriage. Classical science was describing a static world, while human sciences deal with an ever changing situation, where the very idea of reaching an equilibrium is clearly meaningless. It would at best correspond to a nightmare, such as described in the novel "1984" by Orwell: a timeless form of society is imposed through brutal force or sophisticated technology. Anyway, this idea does not apply to human societies as we know them in this century.

Our ideas about the role of time in hard sciences have changed radically over the last decades. A first breakthrough was the formulation of the "Heisenberg paradigm", expressed in quantum uncertainty relations. This was indeed a fundamental step: quantum mechanics was essentially the first science that was forced to give up a deterministic description. Now, this change has led to ideological conflicts. For example, Einstein was opposed to the statistical character of quantum mechanics; in one of his last papers, he wrote that anyway, the statistical character of quantum mechanics is of application for microscopic problems only, while for the macroscopic world, determinism continues to be the rule. This is the point where the developments of the last decades have not followed Einstein's lead.

We now know that the behaviours of systems submitted too far from equilibrium conditions, can only be described in terms of a curious mixture of determinism and probabilities; and this is true even at a macroscopic scale. A well known example is given by the so-called Bénard instability, due to a vertical temperature gradient set up in a horizontal liquid layer. For some threshold value of this gradient, the fluid's state of rest becomes unstable, as heath is then conveyed through convection rolls; this corresponds to the coherent motion of huge assemblies of molecules. This convention is a symmetry-breaking phenomenon: two points which were 'equivalent', being 'almost' at the same place before the instauration of the heath constraint, are now involved in distinct convention rolls. We must even say that for a given region of space, the choice between these various possiblities depends on statistical fluctuations, described by probabilisitc laws.

This is a general feature of unstable dynamical systems. According to our present view, whatever the (finite) precision we have about the initial conditions of such systems, we can only predict the probability of realizing one of the many possible structures. This is not in any way of defeat of the human mind. Far from that. Giarini and Stahel write that "the positivistic dream of achieving omni-science in an abstract static world is essentially a psychological fantasm" (section 4.1.2). Indeed, this dream has theological roots; this can be understood by reading the correspondence between Clarke (speaking for Newton) and Leibniz. As well known, Leibniz starts the polemics by saying that Newton seems to have a poor idea of God, as for him the Creator would be obliged to retune his work from time to time, being thus a bad watchmaker. For Leibniz, it was not conceivable that God would not know at a given time what would happen for an arbitrary far reaching future. In this tradition, a large current of modern physics tried to negate the importance, and even the existence, of time. Therefore, it appears in this perspective that the very proof of valid knowledge was the elimination of time. It is this theological prejudice that is now crumbling.

Modern Science is now in a position to acknowledge the importance of time, as it has given up the myth of omni-science. This is a pre-requisite to be able to speak about events, as an event is something that cannot be deterministically predicted. The position of the earth around the sun in a given amount of years can hardly be considered as an event, while obviously the birth of Mozart is an event for the history of western music.

Clearly, there is no simple transcription of what has been achieved in physics or chemistry to these difficult questions. Men have memories and anticipations; they have value systems which determine their behaviour. As Giarini and Stahel write in their Declaration about a "Center for Reflection on Uncertainty": "a civilization is a certain way of living and of creating facts: it is a specific 'attitude' to living and to the acceptance of uncertainty". Obviously, some ethical responsibility is related to a world of uncertainty". Here is, I believe, one of the main subjects of interest presented by Giarini and Stahel. It permits us to understand better the value of uncertainty and to situtate our action and our decisions in the real world, and not in an ideal, deterministic world which is far removed from the universe we live in. I am sure that their book will be of interest for readers quite outside the field of economy and sociology, as it will lead to many reflections about the decisions of tomorrow.

Ilya Prigogine, Brussels
Nobel Laureate

# Table of Contents

# Foreword

Reports issued under the imprimatum of the Club of Rome are normally commissioned studies, exploring, analysing and delineating particular complexes of problems, in the hope of aiding decision-makers to understand better the paramaters which they are dealing. Orio Giarini's seminal work, "Dialogue on Wealth and Welfare" of 1980 was such a report, introducing new concepts as to how ecological factors might be integrated with economic thinking. The evolution of a number of global trends during the decade has demonstrated the necessity of such an approach. For example, recognition of the existence of a number of macro-pollution phenomena makes it ever more clear that ecological considerations are no longer a matter of concern to Nature lovers but major factors in economic, industrial agricultural and energy policies.

In addition to these reports to the Club of Rome, we endorse from time to time, outstanding studies undertaken spontaneously by our individual members, as volumes of the Information Series of the Club. The present work is one of this series and is a very timely analysis of the development of the post-industrial society which the authors, rightly to my mind, make explicit as the "service economy".

The contemporary world situation is characterized by complexity, uncertainty and rapid change, while intellectually we are witnessing a flight from determinism. Traditional policies, institutional structures and thinking find it increasingly difficult to master this situation. It is important that the leaders of society, whether in governance, economics, industry or education learn to understand more deeply the concept of uncertainty and, within it, of risk. In both individual life and that of corporations and countries, perception of risk is frequently highly subjective and at times so unreal as to suggest actions and policies which are diversionary or irrisponsible. The present volume is an important and lucid contribution to the understanding both of the nature of the oncoming service economy and of the notion of conscious risk-taking within the cloud of uncertainty. It should be of great interest to economists and sociologists, many of whom will no doubt, find it uncomfortable reading, but also to the informed public concerned with the future of society.

Alexander King, Paris
President of the Club of Rome

# List of Figures

# Chapter 1: Introduction

## 1.1. IN SEARCH OF PROGRESS : FROM "THE LIMITS TO GROWTH" TO "THE LIMITS TO CERTAINTY"

In 1972 the Club of Rome published a report on "The Limits to Growth". When it appeared (one year *before* the oil crisis of 1973), the notion of limits to growth was like a thunder-clap in a clear blue sky. It gave prophetic shape to what hitherto had been an intuition that one could not extrapolate the "Golden Quarter-Century" indefinitely into the future: it probably helped, by opening up this debate, in our being able to cope with the problems of the seventies, better than would otherwise have been the case.

But now, in the late eighties, even if some of the major issues of the Club of Rome (in particular world interdependence and the limits of population growth in most - not all - areas in the world hold more and more true, the very issue of the limits to growth needs to be reappraised.

What in the seventies was interpreted essentially as a problem of limits to general economic growth, appears increasingly as the description of the end of the great cycle of the classical Industrial Revolution. This is what the simulations of Jay Forrester and Denis Meadows point to. It is not the end of economic growth as such, but the end of *one sort* of economic growth, i.e. that based on the development of bigger and faster tools, of productive investments essentially in hardware rather than in software, in machines rather than in organization, in tangible products rather than in communication. Obviously, an important part of economic activity will always depend upon tools and hardware, just as we still need agricultural produce. But today, hardware tools and agricultural produce already account for a *minor* part (even if still a relatively large one) of the work actually done in producing wealth and welfare. *Within* the most traditional industries themselves, as *within* agriculture, service type functions predominate. In most of the hardware sectors of activity, technology has been showing signs of diminishing returns for almost 20 years now. But there is evidence of increasing returns of technology precisely in those activity areas which are typically post-industrial, or are designated as service functions.

The foregoing is demonstrated in a dramatic way: agricultural over production in Europe and the U.S. contrasts with famine in Africa and Asia, because the major economic cost is not in producing these goods, but in storing, transporting and distributing them. These services account for 80% of the final cost, hence agriculture has become predominantly a service activity. It is therefore service economy technologies which will have to solve the major problems of our economic development today. The manner of its integration with existing cultural and organizational patterns will be significant.

Like Adam Smith who wrote his book on the Wealth of Nations in 1776, just twenty years *after* the start of the first big cycle in the Industrial Revolution, we have been well into what can be called a service economy for more than a dozen years. Thus it is time to bring our economic interpretation of events into line with what is actually happening.

In this sense, we can consider the "Golden Quarter-Century" (the 25 years of exceptional economic growth following World War Two) the last glorious manifestation of the classical Industrial Revolution; and the seventies as a period of conflict of many features of the new economic reality with our already outdated models of thinking and behaviour. Of course, at this junction we can decide either that *reality* is "irrational" and "incomprehensible", or that *we* have failed to adapt our models of analysis and interpretation. We are firmly convinced of the second option and accordingly propose to consider three major issues in an effort to contribute to the "reconstruction" of the 80's and 90's.

Such a process is closely linked to our cultural ability to detect in our "age of uncertainty" the starting of a new era of challenges and opportunities in the evolution of human society. An era in which an unrealistic quest for certainty will be replaced by an understanding of the limits to certainty.

## 1.2. THREE MAJOR ISSUES IN RECONSTRUCTING AN IMAGE FOR THE FUTURE

1. Recognition of the service economy: the major battlefield for risk taking - where the chances are.
2. Importance and scope of the supply side in the economic process: regaining faith in the "producer" and in his risk-taking activities.
3. Risk as a positive factor and the challenges of uncertainty: an attitude and a philosophy for stimulating progress.

MAJOR ISSUE 1 : RECOGNITION OF THE SERVICE ECONOMY: THE MAJOR BATTLEFIELD FOR RISK TAKING - WHERE THE CHANCES ARE.

In most countries in the world, the Service Economy we inhabit is not just a condition in which service industries such as finance, insurance, telecommunications and transport, maintenance and engineering grow unendingly. Equally significant is the fact that in manufacturing, and even in agriculture, the majority of functions performed - and of jobs done - concern service activities.

Furthermore, many leaders in the fields of electronics and telecommunications as well as in finance state openly that the value of their "products" is "immaterial". In fact, whereas the classical Industrial Revolution concentrated on developing material tools, i.e. "hardware", the increasing refinement, complexity and interdependence of technological development has shifted the center of gravity towards "software" i.e. the ways, conditions and skills through which material supports are employed and are made available, accessible and usable. All services require some hardware, but a lot of services are necessary to let the hardware be of any use.

One of the challenging and attractive consequences of this situation - even if initially it might prove a source of difficulty - is the increasing importance attached to product quality, *human quality* and to better integration of economic ingredients into the wider human and natural environment. The proper maintenance and functioning of complex systems do not depend on a few limited skills: the service connotations of advanced technological systems and their proper use, stimulate and demand a higher and better integration of human values, qualities and motivation.

The Service Economy and in a wider sense, the service society, is the *key frame of reference* for the specific actions of major new endeavours of both an economic and social nature.

## MAJOR ISSUE 2 : IMPORTANCE AND SCOPE OF THE SUPPLY IN THE ECONOMIC PROCESS: REGAINING FAITH IN THE "PRODUCER" AND IN RISK TAKING ACTIVITIES.

A key issue in the current economic and social environment within the new service society) is probably the rediscovery of the fact that the value of the human being is first of all based on his characteristics as a *producer* both for himself and for more general economic and social purposes.

> Even culture is now considered as being first of all a product for consumption
> and not - at first - a productive endeavour.. economic and cultural crisis run
> in parallel..

writes Denis de Rougemont [1].

Up to the end of the last century, classical economics stressed the decisive aspect of supply. From Adam Smith to Karl Marx, all economists have focused on supply. Alfred Marshall achieved a better theoretical balance between the supply and demand sides of the economic process. But subsequently and to this day, the *key school of economic thinking has been demand-side oriented*. Demand and consumption play an important part in the economy: but this approach becomes deceptive when it starts to undermine the essential role of productive activities or of supply. Worse still, when we start to accept the idea that we are what we consume rather than what we produce. Time is probably ripe to reconsider the basic values, the codes of our economic and social development, in terms of their efficiency and cultural acceptability.

These are numerous explanations and reasons for this bias in favour of demand in contemporary economic thinking: up to the 1930's, all economic crises had been crises of *over*production, *de*flation and *un*employment: the efficiency of supply had grown so much, that demand had some trouble in the pre-Keynesian era in catching up with supply. Evidence of powerful advances in technology on the supply side had given further impetus to the idea that we had definitely entered an era of great (almost infinite) elasticity of supply. But this almost hidden, yet fundamental, assumption has been wanting in certain crucial respects in the seventies. Technology, as one of the important conditions of supply elasticity, has varying rates of return (diminishing or increasing) in different sectors and at different times: it accounts for the *quantitative* level of relative rigidity or elasticity of supply.

Furthermore, the switch from an essentially industrial to a service economy, has modified the qualitative conditions of elasticity of supply. How to produce (supply) accessible services in the most economic way is probably now the right and relevant question. How to make available better systems for food delivery (and these obviously include integrated production systems), for health, for housing and shelter, and for education and recreation etc., its almost certainly the key issue that confronts us today. Demand will continue to have the function of selecting from among the available supply alternatives. Demand must become increasingly free to choose. But the primary choice must be made by the producer, who will only later encounter the sanction of demand. Henry Ford exercised free choice and ran a risk as a producer when he decided to manufacture motorcars, just as Mozart or Beethoven produced successful music. In their respective fields many others tried and, subject to demand, failed: just as in nature there is a constant oversupply of possibilities and a selecting of results. Equilibrium between supply and demand comes about *ex-post*, only *after* the whole process of risk taking is complete. At the outset, there is a situation of disequilibrium: at best, a reasonable guess as to the risks we are taking in trying to produce or create something. In other words, a situation of creative uncertainty, the norm of all living matter.

For more than half a century, economics has largely concerned itself with focusing on the utility function of the demand side. It is now time to *reestablish a balance* and, in the context of the new service economy, to review in particular the supply side situation. A supply set up where - and this is the new challenge - services are an integral part of tools and material support systems.

## MAJOR ISSUE 3 : RISK AS A POSITIVE FACTOR AND THE CHALLENGES OF UNCERTAINTY: AN ATTITUDE AND A PHILOSOPHY FOR STIMULATING PROGRESS.

A main, probably *the* most relevant, feature of these changes in the socioeconomic environment is their relation *to the advance of scientific thinking* and of discoveries in this century. More generally, this has to do with the relationship between social and natural (soft and hard) sciences which embody the cultural background of our knowledge, views, attitudes and behaviour with regard to our individual and community life.

When economics became a specific and recognized social science (in a process started by the definition of value by Adam Smith in 1776), its key inspiration and reference were the cultural and scientific assumptions of the day. Economics proved a useful tool for analyzing, understanding and systematizing the ongoing process of the Industrial Revolution. Let us recall just a few of these basic assumptions. Newton had provided a *notion of equilibrium*, as a basic reference for understanding the universe. This equilibrium was a static one, which survived until Einstein started the modern Scientific Revolution by adding *time* as the fourth dimension of space.

Heisenberg and the quantum theory introduced the notion of indeterminate systems, thus overcoming the objections of even Einstein who was still striving for a universal model of scientific knowledge which would eliminate uncertainty. In 1983, Ilya Prigogine wrote:

> We are more and more numerous to think that the fundamental laws of nature are irreversible *and* stochastic: that deterministic and reversible laws are applicable only in limiting situations.

He further wrote that:

> Over the last decade we have learned that in non-equilibrium conditions, simple material can acquire complex behaviour .. Today, our interest is shifting to non-equilibrium systems, interacting with the surroundings through the entropy flow [2].

There can no longer be any "scientific" justification for considering a state of equilibrium in economics (as referred to the Newtonian model) as the premise of economic analysis. In some cases, equilibrium might be desirable, but economic progress could well depend much more on specific and *desirable states of non-equilibrium* in cases where the isolated industrial system opens up to a multiplicity of new functions and interactions typical of the service economy. The key economic question of the future might well cease to be, "how shall we achieve a perfect (certain) equilibrium?" and become "how shall we create or stimulate productive non-equilibrium situations, situations which, contrary to Newtonian philosophy, have a real time dimension?" However, the model still subsumed by the mainstream of current economic thinking has as its fundamental paradigm the hypothesis of perfect equilibrium and of certainty which belong to the static Newtonian scientific model.

Unfortunately, this means that the current economic model refers to scientific premises which science itself has long ago abandoned.

## 1.3. UNCERTAINTY : THE CONDITION TO MAKE A FUTURE

Intuition suggests the idea that modern societal and economic development depend not so much on achieving perfect, deterministic and sure objectives, but rather on developing creative activities, in a world where uncertainty, probability and risk are a given condition, providing a circumstance of real opportunities and choice.

This would not be a step backwards towards irrationality. Quite the contrary, more intelligence, more rationality, more initiative are required to cope with situations of uncertainty, which after all are the daily experience of every living being. The simplistic vision of mechanized pre-programmed robots belongs much more to a deterministic world: the attempt to achieve abstract "certainty" and "perfect information" can only lead to a dogmatic, pseudo-religious system on the one hand or, on the other, to the annihilation of all intelligence, to the destruction of all hope for development and creativity. Hence the prevailing atmosphere of pessimism in the world. The marrying-up of contemporary scientific thinking with social sciences, and in particular with economics, in an increasingly complex world which is interactive even beyond the limits of planet Earth, is providing a rich source of moral and intellectual stimulus for reconstructing an Image of the Future. Learning to face uncertainties and to manage risk beneath these new horizons might in turn lead to a quantum leap in the human condition.

*In economic terms,* the process of production - in a very broad sense - is always decided *ex-ante:* uncertainty as to the outcome can and must be reduced as much as possible. But the reward or sanction beyond the selection process, i.e. the meeting with demand, will always happen *later*, after the initiative to produce (a computer or an opera) has been taken under natural conditions of uncertainty. Whatever the guarantees and precautions, a margin for adjustment will always remain: the more important the endeavour the greater this margin of uncertainty or unpredictability will be, because real time, that of the living beings, is take into consideration.

Even in terms of equity or of social justice, the problem is not to produce or sell or distribute *security,* which is in any case a self-deceiving system in political (look at the dictatorships of our century), as well as economic terms (excessive state or community protection has limited the capacity of social institutions to provide security, and has rendered them increasingly vulnerable, inefficient, and ultimately the agents of greater global insecurity). *Equity* has more and more to do with increasing the physical and cultural capacity of individuals and communities to identify, control, reduce and exploit risks and uncertainties by being able to face them: the very risks which confront all living species and render them creative.

*Definite poverty* is a situation in which no risk can be faced, no choice taken.

And finally *in cultural terms*: no enterprise is built with dreams alone and none without. Action, successful action, is by necessity guided by practical circumstances. But the goal of any action is defined implicitly or explicitly, by the deep nature of the human being, his dreams, his vision of life, his culture. The dynamics of life, the challenge of risk and uncertainty, require from us today a new creative effort leading to the reconstruction and to the re-conquest of the notion of progress, which the philosophies and the ideologies of certainty have shuttered so much and almost destroyed. There is no real human culture other than that to be found in the real-life process of creation, in the producing and continuous testing of each of our many endeavours, of an Image of the Future we would fashion for ourselves.

Notes Chapter 1

1. from: Rougemont, Denis de (1972) Penser avec les mains, Gallimard, Paris, p. 32.
2. quotations from papers circulated at the Seminar on Complexity, organized in Montpellier by the UN University and IDATE, May 1984.
(for notes nos. 3 to 85, see end of Chapters 2, 3 and 4)

## Chapter 2: The New Battleground for Risk Taking : The Service Economy

### 2.1. THE LEGACY OF THE INDUSTRIAL REVOLUTION

2.1.1. <u>Leaving Heaven For A World Of Scarcity</u>. One day, according to the Bible, Adam and Eve were expelled from the Garden of Eden and contrived to start a new life of labour and effort to survive. They had left heaven for a new *economic* world. A world where, although blessed with a large dowry and patrimony [3], directly available resources were scarce. Air for breathing was available everywhere and so was water: water for drinking and washing, but not in all places and not always of the desired quality. Rivers and lakes then became privileged places for human settlements. The problem of finding food could first be solved through hunting and gathering. But all this was of limited efficiency when population density increased. The first economic revolution started with the beginning of agriculture. The descendants of Adam and Eve had learnt by then that most resources do not only exist per se, but also as a consequence of human knowledge and understanding of its environment and of the technologies that man is able to develop.

Knowledge also enabled man to find new energy sources as substitutes for wood. Coal and petroleum have existed under the surface of the earth for many millennia, but it took the development of chemistry and technology services to harness these resources [4] and their derived applications. In fact, the reader is almost certainly wearing one of several garments manufactured with fibres derived from oil.

Discoveries led to the extension of that knowledge, such as the introduction of tomatoes and potatoes to Europe after the discovery of the Americas. It would be quite wrong, therefore, to share a picture in ones mind of an ancient Roman enjoying a plate of spaghetti with tomato sauce! Geographical discoveries, technology and cultural development made a "resource" of these commodities only a few centuries ago. A striking example of uncertainty in forecasting due to a new technology, can be seen in the prediction by Robert Malthus [5] made in 1798. He forecast that resources would be insufficient to feed Europe's growing population. This "reasonable" prediction was defeated by the unexpected: the introduction of the simple potato. It took in fact 150 years from the very first introduction of this crop into Europe to win over indifference and mistrust [6]. However, by the beginning of the 19th century, the potato had gained wide acceptance and diffusion, especially in Northern climates where more traditional crops could not easily be grown.

But this still could not avoid a great famine in Ireland during the first part of the last century, due precisely to the failure of the potato harvest.

2.1.2. <u>Producing Tools And Goods To Increase The Wealth Of Nations</u>. If Adam, with his companion Eve, was the first man to enter the economic world, another Adam, called Smith, was the first to lay the foundations of that body of theories and analysis aimed at understanding and managing economic systems: economics.

Certainly, economic analysis and even economic theories had existed long before Adam Smith. In the Bible, for instance, we can find the first theory of economic cycles, when seven years of abundance are described as being followed by seven years of great poverty. There are plenty of other economic observations in the world literature, in all places and at all times. But it was only Adam Smith, in 1776, who laid the foundations of economics as a specific discipline or science, separated from more general societal or historical analyses.

So why Adam Smith? His impulse was not only an intellectual one. It was essentially provided by a new economic revolution occurring to the descendants of Adam and Eve in their struggle against scarcity. Adam Smith experienced in fact during his life the birth of the Industrial Revolution, the big switch from the agricultural to the industrial economic system [7]. This transition is very well illustrated by his opposition to the views of Quesnay, the illustrious doctor of Madame Pompadour and even more illustrious physiocrate (the French school who made famous the sentence: "laisser faire - laisser aller").

The dispute between Adam Smith and Francois Quesnay focussed on the origin of the Wealth of Nations [8]. Both had an explanation. For Quesnay, looking at the main source of wealth in France, it was obvious that the wealth of nations had to do with a striving agricultural system. Adam Smith, however, was more concerned with the new development of manufacturing activities, as observed around him in Scotland. Since Adam Smith, the industrialization process has appeared as the new key development to fight scarcity and to open the way towards progress or, in a sense, back to the Garden of Eden. After all, Adam Smith was essentially a moralist as many other great economists were going to be, such as Malthus and Marshall.

The Industrial Revolution is characterized by the appearance of distinct manufacturing processes [9], where a source of energy exists (the steam engine) which can propel a multiplicity of equipment (for instance weaving looms) and provide the mechanical impulse to produce the required movements (for instance pushing the shuttle containing the weft yarns through the warp). It is at this moment that the innovation of the flying shuttle became feasible, increasing the rapidity and the precision of the movement of the shuttle, which no longer needed to be pushed by the human arm.

The combination of a central, immobile steam engine machine with many flying shuttle weaving looms requires the organization of a specific space for production: the modern manufacturing plant was born! Whereas in the agricultural society, weaving and any other similar manufacturing activities could be performed at the home of the peasant whenever time was available, the new quantitative step in technology required that labour moved to where the equipment was, for reasons of efficiency.

Furthermore, the concentration of production also meant that the part of production-consumption for own use was more and more reduced: specialization increased and with it the need for trade and exchange of products.

It was this phenomenon of the specialization of manufacturing activities, their growing independence structure (i.e. of a market) to make them available, which provided the background of experience for Adam Smith to define that the real wealth of nations can be built through the development of the manufacturing process; i.e. industrialization.

The key to industrialization was the increase of productivity, i.e. the capacity to use scarce resources in such a way as to produce more goods with less resources. Specialized production technology and new tools with an ever increasing performance (faster and faster, consuming less and less labour and/or capital per unit) are key features.

Industrial technology had thus moved to the centre of the battlefield to increase wealth and welfare, in a situation in which human culture and environment were both capable of developing it and of putting it to use in an efficient way.

It is important to note here that the technological jump at the beginning of the Industrial Revolution was not a qualitative, but a quantitative jump. Technology has always existed in the form of tools since the first activities of human beings. One can also speak of technological performances developed by animals (a bird's nest, for instance). Intrinsically, there is no major difference between the technology of the pre-historic "engineers" who specialized in cutting stones in order to produce arrow heads or cutting tools, and the "engineers" of the first Industrial Revolution who developed tools, which, by contemporary standards, are still extremely simple. In fact, most of the tools of the first industrial revolution are of a nature that each of us, without a specific university or scientific education, could probably reproduce with the tools available in most hardware stores. The "steam-engine" is in fact nothing more than a sophisticated control system of the increased pressure produced by a volume of water transformed by heat into steam in a given space. The common pressure-cooker, which many people now use in their kitchen, is based on the very same principle. The real problem is to produce the materials, pots and related mechanisms, capable of resisting the pressure and of releasing it under control. Similarly, the notion of the flying weaving shuttle is very simple: the problem was to have a fixed hammer capable of hitting the shuttle violently enough to send it to the other side of the loom.

Only much later, towards the end of the 19th century, the manufacture of tools and products started to depend on scientific knowledge, i.e. on research and the understanding of problems which go beyond the immediate perception of our senses. We know how to cut a piece of wood and we understand how boiling water transforms in a larger mass of steam. But we need scientific research in order to find out that the same molecules which are found for instance in cotton fibres, can be reproduced in a similar, but not equal way, using oil as raw material. Scientific research and exploitation of technology based on science, have thus only started to be diffused since the beginning of our century and have come'to full and professional exploitation during and at the end of World War Two.

Up to the middle of the 1920's there was no consistent investment in research laboratories in industry or elsewhere. The cost of production, up to then, could only be accounted in terms of cost of labour and cost of capital. It is only since the 1930's that more and more money has been invested in research and development and that this activity has become a *professional* one. Today, research and investment, anticipating production which might take place ten to twenty years later, can in some cases reach or even go beyond twenty-five to thirty percent of the total sales income of a company.

There has been a tremendous evolution over the period of the Industrial Revolution, punctuated by many discoveries and new technological adventures. The main discontinuity is the changeover from a long period of great development of traditional technology that has lasted throughout human history and up to the end of the 19th century, to a new period in which the main, although not exclusive, impulse has come from the coupling of technological applications with the advancement of scientific knowledge. The full maturation of this new process or marriage reached a peak after World War Two and has been responsible for twenty-five years of continuous high growth rates in most industrialized and industrializing countries. This has been a unique phenomenon in the whole history of mankind in terms of quantitative economic growth.

The legacy of the Industrial Revolution as a whole has then been one of a series of victories to increase the wealth of nations by the priority given to produce new tools and new products in a more and more economic way, i.e. getting more and more output of products for less and less input of resources.

2.1.3. The Monetarization Process Of The Economy : Developing Capitalism. The second essential characteristic of the Industrial Revolution has been the monetarization of the economy. Of course, some sort of money has always existed, either directly as such (gold or silver or copper-coins), or indirectly (in exchanging three goats for one horse, there is an implicit element of ex-change value which is one of the typical connotations of money). But until the beginning of the Industrial Revolution a very minor part of all economic activity had entered the monetarized system.

In a totally agricultural society, the vast majority of production and consumption does not enter the exchange system, where money has its cradle. Trade in fact gives rise to money. Even if we take into account the glorious histories of caravans travelling through Europe and the rest of the world and the many towns in Europe flourishing during the Renaissance period as places of international markets for certain parts of the year, a quantification will show that a very limited part of all the goods produced and consumed in those times were exchanged in a monetarized system.

It has been calculated that up to the 16th century, no more than 1% of the average life of a European was organized in a monetarized system (the time spent in selling his time for money or using his time for trading) [10]. Today, the corresponding percentage would be about 16% or more.

It is also very revealing that, at the time when the kings and the aristocrats were the rulers, they often possessed little money as it was not one of the indicators of real power. The fact that banking activities could often be developed by marginal groups which were not really part of the upper classes, shows that up to the beginning of the Industrial Revolution, money was still a secondary type of tool in the societal organization, a tool which could be left to those who were not really integrated in the same society.

Money has in the past always been linked to limited (by modern standards) trading activities and very little or no recognition was attributed to money as a tool to stimulate production, until the beginning of the Industrial Revolution.

It is not because Pope Gregory XII in the 13th century was particularly conservative or moralist, that the notion of interest on money was condemned by the catholic church. It was because lending money for interest was not linked to a productive function, but sheer usury, which was simply a way of making the poor poorer. Having debts was always "bad" before the Industrial Revolution; in most cases now it is the nerve of investment.

Putting money aside, in other words savings, has often been mocked at in classical literature. Remember the play "l'Avare" by Moliere: If, on the one side the modern spectator will still laugh at and condemn the tightfisted attitude of the hero of the drama, on the other side, he will miss the fact that saving money was, in those pre-Industrial Revolution days, a socially unproductive activity condemned at a moral level. Moliere's play lost a great part of its social significance in the modern world; if somebody sets aside a lot of money, his bank will find a way to channel it into productive uses. And even if a lot of people put wealth and money aside without putting it in a bank, some sort of deficit spending system will socially equilibrate the situation.

Here again we must recognize the importance of Adam Smith and the social weight of his moral convictions. In his book on the Wealth of Nations, he is completely reversing the "moral" attitudes of the past centuries as exposed by Moliere. He clearly states that the God-loving person, a person avoiding sins and trying to nourish the most morally and socially acceptable attitudes, is the person capable of saving. Savings which were potentially a sin before the Industrial Revolution had become a moral merit at the beginning of the new era, especially in those countries starting the first waves of the industrialization process.

Saving, hard and virtuous saving, is then the virtue of the capitalist: through his accumulated money, he is able to buy the machines or tools, which the new Industrial Revolution needs to develop in a specific environment outside the farm or the house of the peasant.

Increased specialization depends on more trade; and trade increases require more money. A greater availability of money makes it possible to save more and therefore to create capital for investing in new production activities. This is how the mechanism works, which increased the generalized monetarization of the industrialized world to the great extension of today.

As we have seen, new moral and cultural attitudes have to develop parallel to the emergence of new production processes and technologies. Adam Smith definitely made saving a virtue. One hundred and fifty years later, with John Maynard Keynes, even dis-saving (making debts), will be considered in some circumstances (when we are in a clearly deflationary situation) to be more of a virtue and less of a sin.

The banks, which up to 1800 were mainly involved with trading, started to contribute to the saving and investment functions of the Industrial Revolution only during the second part of the 19th century. At the times of Adam Smith, the amount of money used for investments out of the total sales in an industrial activity, was not more than 5%. In the 19th century, this percentage grew (as a function of the increase in the concentration and the productivity of new technology) to about 10%. Various savers (capitalists) joined together and shared the ownership of a new industrial venture: they created in this way the "corporation" (sharing the ownership). Corporations grew and started to spread their shares outside the initially restricted circle of the initiators of a new enterprise. Banks then entered the picture as a professionalized system of collecting savings from all sectors of the population and then playing an intermediary function in channelling those savings to productive activities.

It is important to distinguish the phenomenon of monetarization before and after the Industrial Revolution. Before the Industrial Revolution, the monetarization of the economy was a relatively marginal phenomenon. It is typical of the Industrial Revolution to accelerate and to develop monetarization as an essential element for the functioning of the manufacturing process.

In parallel, there was a shift of power in the transition from a society which is not yet industrial to an industrial society. In the latter case, the very control and availability of money is an instrument of power, both social and political, whereas in pre-industrialized society, power could be exerted and was exerted outside the direct control and availability of the few activities in social life being directly monetarized.

In this sense, capitalism just means studying the sociological and economic facts of this fundamental phenomenon: the monetarization of the economy as an essential part of the Industrial Revolution. Therefore, the Industrial Revolution cannot be but capitalist. The only important political question is then to determine to what degree capitalism (the monetarization of the economic activities) is a phenomenon compatible or even requiring a specific degree of political democracy. In any case, even a communist society developing the Industrial Revolution, is by necessity a form of capitalism.

This analysis of the process of monetarization stemming from the Industrial Revolution also suggests that there is an equilibrium somewhere between those activities which are more efficiently developed and managed through a monetarized system and those outside.

Clearly, the process of improving and diffusing monetarization still has a long way to go at the planetary level. Nevertheless, we can today put forward some new questions: which type of *productive* activities (in a general sense) can be better stimulated through a monetarized system and which through a non-monetarized one? Which is the best blend of monetarized and non-monetarized contributions for each type of productive activity? How far should and can monetarized (and non-monetarized) systems go?

The Industrial Revolution was a situation where priority was given to the production of tools and products and to the monetarization of the economy There is still a long future ahead, at the level of the globe, for developing industrialization processes. But the service economy, as we shall see in a later chapter, is already providing new answers to some of these questions.

2.1.4. <u>The Utopia Of Certainty</u>. The history of ideas, of utopia, of philosophy, is closely interlinked with the history of facts of all sorts and in particular with the history of economic development. Some type of mobilizing ideology, some kind of expectation of future happiness or achievement expressed in various forms appealing to more spiritual perfection, to sheer power or wealth, is the emotion or nerve which makes historical movements strive.

The renewed and increasingly efficient struggle against scarcity initiated by the Industrial Revolution, can be traced back to the search for a paradise lost, free of any anxiety because it is freed from any need to fight for survival. The idea of progress is in most cases defined as utopia, where the normal uncertainty of real life will have been replaced by the dream of achieving some form of eternity through universal truth based on definitive certainties.

Before the European Renaissance, this type of progress was essentially linked to a religious vision, where the churches played various forms of intermediary roles between the ultimate certainty (in fact the problem of death) and uncertainty (the reality of life).

With the diffusion of cartesianism, i.e. the development of scientific knowledge verified by experimental evidence, with the further development of positivism and benefitting from the evidence of the great advances in scientific discoveries of the last centuries, western civilization has lived a specific type of dream. It consisted in believing that mastering the reality, "scientifically", piece by piece, one would one day come very close to the universal truth. By the time of Descartes, some theologians in Utrecht considered that in fact, he was setting up a counter-religion: instead of starting from a universal truth revealed directly by God and administered by the church, Descartes, in his "Discours sur la methode", started by saying that he will only consider those realities, which are clearly verifiable and distinct. Everything which goes beyond, he wrote, belongs to the church to which he was fully submitted. But whereas most of the theologians of his time thought that there was no danger in somebody limiting himself to verify that water is liquid and that one plus one equals two, the Utrecht theologians saw very well that with this method, one could advance the idea that all reality could gradually be uncovered by the scientific inductivist method and inoculate the metaphysical idea that one day, all this construction would cover the whole of reality.

The method symbolized by "Cartesianism" has in fact been a tremendous cultural change which was at the root of the Industrial Revolution: it does not only concern essentially limited material experiences, but has had much wider ideological or metaphysical implications.

Even in the common language of today, the word "science" is very often used to define something which is certain. When one wants to add credibility to a report or to research, the first thing usually done is to add to it the word "scientific". In fact, this word only refers to a consensus as to the method used, but *never* to the fact that the results are necessarily certain beyond any doubt.

Particularly during the last century, the notion of science, of positivist and inductivist science in particular, was linked to this ambition to pave the way for achieving a verifiable universal truth, starting little by little to collect limited but definitive evidence.

Pascal once said:

> Science is like a ball in a universe of ignorance. The more we expand knowledge, the more the surface of the ball gets in touch with more ignorance.

In fact, we measure the advancement of science by the increasing amount of questions to which we are looking for an answer. Science is about the ability and capacity to put questions much more than it is a guarantee on the answers given.

In addition, the so-called scientific observations and analyses always come to a point at which they show their limits and they fail to be applicable under changing conditions. When philosophers, who are after all the fathers of physics, believed that the earth was flat, this theory was perfectly valid for a humanity moving by foot, at low speed and on a limited part of the earth. The fact that the earth was round was of no practical use during the Roman Empire. The knowledge that the earth is almost round and that it is rotating in a certain way, is clearly a necessary knowledge for organizing air traffic. In the same way, as a further step, the knowledge that outer-space is curved is of no immediate interest for local air-traffic on the earth, but it is essential to organize space travel. From the point of view of its application, no knowledge needs to be the definition of a universal truth: it is its relevance and application in given space and time conditions, which make it valid and valuable.

We can never really "know" but we can always "know more". It was part of the culture and the implicit or explicit ideology of the Industrial Revolution (be it marxist, liberal or conservative), to define a future of progress, aiming at ultimate certainty by adding specific pieces of knowledge of universal value, like in the process of adding bricks in building a house. The problem is, referring to the possible completion of such a building, that each new discovery or advancement in understanding re-defines and very often restricts the meaning and the application of previous knowledge. Some previous knowledge might of course be completely discarded, but in fact, this is not necessarily so because, after all, we still do a lot of things as if the earth were still flat.

At the political level, the Industrial Revolution has introduced an assumption that every nation should have its independent state. It is too soon to judge, but overall this has probably been a useful historical step. On the other side, the definition of a nation in modern times is probably less clear-cut than it was when nations were simply tribes. In the modern world, nations are more and more an indeterminate concept: the difficulty is that nationalism grows in particular among those who do not feel integrated among the people they live with and try to compensate by over-doing it. This shows that there is always a pulse going in the direction of looking for certainty instead of accepting uncertainty.

After all, the principle of certainty, in the course of the Industrial Revolution, has been - in its political and ideological forms (in particular in many cases of nationalism and communism) - the justification for releasing the greatest movements of barbarity during the whole of human history. The mass-production achievements of the Industrial Revolution have become awful mechanisms, when at the service of the barbarian impulse. And this could also happen because of the habit of looking for certainty and universal truth, which are too easily used as instruments to select those which are "on the other side of the barrier", out of "truth".

Enthusiasm and idealism for achieving new goals is essential for the development of mankind, provided the search is always for doing "better", leaving some allowance for changing the conditions under which one will be able to "even better" later on. The quest for "The best" possible solution which automatically discards any change and any other alternative, is the desperate attempt to eliminate human anxiety applying the principle of certainty beyond its limits of applicability in time and space. The search for certainty, which has been part of the mobilizing utopias of the Industrial Revolution is also the source of nihilism. Certainty and nihilism are twin-brothers: both do not accept reality, the possibility of change, of contradiction, the change of even the most advanced scientific ideas, those of Einstein included. The utopia of a worldly certainty appears now, at the sunset of the traditional western born ideologies, which have conditioned the world in the last two centuries, as the means to finally secularize religion or metaphysics.

But life is such that when a dream really comes true, in the best of circumstances, it means that the dream itself is killed. And in the worst it is a dream that kills. The quest and the interest of life is in searching and in finding out what one can search for more effectively. It is uncertainty which is the raw material for searching, for asking, for developing, for creating, for doing. When uncertainty reaches intolerable levels, of course, it must be reduced. But the most intolerable level of uncertainty in life, is the level of full definitive certainty, because this is the point of death and the choice here depends on the individual beliefs of each of us.

## 2.2. THE LIMITS OF THE INDUSTRIAL REVOLUTION

2.2.1. <u>Production Is Not In Isolation From The Non-Monetarized World</u>. Common sense people, and even economists, have always admitted and considered the fact that a substantial part of the productive activities in life and in society are performed in a non-monetarized form. Most of the great classical economists from Adam Smith to John Stuart Mills have devoted a considerable part of their writings to the notion of productive labour and to the notion of value largely including non-monetarized activities.

But in fact, the very notion of value upon which Adam Smith founded the first comprehensive synthesis of economic theory, has led to the exclusion in fact of the non-monetarized contribution to the creation of wealth in industrial societies.

Taking into account the priorities and the functioning of the Industrial Revolution, this attitude was finally both legitimate and theoretically justified, given the type of scientific and philosophical ideas dominant up to the beginning of our century.

First, it was the problem of managing a clear priority: it was obvious that the wealth of nations could be developed in an unprecedented way thanks to the progress of the industrialization process. The main social mechanism of diffusion of the process, which meant specialization, increase of trade and investment, was the development of the monetarization of the economy. Money was clearly the tool in social engineering solving the complex logistic problems which go along with the development of industrialization.

Second, at a more theoretical level, the notion of value proposed by Adam Smith was derived from a measurement system dependant on the price provided in the market by the interplay between supply and demand. The price, the monetarized value of goods, is the clear, easily quantifiable yardstick, by which economics has seemed able to measure its own performance in an unambiguous way. Even more so: the price of reference of a good, defined by its monetarized value, is a type of measurement which has had a great advantage over other types of measurement in social sciences. It is a quantified, apparently precise reference, avoiding the more vague statements, indicators and performance evaluations used in other social sciences. In this way, economics could come very close to the dream of having at hand an instrument to measure value (price), which would put this science much closer to natural sciences where phenomena are normally more clearly defined and most often dispose of self-evident systems of measurement. In this sense, the monetarized economic value derived from price could look like the equivalent of measuring the speed of sound or of light, the weight of a body, the boiling point of water or the thermal inertia of a metal.

To summarize, convenience, practicality and the reference to the scientific method of analysis, have combined to focus attention on the monetarized activities as the key tool for developing the wealth of nations during the industrial revolution.

And even if now, in the new service economy, the predominance given to the monetarized activities, has to be put in a broader perspective, the mastering of the monetarized phenomena and the smooth functioning of the monetarization process is a key condition in those situations where increasing the absolute quantity of tools and products is the very first priority.

One has also to consider the fact that criticism against "money" during the industrial revolution very often derived from pre-industrial attitudes, philosophies and cultures of an essentially conservative nature, even when they are presented in a "progressive" way, but always referring to some abstract reference to the past. As a result, many socialist movements and even the young Karl Marx, tried to envisage a society "without money": these openings, instead of addressing the future were a sign of social inertia, of nostalgia for a time when - before the Industrial Revolution - monetarization was limited to a small part of the economic life, and where the accumulation of money was socially unproductive. However, it was the more mature Marx himself who, as one of the last classical economists, terminated the discussion on the use value (including both monetarized and non-monetarized activities). In "the Capital" he reduced it to the idea that "use" simply means destination of goods and eliminated finally, any interest for the actual non-monetarized activities in economic life.

Later, neo-classical economists did from time to time come back to the notion of non-monetarized economic activities, but always explained them with analogies to the monetarized system (as in the case of those non-monetarized transactions having "ghost" prices).

The transition to the modern service economy also represents a basic transition in the notion of value: we witness the re-emergence of the importance of considering the value of non-monetarized activities in a full economic sense.

"There is a price for every good which is scarce. If it has no price, it means that it is not scarce and freely available". This typical economic assertion is true in many cases: air is essentially free whereas a piece of bread costs money. But this assertion completely hides the process by which a good might *become* free or, on the opposite, become scarce. For instance, one can assume that water-pollution was much less extended at the beginning of the Industrial Revolution than it is nowadays. The same water for drinking, washing and pleasure (swimming), that in the past was in many cases free, in many places of the world, in the meantime has become costlier, not necessarily by an increased consumption, but because of pollution. The same water, in addition, has a very important contribution to play in the production system (in many countries of the world, the consumption of water by industry is much higher than the quantity of water consumed by the population). When today money has to be spent to de-pollute water, to build swimming pools along the seashore in order to allow tourists to take a swim, then these costs are indicators of a scarcity - of an increased poverty of available resources - which have been induced by the development of industrialization. When resources, which were free or available at a very low cost become an increasing element of costs of the industrial production system we realize that after all the monetarized economic system has had and is having effect on the non-monetarized one. And that in the drive to reduce scarcity through increases in productivity in the monetarized system, sometimes scarcity is produced in the non-monetarized sector (and is in most cases "internalized" - if ever - *after* the scarcity producing process has started).

The limits of the Industrial Revolution - as an efficient system to increase the overall wealth of nations - become thus apparent when the increase in scarcities in the non-monetarized world offsets or overcompensates the decrease in scarcities in the monetarized one. This also means that the two worlds are interdependent. Clearly, there should be a system of accounting and monitoring increasing scarcities in the non-monetarized sector, which should be integrated, more than it is today (through the existing taxation systems on pollution for instance), in an overall accounting system.

2.2.2. Production Is Increasingly More Dependent On "Non-Productive" Service Activities. A common sense reference in the Industrial Revolution is made to the fact the humankind needs first to satisfy the basic needs such as food and shelter to a reasonable level of satisfaction before looking for other types of needs. This type of common sense fits pretty well with the priority given to the production of goods and tools in the Industrial Revolution.

But this image and this type of common sense correspond to a very early stage of the Industrial Revolution, where the major problem is, in absolute terms, to make a product. It is assumed that "the rest" will always be solved in one way or other.

Adam Smith, for example, and others have discussed at length "non-productive" activities: they might be acceptable ones, but they do not really contribute to wealth even if they are honourable professions like scientists, lawyers, retailers, planners, financial experts, etc..

In fact, reality today has completely reversed this thinking. The mature Industrial Revolution has produced an economic system where the costs of production are only a very minor part of the costs involved in making a product available to a consumer. Two studies at the Battelle Research Institute in Geneva, during the late sixties, illustrate this matter.

The first case concerned a machine capable of producing 500.000 blankets per year. The cost of production per blanket would have dropped to a very low level, provided of course that all the blankets would have been of the same size, use the same type of yarns and be of the same colour. At that time, the whole market for blankets in Switzerland in one year was of about the same quantity of 500.000. But given the very specialized type of blanket available through that machine, it was obvious that one could only sell them through a worldwide distribution network. It then became apparent that, for such a high volume production, specialized on one type of blanket, great costs would have arisen in storing the inputs for the production itself, storing the blankets once produced, sending them to the different markets, organizing the distribution and so on and so forth. The total costs of the service operations alone would have been more than 90% of the price that the consumers would have spent. Pure production costs per blanket would have decreased to less than 10% of the final selling prices. The product was not competitive because the increase of the service functions would have been greater than the increase in productivity through the super-specialization of the available machine.

This case study was a blow to the traditional theory of "economy of scale" as it is still presented to most students. New technology and increases in specialization do increase productivity in a continuous upwards way, even if it is very often admitted that beyond a certain point, the gain in productivity can be very low. In fact, if one does take into account not only the costs of the production process, but also the increase in all the functions necessary to make the product available to the customers, one does not obtain a curve which is S-shaped, but a curve shaped as a reversed U (see *Figure 1*). When the costs of all the services necessary for distributing and using the product are increasing much faster than the increase of productivity on the pure production side, the curve points *downwards* and before reaching the top of the S-curve, as a result of the growing costs per unit of the product involved, both in production and the service to make this product available.

In the second study, the chemical industry was striving to find new products for the textile industry with which it was hoped to relaunch a very soft market. During the decades before, the development had always come from a very successful new product like nylon, polyester

18

Figure 1. Increases in productivity,
  a)  regarding the effects of new technologies and specialization only (*),
  b)  and, in addition, taking into account all service functions necessary to make the
      product available to the customer (**)

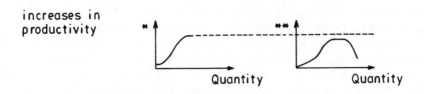

fibers, or acrylic fibers. This time, an enquiry was made on how far consumption could be increased in the textile sector by reducing the life-duration of products and therefore eliminating the need for users to wash products. This study was done just a few years before ecological and environmental issues became popular.

A typical issue of the study was to test the idea of disposable bedsheets. On average, a bedsheet is washed about fifty times before being thrown away. For production, it would thus have been fantastic if consumers had bought fifty bedsheets instead of one, attracted by a much lower price and by the elimination of the necessity of washing them. It would have meant storing an enormous number of bedsheets at each home, the destruction of the same amount of bedsheets either at home (at a cost very near to washing them) or through an addition to the domestic waste disposal systems (which would certainly have provoked either restrictions from the city services and/or increases in local taxes for collecting and destroying the bedsheets). The only positive outcome of the study was the identification of a very specialized market of bedsheets used in hospitals either for heavily wounded patients, mainly victims of road accidents, or for patients suffering from infectious diseases. The lesson of this study was that the obvious key economic problem was to consider the optimum product-life of a bedsheet, taking into consideration the costs of storage, of washing and cleaning, of disposal. The *utilization* of the product was the real issue.

These two examples stand for a period when the key transition was taking place from the Industrial to the Service Economy. They show the key importance of distribution, storage and handling systems; products are not economically useful until they are made available. And in the service economy, all the functions making the products available absorb by far the greatest part of resources in comparison with the effort to manufacture the product.

There are other macroscopic examples: research and development are service activities which may absorb up to 20 or even 30% of the total sales income of a technologically advanced sector, such as electronics. Nobody today would imagine being able to develop any electronic product without a substantial contribution from a complex and extremely diversified financial sector.

The same goes for insurance: at the time of the Industrial Revolution, economic theory was dominated by the notion of Engel's law. For Engel, insurance as well as most other services, were "secondary" types of consumption to be taken into consideration after having satisfied the "basic" needs. This was true in a simple industrial society. But during the last ten to twenty years, when the insurance market in the world has continued to increase in most countries at an average rate above the rate of GNP, this sector is no longer representative of a secondary type of consumption. It has become an essential tool to guarantee the *functioning* of production and of a distribution system which has become very complex and in many cases very vulnerable. Insurance is guaranteeing the *availability* or substitution of products and services and is, therefore, of the same order of importance, not only as most other services, but as the traditional production system itself.

2.2.3. The Pace Of Discoveries And Innovations Against The Diminishing Returns Of Production Factors : The Long Cycles. The Industrial Revolution not only had to fight against scarcity in order to increase production, but also against the law of diminishing returns of production factors. Technological development is then essential in order to maintain the possibility of a continuous development.

The law of diminishing returns plays a role in all human activities and experience.

Let us take the case of our efficiency to cover distances by walking. We are efficient in walking distances of about one hundred meters, less efficient if the distance to cover is one mile, much less if the distance is fifty miles. Thus as the distance increases, our performance in walking diminishes as compared to other possibilities. We can then introduce a higher level of performance by using a bicycle. To cover one mile, the bicycle will clearly be superior to walking, except in rough terrain, and it will still be quite valuable for a distance of a few miles. However, the bicycle will become impractical if we have to cover more than a few dozen miles every day. For these longer distances, we fight the diminishing returns or performances of the bicycle system by introducing a higher level of technology: the automobile, which will be adequate for distances covering dozens or even hundreds of miles. But when we are facing even longer distances, the same phenomenon will start again and the airplane will become more efficient than the car.

This type of sequence can be observed in the great majority of production systems within the Industrial Revolution: it applies to the different generations of weaving looms, of machine tools, of transportation systems, of distribution and information systems. In each case, when a machine or a type of performance reached its limits, a qualitative jump intervened (if it was possible), which enabled a further development.

In addition, during the Industrial Revolution, some quantum leaps in technology became feasible thanks to discoveries made by the advancement of science.

However, each technological development meant not only the capability of pushing back the limits of what we were once able to do: covering distances, transmitting signals, producing any sort of goods; it also meant a more and more specialized performance! And this specialization by a series of qualitative jumps has its own limits.

For specialization also means loss of versatility: with our body, we can walk back and forth, turn right or left, make little jumps, climb mountains, swim and dive. All these performances are not done very fast, but we can do all of them. By using an automobile, on the other hand, we cannot climb a mountain or swim: we need a specialized vehicle to do that. In order to walk or to run on snow, we invented the ski: following the same path of development, we today have at least five different types of skis available for walking or running on snow. And each of them tends to be rather inadequate if used in conditions other than intended, such as a pair of cross country skis used for a slalom competition.

In the chemical industry, when new products were sought during the sixties in order to relaunch the market, new fibres were developed that are capable of resisting temperatures of up to five hundred degrees centigrade. But this performance was only of interest in a limited number of applications such as the nose of airplanes flying at supersonic speed. There is little use, in economic terms, for having shirts with fibres resisting temperatures of five hundred degrees centigrade with the exception perhaps of clothes for racing drivers, similarly to the lack of demand for the machinery producing five hundred thousand blankets per year which we described in a previous chapter.

It was precisely during the sixties that evidence accumulated pointing towards the limits of the simple linear development of *production* processes in the direction of more specialization and more productivity. Technology per se was not really reaching its limits, but the possibility of its economic utilization was either beyond the interest of the market, or was increasingly conditioned by costs caused by either services or environmental factors.

Simultaneously, the growing dependence of modern technologies development on fundamental research had also made apparent some new problems: fundamental research is a process where discoveries depend largely on chance. One can reduce the number of directions from which one can expect a new discovery to surface, but this will always depend on a very high degree of uncertainty. Advancements in new materials increasingly depend on such discoveries and in some cases can lead to bottlenecks in development. This is the case for example for batteries storing energy in a concentrated form, which today are hardly more efficient (only a few times) than at the beginning of this century: after all, the first automobile was driven by electric batteries and not by the later combustion engine.

Similarly, after the oil crisis in 1973, many people expected the cost of extraction of further oil for instance from the North Sea to drop dramatically, due to our powerful research capabilities and adequate investment in new research and technology.

More than twelve years later, the tension in the oil market had changed, but not so much because of the effects of overall cheaper supply but rather because of an overall diminishing demand for oil as the result of a long term adaptation phenomenon. It is important to underline here that the key factors in the modern economy have reaction times which are long and will increase and which do not fit the hypothesis (or rather the wishful thinking) of instantaneous or short term adaptation.

Parallel to the experience of the relative rigidity of oil extraction costs and technologies, we have lived through an authentic new technological revolution in the field of electronics. In this sector, the manufacturing production costs of all products from TV sets to calculators have dropped dramatically.

If the technologies in traditional fields such as oil extraction or car manufacturing had made the same jumps in productivity as the technology to produce computers and calculators, the cost of oil produced in the North Sea today would be lower than the very low cost of oil produced in Saudia Arabia fifteen years ago, and cars would be bought for the price of an expensive dinner.

This evolution has taken place despite the fact that political attitudes and public demand in the 1970's and 80's have been more conscious of a need for improving the situation in the production of energy rather than in the field of electronic products. And yet, great technological advances have been taking place in this latter sector.

All these examples serve to underline the fact that in economic history, the great advances in scientific discoveries and technological development represent a factor which is largely exogenous to the economy. In other words, even if modern technology is more and more dependent on scientific advances, it is only once all necessary knowledge is ripe and available that the products can be launched onto the market and sold. The period of ripening or development is a process where pressure from the demand side is only one of many conditioning elements, and surely not the determining one.

When a cycle has started based on a new class or type of product, then economic pressure (cost of production, type of demand) becomes more and more important. But at the starting stage of the necessary quantum jumps, the process is largely autonomous and the key scientific and technological innovations are largely exogenous from the functioning of the economic system per se. In many cases, this has *not* been understood by traditional economics, who have followed another line of assumptions and hypotheses, such as: never in history has there been so much money invested in science and technology. Therefore, when market forces change and products become rare, the increased prices will stimulate technology and development, and new innovations will relaunch production under better conditions. This assumes that science and technologies have very little rigidity and are not themselves subject to the law of diminishing returns.

Yet another point should be stressed. Investment in technology today, and even scientific discoveries made today, will have economic effects only after a certain period of time which is different in various cases and sectors. This lead time can be more than ten years, in some cases even more than twenty or thirty years. There is therefore no possibility of a correlation between money spent today in science and technology and economic outputs produced *at the same date*. All statistics making correlations for the same slices of time between production costs and research expenditures are thus per se meaningless. The consequence of this should be the return of economic research to a sound empirical basis, where economists together with engineers should try to develop models that take into account the various lead times. Only then would economists have an adequate (or at least less inadequate) understanding of the impact of science and technology on economic development. They would then be able to monitor periods of increasing or diminishing returns of technology, which are quite different phenomena and have a quite different behaviour from the performances in productivity during the same periods, related to actual production.

The classical Industrial Revolution was able to develop rather well for two hundred years, in a period of time when new clusters of inventions and later on of inventions and discoveries have taken place with a *predominant* impact on manufacturing activities. *Figure 2* gives a graphic idea of these sequences.

Figure 2. A schematic view of the effect of the technological revolution on global economic growth through successive sectorial advances.

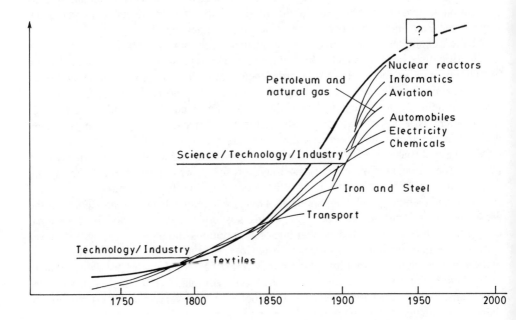

Source: Giarini, Orio and Louberge, Henri (1978) The Diminishing Returns of Technology, Pergamon Press, Oxford.

This leads us to consider the theory of the emergence of long cycles in the Industrial Revolution, a question which has been dealt with in 'several books [11].

In fact, the large clusters of innovations taking place first in the textile industry, then in the transport sector, then in the chemical industry and later on in computers electronics and other sectors, are key events introducing great periods of change, of innovation and economic development. Some authors have tried to derive perfectly regular laws of repetitive cycles, which would be expected to continue more or less indefinitely. This is a hard-to-die determinist analysis. It does not take into consideration that even long economic cycles covering thirty to fifty years (like the Kondratieff cycles) have to be inscribed within higher levels of still longer cycles, the longest of which is probably the history of Man. It is a matter of faith rather than scholarly analysis, to believe in identical long term economic cycles reproducing themselves with the precision of a giant pendulum [12].

It is psychologically understandable that in a period such as the 1980's, where the origin of the present changes in the economy are not yet adequately perceived, there is a recourse to mechanical explanations which would "guarantee" for instance that if the forty year Kondratieff cycle should really exist, we could count on a general resurgence of the industrialization process everywhere around the year 1990. Reasons are not given, and analyses are not made, but a sort of magic ritual is proposed as a substitute.

As a rational alternative, the two fundamental cycles characterizing the Industrial Revolution could be studied in detail: the first one being the period during which traditional - non science based technology - allowed consistent advances in wealth making; the second one covering the period when scientific knowledge gave a fundamentally new impulse to technological development for the first time in history.

But even these two cycles or key periods of the Industrial Revolution are contained in a higher cycle or period of the Industrial Revolution itself.

2.2.4. <u>The End Of The Megacycle Of The Industrial Revolution</u>. Most of the points already discussed are indicators or connotations of the end of the megacycle of the classical Industrial Revolution. A megacycle which made essential and unique contributions to increasing the wealth of nations by giving absolute priority in developing more and more efficient production systems. We now consider the end of this megacycle, which is not due to economic development coming to an end, but to a fundamental change in priorities taking place in the way in which this old goal of increasing wealth is now attained.

The process of diminishing returns of technology is not only one of the "important" elements to appreciate the situation, but also a key to bringing economic analysis closer to scientific and empirical requirements. It does not mean that technology has ceased to develop or produce useful results. Quite the contrary: it means that the main result of modern developments in science and technology do not apply *in priority* or exclusively to manufacturing systems. They now apply to a system of production which is no longer the simple one that characterized the Industrial Revolution: one day, some unexpected scientific discoveries may for instance revolutionize the production of energy, at a pace which could be as astonishing as the increase of productivity in the computer and telecommunication sectors. But any fundamental innovation even at the manufacturing level in the future will take place within the framework of the service economy, where the main economic target will be that of making products available throughout their life cycle of utilization: the "Service Revolution".

The technological advances of the last fifteen years have started to reshape the modern manufacturing economy and the world of high technology in terms of a service economy as we shall show in detail in the later chapters.

Specialization combined with integration of activities into a wider frame (products and environment) and new complexities and networks (functioning of systems) are characteristics of this new challenging reality into which the so-called industrialized world has already entered in the course of the last decade.

This change of a very long cycle is of course not only a matter of technical, scientific and economic tools: it is also a question of cultural adaptation and thus presents a fascinating challenge.

Not so long ago, during an economic debate broadcast by French television, a sociologist returning from the United States was firmly asserting that the new jobs developed in that country in the service sector during the last ten years were not really "true jobs". "The true, economically valid new jobs that can be created", the speaker said, "are for instance those in the iron and steel industry". This is obviously a case of lack of cultural adaptation: the increase in the wealth of nations which once was measured by the increase in tons of iron and steel consumed, is still conceived today in the same way. Similarly, many journalists are expressing fears about "the de-industrialization" process. These fears can be compared to the anxieties of owners of horse-and-carriage systems during the last century who could not distinguish the decline of their production as being separated from the vision of a globally declining economy. The difference from today's situation is that whereas in the past the substitution was of one production system for another, i.e. the automobile for the horse-and-carriage systems, the priority today is the improvement in the productivity and performance of service functions as partial substitution for the manufacturing of goods.

For each product which we buy, be it a piece of meat, a pair of shoes, a perfume or an automobile, the pure manufacturing costs are a maximum of twenty-five percent of the total price we pay. The largest share of the cost is linked to services such as product development (research and development, and planning), storage and distribution, marketing and publicity, financial and insurance services, waste management and disposal systems. Herein lies the great challenge for today's economist, to stimulate a better use of resources in order to get more and more performance with less and less effort. This development concerns the vast majority of the working population in all "industrialized" countries, and even in most of the industrializing and less developed countries. It is only a question of changes in demand, but it is the normal evolution of a maturing Industrial Revolution in which the development of production technologies, their greatest efficiency, has paradoxically led to a reduction of the manufacturing processes to a still important, but definitely minor part of a larger service system from which our wealth depends. A similar changeover had of course occurred between the agricultural and the manufacturing sector during the Industrial Revolution.

Furthermore, a service system which is primarily concerned with performance in use and over time also needs to account for the non-monetarized productive activities.

2.2.5. <u>The New Dimensions Of Risk And Uncertainty</u>. In an overall balance, it would be difficult to establish if the uncertainties of modern life are greater than those of life 100, 1.000, or of 10.000 years ago. It would require deep research based on a clear agreement on the points of reference or parameters, in order to approximate an answer on this point.

It is indeed difficult to balance out the reduced uncertainty of dying from one of the great plagues which were recurrent in Europe up to a century ago, and the increased uncertainty of dying from a major war-produced nuclear disaster.

In fact, a feeling of uncertainty coupled with anxiety has been spreading, particularly in western civilization, in the last decades. These perceptions and attitudes are probably linked to the final failure of the basic cultural and philosophical assumption that was nourished during the two hundred years of the Industrial Revolution: that our knowledge and our capability of mastering nature had produced a sort of heaven without uncertainties, that the spreading of "scientific" methods had enabled us to reach certainty on earth.

However, the problem does not lie in the persistence and even multiplication of situations of uncertainty despite the scientific advances. On the contrary, the evidence of uncertainty is the evidence of life. The problem is to adapt our culture to the idea that the search for certainty is and will always be a negative utopia, based on the wish of a future of certainty, freed from all material and spiritual anxieties of life. Life can of course be destroyed by totally uncontrollable uncertainties but also by the idea or hope that uncertainties could be totally eliminated. But the only way to eliminate uncertainty in life is by dying, by giving up the possibility of further development, of discovery, of adaptation, of participation in a world of evolution. Life constantly recreates uncertainties and risks.

The essence of life cannot be to avoid risks: we take risks by the very fact that we live. The choice must be to live our risky situation in a more or less conscious way, as we live in risk whether we like it or not. Only with the growth of our understanding of our human condition, might we avoid falling into the trap which once led Huxley to say (reversing a famous sentence of Karl Marx) that "opium is the religion of people". Any sort of chemical, natural, ideological or cultural drug is a way to try to escape, or to get the illusion of avoiding uncertainties and risky choices. But the very fact of their existence is proof that we live. And the real question is to reinforce our cultural and material capability to face them, as individuals and as society.

Cultural and material problems in facing risks and uncertainty in modern life are closely linked. The passionate debate following the publication of the report by the Club of Rome [13] in 1972 on the Notion of the Limits to Growth is a clear example.

The success of that report, which has been translated into some twenty languages and has sold over three million copies, was due to the "scandalous" assumption that despite all our industrial and scientific capabilities, we could fall back into a situation of slower or even zero economic growth. As if we could lose our capacity to master nature and the organization of the industrial society. It was quite obvious, because of the extremely passionate level of the debate, that the real scandal - as it was felt for instance by the majority of economists - did not lie in the fact of a somewhat puzzling economic forecast. Many economic forecasts pointing all directions are made every year which do not produce the slightest reaction and which in general are never verified to measure by how far they were wrong. The Report of the Club of Rome, although by intuition more than by scientific methods, was less wrong than most economic forecasts produced by experts during the 70's. Some members of the Club of Rome had already explained in advance, before 1973, why there would be an economic slow-down, not necessarily as a vision of an utopian ecological world, but as a result of under-standable and empirical reasons. And yet: it is very common to read today that nobody had foreseen what would happen during the seventies. This shows that there are problems of culture, of ideology (which very often are not admitted as such), and of social control at stake: predicting in 1972 that economic growth could slow down and even reach zero level (which after all the Club of Rome had initially forecast as something which would happen somewhat later than it actually did) was not perceived as an act of simple economic analysis on the growth trends of the National Product, but was immediately and directly perceived as questioning the real validity of the ideology sustaining the Industrial Revolution, i.e. of the ever increasing mastering of nature and human and economic wants by modern science. Doubts about economic growth were then first of all interpreted as an act of doubt about some basic ideological and cultural assumptions. Furthermore, these doubts were politically disturbing because the idea that wealth would increase in an uninterrupted way and at a high rate allowed many social conflicts to be solved. If the cake was constantly becoming bigger, the problem of the distribution of the cake itself was less urgent and less of a social problem.

For all these reasons, the famous first report of the Club of Rome was much more than an economic forecast, it was a cultural event. It is amusing to consider today that the furore of those attacking it was conducted as if reality itself could be changed by demolishing the scientific basis of the report. But the campaign, by absolutely all political groups, only served to make the report more famous and could not prevent the world economy from entering into a period of slower growth for the reason which we are examining in this report. Today, we can also say that the report by the Club of Rome became *by accident* the reference point for signaling the end of the classical Industrial Revolution. It was itself, after all, a product of that Industrial Revolution, extrapolating its results a long way ahead.

But from now on, economic, social and human development is no longer dependent on the development of the Industrial Revolution as a priority assumption. From the end of one secular cycle, we are progressively passing to another: a cycle of more mature perception, more scientific knowledge (less manipulated by ideologies), more understanding of the dynamics of our human and economic condition, more acceptance of the reality of risks and uncertainties as a tool and as a basic assumption.

The growing complexity of social and economic life, the continuing trend to a growing world of interdependence, complexifying patterns of behaviour and rules of co-existence, the first timid extensions of our civilization to outer-space, are all pervaded by a sense of uncertainty. But this is precisely because they are processes in the making, opportunities for explorations, possibilities to restore the value of the notion of progress, after the many failures and the dead ends to which this ambition has been condemned by an age which has unveiled the many and often tragic limits to certainty.

2.3. THE "SERVICE" ECONOMY

2.3.1. The Growth Of Services In The Production Of Wealth. The growth of service functions is the direct consequence of the development of production technology through the Industrial Revolution. Let us follow it step by step.

Up to the beginning of the 20th century, new technologies and changes in production resulted mostly from improving practices on the spot and through work experience. Very rarely were such changes or improvements the consequence of an organized work programme specifically financed in a particular research department or division, inside the company or in a specialized research organization outside. The professionalization of research only started during the 1920's, reflecting the growing complexity of new technologies and the need to carefully plan their development and manage their achievements. This research service function, which developed over the last 60 years, includes today millions of persons and substantial budgets at company and at State level.

Maintenance and storage of incoming raw materials and storage of outgoing products have always been part of even the most simple production processes. But the increasing specialization of production units, more and more complex and advanced technology, the growing need to protect the more sophisticated products against damages over increasing transport distances, have among other factors contributed to the continuous increase of the cost of organizing such functions. At the same time the pure costs of production were decreasing.

The distribution of products to more and more people in an increasing number of countries at great distance from the point of production requires the organization and operation of complex marketing functions without which the product simply cannot reach most of the consumers. The financial activities as well as the insurance functions linked to the performance of production and distribution become essential and ultimately indispensable. When investments for one "machine" such as a nuclear power plant or an oil rig routinely are higher than a billion dollars, the requirement of an adequate functioning of all financial and insurance institutions becomes crucial.

As our society becomes more complex, so do the regulations governing the interaction of people including product utilization and safety limitations.

At the beginning of the Industrial Revolution there was little need for a bakery or a textile mill to do any research in order to define the qualities of its product and to target the market. Today, selling e.g. video-recorders inevitably requires detailed analyses of the potential consumer profiles in terms of regional markets applications, product pricing policy, age groups, etc.. A variety of liberal professions, from doctors to lawyers, from market researchers and economists to consulting engineers, perform a large number of professional services, either *within* or attached to the production complex.

Electronic engineers or physicists working in a laboratory clearly have a higher education than the technicians who operated the simple looms used at the beginning of the Industrial Revolution, leave alone the great majority of labour functions performed before the Industrial Revolution which required a very basic level of education. In pre-industrial society, very few people really could and needed to read but in the service society, most people will need to have "computer literacy". Mass education has been among the service functions which have passed through a period of rapid expansion, throughout the Industrial Revolution, and today it is a large sector with great possibilities of improvement.

As important and in some cases even larger than the education services in the modern economy are the sectors of health services and national defense.

In order to properly understand and evaluate the modern service economy, it is essential to consider that the growth of services is the result of the specific, successive evolution of the production process itself. The development of technology which changed production processes in order to increase its efficiency, has produced the great development of service functions at all phases of the transformation processes.

Figure 3. Services and maintenance in the production sector.

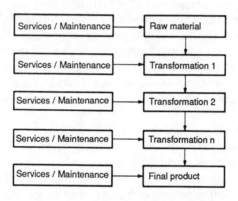

Source: Giarini, Orio (ed.) (1980) Dialogue On Wealth And Welfare, An Alternative View Of World Capital Formation, a Report to the Club of Rome, Pergamon Press, Oxford.

All the services which we have mentioned are essential in planning and accompanying and supporting production up to the point-of-sale as well as the products during their period of utilization. However, the maturing industrial revolution has put in evidence another important service to be added: the management of waste.

Waste has always been a by-product of any type of human activity and production: by peeling a banana, we produce waste; by cutting an arrow from a piece of wood, we produce waste. When the Industrial Revolution started a large movement towards the concentration of production and its specialization, waste inevitably also started to be concentrated and accumulated. This is not necessarily a negative point. During the history of the Industrial Revolution, waste had often been turned into usable by-products and even major new products as, for instance, the case of nitrogen fertilizers as by-products originating from the industry producing explosives, or phosphorous as a base for detergents and fertilizers, stemming from waste produced by the iron and steel industry. In the most advanced stages of the Industrial Revolution, when the principle of the specialization of products had been stretched to its limits, more and more problems appeared involving waste which could not economically be transformed into usable products. Furthermore, the fact that more new products were derived from a manipulation of matter benefitting from a deeper knowledge of physics and chemistry, resulted in an increased complexity of waste and a higher level of potential hazards such as poisoning by a greater number of products.

Concentration, specialization and increased levels of dangerous secondary effects are therefore the negative outcome of the use of more sophisticated and advanced science-based technology in various sectors. Parallel to the increase of industrial waste, the extension of conspicuous consumption to a constantly increasing number of people has also meant an enormous increase in the amount of waste produced by millions of consumers, in both quantitative and qualitative terms. A plastic bottle cannot always be burned similarly to a piece of wood or paper: it may produce smoke of a corrosive or even poisonous nature. This requires even more investment to organize an efficient and appropriate disposal system.

Every product finally becomes waste! Most materials, including our bodies, become waste at the end of their production and utilization cycle and some waste is transformed into new raw material. This transformation process happens in some cases naturally (e.g. in the case of organic waste), sometimes only after a delay involving a recycling intervention by man. The recycling of waste is in most cases limited, either by "economic entropy" (when the cost of full recycling would be prohibitive) or by physical (absolute) entropy (when full recycling cannot be done for physical reasons).

Waste handling and disposal is therefore one of the key economic subjects of the service economy.

*Figure 3* indicated that, in a situation typical of the Industrial Revolution, the production process was considered as terminated at the moment when a product or a tool was available and sold on the market. In the service economy, the real issue - in terms of economic value - appears to be the maximization of the utilization of products and services together during their life time, taking into account a series of costs which first precede, then accompany production and finally follow it.

On one side, the traditional notion of economic value is linked to the existence and marketability of a product. On the other side, the notion of economic value in the new service economy is extended to include the period of utilization.

As we shall see in more detail in *paragraph 2.4.*, the notion of value in the service economy is in essence not so much linked to the service functions now predominant in the production of a product, but rather to the value of any product (or service) as looked upon in terms of its performance or result over time. It is this utilization value during the utilization period of time which is the point at stake: the effective performance (value) of an automobile as a

Figure 4. The real final outcome of the production process.

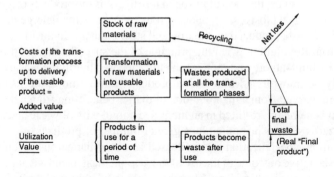

Source: Giarini, Orio (ed.) (1980) Dialogue on Wealth and Welfare, a Report to the Club of Rome, Pergamon Press, Oxford.

transport system has to be accounted in terms of its period (and frequency) of utilization, and the effective benefit (value) of a drug has to be accounted in terms of the level of health achieved. Whereas in the industrial economy the key question was: "what is a product's "monetarized" value?", the service economy asks another question: "what is a product's "utilization" value; what function does it serve, how well and for how long?"

2.3.2. The Growth Of Industrialization Within The Service Or Tertiary Sector. The development of the service economy ahead of us has to be considered as a global process of the whole economy following from the Industrial Revolution, rather than simply as the result of growth of the traditional tertiary sector.

In fact, service function are integrated into all productive activities in the industrial and also the agricultural sectors. It is essential to note that modern technology has forced the traditional service or tertiary sector to radically change some of its ways of functioning, by the introduction of processes which are very close to the capital-intensive processes in manufacturing. The distinction between functions performed in a modern computerized office, and a control centre in a production factory, is rapidly disappearing. This fact has led some authors, writing about the characteristics of the contemporary economy, to speak about a "super-industrial"economy or a "third Industrial Revolution" instead of speaking of the "Service Economy". Looking at the most advanced technological sectors, these authors point out that what is in fact happening is a process of industrialization of the traditional service sectors [14].

This is clearly an important phenomenon but it overlooks the spectacular increase of service functions within the traditional productive sectors. It would be inadequate to believe that the development of telecommunications, of banking and financial services, of insurance, of maintenance and engineering services, is simply a new kind of "production", an extension of what has happened in the field of textiles, iron and steel and the chemical industry. Selling a shirt (once, in a given moment of time) is a different business to fulfilling a maintenance contract over an extended period of time, during which the seller remains contractually engaged to the consumer for the utilization of the "product". The point of relevance really concerns understanding, what the selling of shirts in a service economy actually means: we switch from an "Industrial Revolution" mentality to a "Service Economy" mentality, when we add to the costs of their production the costs of maintenance (washing and possibly repairing) during their period of life, plus the costs of their disposal and replacement and we appreciate their value in terms of their actual utilization.

2.3.3. The Horizontal Integration Of All Productive Activities : The End Of The Theory Of The Three Sectors of Economic Activity And The Limits Of Engel's Law. Traditional economic theory still distinguishes between three sectors: the primary or agricultural one, the secondary or industrial one, and the tertiary one including all services (sometime subdivided further in a quaternary one) [15]. This sectorialization is a "vertical" one and has produced theories of economic development according to which there would be a historical transition from agricultural societies to industrial societies, and there could now be a transition towards a society with a predominant service sector. Such a theory is essentially centered around the industrialization process, where the predominantly agricultural societies are those which are not yet industrial, and where the tertiary sector very often is simply a "trash can" used to classify all those economic activities which simply cannot be called industrial.

In reality, for the three types of society, the agricultural, the industrial and the service one, the relevant point is the reference to the priority to be given to better stimulate the production of wealth and welfare. In an industrial society, agriculture does not disappear, quite the contrary: agricultural production becomes more and more efficient thanks to its *industrialization*. Industry does not develop as a completely separate productive activity from agriculture, it also penetrates the traditional way through which agricultural products are produced and distributed. In the same way, the service economy is not the outgrowth of something completely detached from the industrial productive structure, but penetrates the very industrial production which becomes predominantly dependent on the performance of service functions within (as well as outside) the production process. The real phenomenon therefore is not the decline and growth of three vertically separated processes or sectors, but their progressive horizontal inter-penetration and integration. In other words, the new service economy does not correspond to the economy of the tertiary sector in the traditional sense, but is built on the fact that service functions are today predominant in all types of economic activities.

A Finnish economist, Pentti Malaska, has expressed this idea as shown in *Figure 5*.

With every fundamental switch from one priority way to produce wealth and welfare to another, there is a modification in the perception of needs or demand. The definition of what is a basic need also changes.

Figure 5. Changing society: growth of the dominant sector.

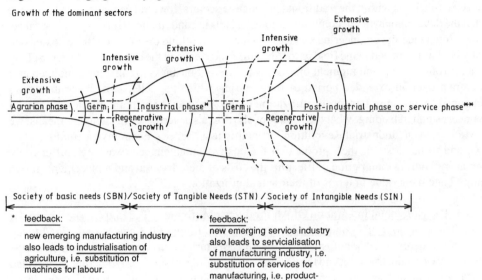

Source: Malaska, Pentti (1985) "The Outline of a Policy for the Future", in UNU, The Science of Complexity, The United Nations University, Tokyo, p. 343.

In an agricultural society, it was obvious that the agricultural (pre-industrial) system of production was perceived as facing the problems of satisfying basic needs. After the start of industrialization, and in line with the history of economic theory which until now coincided essentially with the development of industrialization, primary needs have been defined in terms of what basic needs the manufacturing system (integrating key agricultural productions) can satisfy. Engel's law states that services are secondary in most cases, because they only fulfill non-essential needs. The Industrial Revolution, in the same optic, is supposed to be an efficient method to provide food, shelter and health to people. Only once such basic needs are fulfilled will a number of "services" be consumed.

But the real changes towards the service economy stem precisely from the fact that services are becoming indispensable in making basic products and services which fulfill basic needs, available. Services are no longer simply a secondary sector, but they are moving into the focus of the action, where they have become, *indispensable production tools* to satisfy the basic needs and to develop the fundamental tools to increase the wealth of nations.

The insurance industry is a typical example: until a decade ago, everybody, including people in the insurance industry, accepted that insurance policies covering e.g. life risks, or material damage, were a typical secondary product in the traditional economic sense that they could only expand once the basic needs were satisfied by material production. However, during the ten years following 1973, when the growth of GNP in the world dropped from an average of 6% to less than 3% per year, the overall sales of policies continued to grow about 6% per year. If insurance consumption was of secondary importance, the slow down in other activities and in particular in manufacturing would have produced more than a proportional reduction in the sale of insurance, according to Engel's law.

The explanation for this continuous growth of insurance activities, even in periods of declining growth, lies precisely in the nature of the modern production system which depends on insurance and other services as key tools to guarantee its proper functioning. At a very advanced technological level of production, where risks and vulnerabilities are highly concentrated and represent an essential managerial challenge, insurance has become - increasingly so in the last decades - a fundamental pre-condition for investment. Similarly, at a more general level, social security, health and life insurance have by now achieved the status of a primary good in most "industrialized countries".

2.3.4. <u>From The Value Of A Product To The Value Of Systems</u>. Another key difference between the industrial economy and the service economy is that the first one gives value essentially to products which exist materially and which are exchanged, where value in the service economy is more closely attributed to the performance and real utilization (in a given time period) of products (material or not) integrated in a system. Whereas during the classical economic revolution, the value of products could be identified essentially with the costs involved in producing them, the notion of value in the service economy is shifting towards the evaluation of costs incurred with reference to obtained results in utilization.

The first approach considers the value of a washing machine per se, the second one evaluates the actual performance of the washing machine, taking into consideration not only its cost of production but also all other sorts of costs (learning time of the people using the machine, maintenance and repair costs, etc.). The applicability of the two approaches is inherent in most cases in the technological complexity of the products: in the case of simple products and tools, the assessment of value can be limited to the tool or the product per se: nobody buying a hammer would think it necessary to take courses to learn how to use it. In the case of a computer, however, the cost of learning how to use it tend to surpass the purchase cost of the machine, especially when the cost of all the necessary software is added.

Similarly, people buying goods such as dishes or even a bicycle will not consider signing a maintenance contract. With purchases of electronic typewriters, photocopying machines, or even television sets, however, maintenance contracts - even for individual consumers - are more and more common. In the service economy, the functioning of a tool is not what is being purchased: people are buying functioning systems, not products.

The same type of concept can be found for instance in the health sector. For reasons which are clearly linked to the development of the service economy, institutions called "Health Maintenance Organizations" (HMOs) are growing in importance in the U.S.A. These organizations combine various elements: incentives to doctors to produce healthy patients rather than major consumers of drugs and hospital services; generalists integrating the collaboration of specialists; the use of new technologies to record all useful data of the patients' medical history; reduced social health expenses. The good functioning of these HMOs in the United States has provided better treatment for patients and cost reduction in the health sectors, because the target is an optimal system operation and the value of the HMOs is not identified with the amount of money spent on drugs or hospitalization [16].

Money is more efficiently spent *because* the economic value has been shifted to the problem of performance and results (increasing health) rather than a pure "industrial" vision (equating more drug consumption with an increase in health and wealth in all cases).

The "Service Economy" is thus influencing a traditional service sector to really operate as a service (providing the best possible utilization value), rather than as an industrial production machine (interpreting the increase of costs and money spent as an increase of wealth).

If the accent is put increasingly on measuring the results of how systems work, qualitative and non-monetarized considerations will obviously become more relevant. Self-service restaurants or shops are systems that can reduce prices by asking the customer to do non-monetarized work himself, rather than to pay someone else to do it.

The self-service type of economic system contains a clever combination of monetarized and non-monetarized activity. HMOs are sometimes criticized for not being of use for the less healthy part of the population (they have a "selection effect"). However, it is here that social programmes might have a positive complementary role.

Evaluating the working of systems and their actual results also allows an easy identification of the part of the non-monetarized performances and contributions.

Systems evaluation, i.e. the organization of tools and persons in a given environment to obtain desirable and economically valuable results, has to take into consideration various degrees of complexities as well as the vulnerability in system functioning.

2.3.5. Systems Operation : Complexity And Vulnerability.
2.3.5.1. The growth of complexity from the Industrial Revolution to the modern information society.

During the initial phase of the industrial revolution, everyone's attention was focussed on increasing production within a relatively specialized environment. In the course of its various development phases, the industrial economy has grown more and more complex, both vertically and horizontally [17].

Vertical complexification is concerned with the multiplicity of stages in the transformation of raw materials into finished products, whilst horizontal complexification deals with the development of all services activities which go with and support the actual production process.

Let us first examine vertical complexification: One result of specialization is that each new product or each new generation of machines which replaces an earlier one has a more limited range of application. Thus, the gain of productivity is in most cases compensated by a reduction in the scope of the product. For example, it was possible on an early weaving-loom to use either wool or cotton and to produce fabrics for either clothing or bed-linen. Today, the most advanced looms can only be used for one fibre and are limited as to the range of dimensions of the cloth produced. Each event in the production line, from raw material to finished product tends to become a distinct operation (tied to a special tool or machine) just as soon as the boundary conditions enabling certain improvements can be determined. Thus, specialization signified the multiplication of means and methods, each one of which adapts itself to more and more precise purposes. And for each new technology or method introduced, the number of intermediate stages of transformation increases.

At this stage we can conclude that the degree of specialization has to be conceived in terms of optimization and not in terms of linearly increasing development. Specialization is inevitably linked to the goal sought after, and there may be specializations the purpose of which become insignificant and even cease to exist.

In parallel with the processes of specialization and vertical complexification of the system of production in the Industrial Revolution, the supporting service activities such as insurance, storage management, research, training, finance, sales and marketing, security, recycling of waste, grow more and more important. At the beginning of the Industrial Revolution, many of these functions already existed, but often in an unidentified and unclassified way, or were considered utterly secondary: when we are dealing with a small artisan-type production, problems of storage, distribution and the elimination of waste exist of course, but they are of secondary importance and never constitute a so-called "job". The transformation of textile production from tens and hundreds of thousands of small units in the 18th century in Europe into the huge concentration of production that we know today has caused the emergence of the need, among others, for the professional management of stock control and distribution. In terms of insurance, this transformation creates problems as to the question of insurability: a risk is in fact more easily insurable when it has a smaller average cost and a higher loss frequency [18]. This is a fundamental factor for the definition of the optimization of the economy of scale, which most economists have unforgivingly forgotten until now.

As scale and specialization increase in size and scope, more measures have to be taken to ensure a smooth inflow and outflow of materials. Whereas a small baker can if necessary buy flour each day to produce his daily output of bread, a synthetic-fibre factory has to provide far in advance for the proper inflow of raw materials necessary for its operations.

The same is true for the provision of capital finance: at the beginning of the Industrial Revolution, this was essentially the role of the wealthy individual, who was in a sense his own banker. Later on, in the course of the last century, joint-stock companies grew up because of the necessity for the aggregation of the financial resources of a number of individuals. It was only towards the end of the last century that banks started to develop their function as collectors of savings and the channeling into industrial investment began. Today, the most important investment projects have reached such a gigantic scale that they need international consortia of banks world-wide.

The flow and quality of output arising from the new technologies was such that it began to give rise to the need for specialized new professionals, whose task is to check the concentration of waste products and dangerous characteristics of certain processes. This phenomenon has become particularly important during the last 20 years although in fact, "waste management" always existed beside every production system, albeit in an "undifferentiated" way and with fairly limited consequences.

These service activities can take the form of functions performed within industrial firms, or of autonomous activities carried out by special outside firms.

There is a third dimension in the process of complexification which today has become even more important: with the multiplicity of stages observed in the processes of production and distribution it becomes increasingly necessary to coordinate all these separate activities. In other words, we have not only encountered a progressive development of specialization in an increasing number of fields, but also the corollary of that phenomenon in the form of the problems posed by the needs for information, coordination and organization between all the parts of the system. This is a kind of horizontal complexification, which added to the vertical one clearly indicates that the economy has become a system, or rather a network, of increasing complexity.

Compared to biological systems, this complexity may appear rudimentary, or embryonic. The present day economy must be perceived nevertheless as a network of increasing complexity, with both vertical and horizontal lines of communication, in which the components have to be able to integrate with each other. Within the system itself the problems of information and organization have become more and more dominant.

This same perspective allows the best appreciation of the contributions made by contemporary technology: the latest technological advances have their greatest impact on systems concerned with the communication and organization of information, which is exactly what is needed in order to better manage the development of the present day economies. All this is quite different from the direction which technology had taken during the classic Industrial Revolution, when all that appeared to matter was how to investigate and improve the stages of production which transformed raw materials into finished products.

One can thus define the contemporary economy as a service economy in the following way: as a situation in which resources (or factors of production) are used in service functions of which those relating to storage, transmission, and the processing of information represent an increasing part of the whole. It is at this stage that the notions of vulnerability and of risk management become economically extremely relevant.

2.3.5.2. Uncertainty and the vulnerability of systems.

The notion of systems becomes essential in the service economy. Systems produce positive results or economic value when they function properly.

The notion of system operation (or functioning) has to be based on real time and the dynamics of real life. Whenever real time is taken into consideration, the degree of uncertainty and of probability which conditions any human action becomes a central issue.

The economics of the Industrial Revolution could, in contrast, rely on the fiction of a perfect equilibrium theory (outside real time and duration), based on the assumption of certainty. During most of the economic history of the Industrial Revolution, risk and uncertainty have been a subject for historians and sociologists. The first systematic study to take risk and uncertainty into consideration, and with great timidity, was made by Frank Knight during the 1920's [19].

Any system working in order to obtain some future results is by definition in a situation of uncertainty, even if different situations are characterized by different degrees of risk, uncertainty or even indetermination. But risk and uncertainty are not a matter of choice: they are simply part of the human condition.

Rationality is therefore not so much a problem of avoiding risks and eliminating uncertainty, but of controlling risks and of reducing uncertainty and indetermination to acceptable levels in given situations.

Furthermore, the very systemic nature of modern economic systems and the increasing degree of the complexity of technological developments require a deeper and deeper economic understanding and control of the increasing vulnerability and complexity of these systems.

Unfortunately, the notion of vulnerability is generally misunderstood. To say that vulnerability increases through the increase of the quality and performance of modern technology might seem paradoxical. In fact, the higher level of performance of most technological advances relies upon a reduction of the margins of error that a system can tolerate without breakdown. Accidents and management mistakes still happen even if less frequently, but their effects have now more costly systemic consequences. Opening the door of a car in motion does not necessarily lead to a catastrophe. In the case of a modern airplane, it will. This shows that the notions of system functioning and of vulnerability control become a key economic function where the contributions of e.g. economists and engineers must be integrated. In a similar way, problems of social security and savings for the individuals have to take into account vulnerability management.

Thus, the notion of risk and the management of vulnerability and uncertainty become key components of the service economy.

### 2.3.6. The Notion Of Risk In The Industrial Revolution And In The Service Economy - Moral Hazards and Incentives.
A risk taking attitude was not studied in detail by the first great economists: it was rather taken for granted in a given cultural environment, even if Schumpeter made some more explicit references to the risk-taking entrepreneur. Only in 1921 wrote Frank Knight a first comprehensive book on the subject of "Risk, Uncertainty and Profit" [20]. But again, the risks that he discussed were more or less limited to the "entrepreneurial" type. The field of the pure risk linked to the vulnerability of systems, was still considered too secondary to be treated as a priority among the managerial objectives of the firm.

Only more recently have economists such as Kenneth Arrow [21] begun to take a closer look at the reality of the uncertainties that may undermine any economic policy or managerial decision. Just as Ricardo and Smith drew practical examples of their theories from agriculture and small-scale manufacturing, and as the later generation of economists up to Samuelson took their examples from large-scale industry, the most advanced economists of today use the management of risk and uncertainty by insurance institutions and in the social welfare or health sectors as natural reference points.

This has led to a widespread reconsideration of some basic concepts in economic activity, where the fundamental point is the need for a better understanding of the conditions and reasons for modern economic risks and uncertainties that enable the human entrepreneurial talent and creativeness to meet the present challenges in a more successful way. The world-wide discussion on Risk Management is a sign of this process. Basically, it represents a reaction to the new nature and dimension of the risks that condition our economic and social environment.

2.3.6.1. Non-entrepreneurial risks during the last 100 years.

The activities of the service sector, and of insurance in particular, have been regarded as secondary or marginal in the national economy, even if they have existed for centuries. Theories and even attitudes have not yet adapted to the new facts in this field. Some types of non-entrepreneurial risks have nevertheless become more important due to changes in social philosophy: this applies to risks covered by social security and workers' protection in industrialized countries. As early as the 1850's, the government of Prussia had in fact organized the first compulsory insurance schemes for miners. But at the time of the great depression in 1929, this type of risk management was still in its infancy.

After the end of World War Two, one of the greatest silent revolutions of history had started to happen: at present the social security "turnover" in all Western European countries is above 20% of GNP. While authors such as Peter Drucker have labelled this type of development for the United States as the "Unseen Revolution" and "The American Way to Socialism", traditional economic thinking has only recently started to consider this phenomenon in depth [22]. The development of social security can be attributed mainly to changes in social philosophy, which in turn is conditioned by the changing levels and characteristics of risks and vulnerability produced by the modern environment. Indeed, the growth of risks and vulnerabilities interwoven in the functioning of the economic system largely explains why we are now living in a new risk dimension and why we are facing a fundamental change in the expectations and possibilities of traditional growth.

During the last thirty years, statistics of insurance losses and insurance activities show increases at a rate often twice as high as the rate of growth of GNP in almost all the industrialized countries [23].

Unexpected events are increasingly producing unexpected results. The view of Professor Jay Forrester [24] on the behaviour of social sciences and activities is clearly applicable to the present trends in risks and uncertainties, where the indirect effects of an event become more important than the direct consequences of that event.

Where does this increased uncertainty come from? Is it a purely psychological and cultural phenomenon?

The period we are living in, which is characterized by a slower growth of GNP and an increasing growth of vulnerability and risks, is largely influenced by that complex phenomenon which we can define as the "Diminishing Returns of Technology".

2.3.6.2. The diminishing returns of technology and their impact on risk and risk management.

Modern technology has been at the source of increasing risk management problems in many ways:

  a) Increases in the economies of scale have been due mainly to progress in technology. The gains in productivity throughout the period of the Industrial Revolution were enormous, but the increased concentration of production also increased its vulnerability to small disturbances. This is the area where risks and vulnerability are increasingly of the "pure", insurable type.

  b) Specialization has been a key factor in this progress, but an excess of specialization has today resulted in systems that are increasingly interdependent and vulnerable, leading to a high growth of consequential losses (losses deriving from the non-functioning or malfunctioning of a system). Furthermore, specialization can reduce the adaptability to changing market conditions of a machine or installation, and can impose more severe maintenance and repair requirements that may be difficult to implement in some operating conditions. Gains from specialization may be partly offset or even outweighed by the lack of flexibility which results.

c) Operating reliability has made great progress due to advances in technology. However, minor variations and small accidents in one component can lead to disasters in a complex system, even if these accidents occur less frequently due to the higher operating reliability.

d) The quality of many products has been improved by modern technology. However, this same improved quality for a specific task may increase the problem of its recycling when a product is thrown away. The human and economic environment, as Alfred Marshall puts it, is much more like a biological process than a mechanical one. An improvement in one sense may introduce disequilibria in another: this is the lesson brought home by the problems of pollution and hazardous waste management control.

These examples have in common a shift of emphasis from the traditional entrepreneurial risks to pure risks of the "insurable" type. We can thus expect to find a reflection of these developments in the insurance field, and, in fact, there are many examples, such as the following:

- The total cost of damage caused by fires in Europe is now about 1 percent of national income and is growing more than proportionally (the part dealt with by insurance is about one-third of the total).

- The economic cost of crimes is several times higher than that of fire. This is due not only to an increase in the number of criminal offenses, but even more to the vulnerability of systems to criminal activity. The same applies to natural catastrophes: losses from earthquakes and floods are higher today not necessarily because they are becoming more violent, but because they affect more vulnerable systems.

- According to a study [25] by the Geneva Association in Europe and by Skandia in the United States, the total economic costs of *indirect* damages made possible through the utilization of computerized systems is of the order of $5 billion per year. This has, of course, to be compared with the much higher benefits from using computers: but nevertheless, there is plenty of scope here for proper risk management.

- The Statfjord platform in the North Sea is an example of a trend towards increasingly complex and sophisticated industrial activities: in the 1960's, it cost $1 billion to build, without taking into account the infrastructure and the cost of disposal of the platform at the end of its useful life. Further developments and new projects in this area indicate that the levels of investment from the financial or from the insurance coverage point of view are very difficult to fulfil [26].

This shows that risk is becoming concentrated at levels where the vulnerability is such that the overall uncertainty of the economic process increases. How many Boards of Management today dream of the decision possibilities experienced twenty years ago? Consumers are also reluctant to become increasingly consumers of "risk". The unique situation in the field of product liability and malpractice in the United States although amplified by a specific legal environment, starts to have its effects on other parts of the world. This is a typical trend of the service economy; the consumer is increasingly conscious that tools and products which exist for given purposes, and even experts, are only of value when the results of their "utilization" is positive. The fact that their utilization might give negative results, is refuted and gives rise to requests for compensation. Product liability is a great issue in the United States where litigation has led in some cases to extremely high and even excessive compensation. Chemical and pharmaceutical companies have a special problem [27]. Doctors, lawyers and other experts are sued in court for "malpractice" and have to compensate their clients if found guilty. At the European level, a recent Directive [28] is the result of ten years of discussion and preparations to manage the expanding phenomenon of the increasing perception by the public that producers of economic wealth have to be liable for delivering a "product" yielding negative results. Once again, in the contemporary economy, it is the "performance" which has economic value, which counts, rather than the simple "existence" of a product or service.

The problem of environmental hazards, which very often is linked with the question of transportation and storage of dangerous materials, is part of the same type of risk and vulnerability that our modern society has to face [29].

### 2.3.6.3. Pure and entrepreneurial or commercial risks.

The connotations of the notion of risk in the Service Economy cover a much larger ground than the notion of risk represented in the Industrial Revolution. In the latter case, the key risk normally referred to is the so-called entrepreneurial or commercial risk; in the Service Economy, it is extended to the so-called pure risk.

The entrepreneurial risk is one where the people involved in an action can influence its goal and the way the action develops by deciding to produce, to sell, to finance etc.. The pure risk is out of reach to those involved in an action. It depends on the vulnerabilities of their environment or of the system they are working in, and it will materialize by accident and by hazard. This notion of pure risk is strictly linked to the notion of the vulnerability of systems which we have developed in the preceding paragraphs and its relevance is distinctive of the Service Economy.

One of the great differences between neo-classical economics and the new Service Economy is that not only the "entrepreneurial" risk is taken into account (as in the case of Frank Knight), but that the notion of economically relevant risk is extended to include the notion of pure risk. The notion of risk, globally, has therefore two fundamentally different but complementary connotations.

Today, for any important economic endeavour, the consideration of both notions of risk must be on an equal strategic level (again linked to the notion of systems and of vulnerability).

Many people talking and writing today of risk management [30] (meaning the management of pure risk) do not make a clear link with the global strategy of risk. Therefore, instead of showing clearly how the two risks are correlated, they tend to confuse or merge them.

2.3.6.4. The notion of moral hazard and the economic incentives.

The demarcation line between pure and entrepreneurial risks is the notion of "moral hazard" [31]. This notion has long been understood by insurers when they have had to face damages produced by those suffering risk with the purpose of making money out of it. Take for instance the case of somebody burning his own home in order to collect the insurance: such cases concern more than 20% of fires [32]. Economists look at this notion from the opposite side as a spin-off of their studies on economic *incentives*: moral hazard is equivalent to studying the *negative* results of incentives. One important case concerns the level of social insurance for unemployed people who might stop looking for another job if the level of compensation is too high [33]. Many economists who have dealt with *public policy* are entering into the field of moral hazard (= negative effects of incentives) and could profit from the old experience of insurers in this field [34].

2.3.6.5. The new entrepreneur in the Service Economy.

Managers and entrepreneurs in the Service Economy should be prepared to have an overall view of risk in its two forms (entrepreneurial and pure). Even the most advanced management schools today (Harvard included) are often lagging behind in this respect, when reality is imposing big burdens on managers with regard to pure risks.

Risks have to be understood at all levels and have to be controlled as to their level of manageability. Vulnerabilities can, and have to be, diminished and checked. A strategic vision can then be developed and new challenges discovered.

If this vision, by both the entrepreneur and the public at large, is partial and inadequate as to the reality in which we live, the feeling will be that the risks and vulnerabilities of modern life are overwhelming us, whereas it is the consequence of a cultural inadaptation to identify and accept present realities.

Thus, it is very much a question of attitude. The incapacity of adaptation leads to pessimism and fatalistic attitudes, like those of a sailor who, instead of using the winds to steer his boat, lets the wind determine the direction in which his boat is pushed.

It is vital to recognize the new winds blowing in the Service Economy, to recognize how the challenges of the new risks, of the increased concern for product quality and the value in use provide an opportunity to define new directions for stimulating action towards real economic and social growth.

2.3.7. Tradability And Homogeneity Of Services. Many papers dealing with the Service Economy quote two specific issues reflecting the present difficulties in defining the characteristics of the Service Economy. In most cases, these difficulties are linked to the underlying psychological attitude of looking at services, or more precisely at the Service Economy, as a kind of new "product" produced by a new type of "industry".

The difficulty of having a clear perception of the problem is then once again linked to the cultural or theoretical frame of reference which is used for the analysis rather than the problem itself.

A particular point in case is the notion of tradability and homogeneity of services. It is often said that an analysis of the Service Economy is almost impossible because services refer to such different things as hair-cuts, telecommunications, maintenance and health activities. But the same thing can be said of products, as there is little homogeneity between a pullover, an airplane, an orange juice and a watch. In fact, all "industrial products" are homogeneous only in the sense that they are considered from the point of view of the production system, i.e. the manufacturing methods of production developed and improved by the Industrial Revolution. If one looks at services with an "industrial" mentality, one will inevitably discover that some of them can easily be assimilated to an industrial product while others cannot. However, this exercise is pointless as it tries to fit empirical evidence into a framework of reference which is no longer relevant.

The real difference between the industrial economy and the Service Economy, upon which homogeneous theoretical references can be built, is economic value: during the Industrial Revolution, economic value was linked to the existence of a product, and to improvements in productivity that came essentially from improvements in the manufacturing process. On the other hand economic value in the Service Economy is derived from the functioning of a system, the productivity of which can only be measured in terms of improved and increased performance as related to the final result. The reference is not the "product" but its "utilization". Its proper and useful functioning process.

Increases of productivity in the industrial economy are measured by the cost of the inputs used for producing a tool or a product. In the Service Economy, measuring the same cost of inputs without a reference to specific performance (not necessarily products), is very close to nonsense. The productivity of a health system is in "producing" healthy people. In both cases, the measurement of the result inevitably has to integrate qualitative parameters of the "stock": this can be done with reasonable effort based on common sense and requires a minimum of consensus. Measuring the performance of educational systems is inevitably linked to the evaluation of the quality of students formed in relation to the purposes of their learning; no indicator of the salaries paid to teachers or the investment in school buildings will ever be sufficient to properly measure educational productivity.

Being in a Service Economy also means looking at industrial products from a service point of view, i.e. looking at functions of tools and at how well such tools are really used and the results that they are supposed to produce.

In economic terms, the industrial economy is about the evaluation of production and wealth in terms of added exchange value, whereas the Service Economy is about evaluating the utilization value.

If, therefore, the notion of homogeneity and dis-homogeneity is used in the analysis of the industrial and the Service Economy, these notions reveal an inadaptation of the *conceptual* framework. It might of course be quite legitimate to choose one or the other. But it all depends on how *efficient* one or the other system of evaluation is and in which direction the empirical evidence is moving. By looking hard at services as functions and performing systems in the Service Economy, one can observe a great amount of variety in activities (and this is as normal as the variety of goods was normal in the industrial economy), but not necessarily any dis-homogeneity. In the Service Economy, a restaurant performs the function of providing food to clients and this function is of course different from the function of teaching or entertaining. But it is always a function aimed at results which can be rather easily identified in each case.

The same problem arises on the question of tradability: many service functions are tested or considered as if they should fit into the analytical framework developed to analyze trade of industrial products.

As the Service Economy is about producing results *where* the customers or the users are, it is clear that the question of trade undergoes a fundamental change: we can no longer distinguish between trade in services and movement of production factors or investment as was the case in "industrial" economic theory. Trade in the Service Economy inevitably mixes the two in many cases. For many companies, and especially those of the traditional "service sectors", the equivalent of local or international trade in products is the organization of delivery systems where the customer is.

Whereas a traditional industrial producer of a machine will export a "product" to any place in the world, the exporter of a service will have to rely much more upon an established office or point of distribution at the point of use. The transition from the industrial mentality to the Service Economy in these two cases arises when the export of the machine must be accompanied by so much software, that the former simple transfer of the "product" turns increasingly into an investment on site to guarantee the functioning of the product where it will be used.

Therefore, there is no particular reason per se why a service should be more or less tradable or sellable than a product. An hour of learning how to use a computer might be the perfect equivalent, in terms of value and in terms of money, of the price of a small pocket calculator.

The latter is still very much a product in the old sense, i.e. it will probably need little local maintenance, whereas the hour of learning has to be delivered integrally where the student and the teacher are. In this case, we can also see a further interpenetration of products and services in the sense that e.g. video-cassettes, which one can produce and transport like a traditional product, will carry and contribute to the learning performance in the same way as books already do.

The question of trade in services and of tradability in services, is a connotation of a more general movement which has characterized the development of society and of the economy in the last few centuries: from locally closed and largely autonomous productions with small markets to ever greater interpenetration around the world. In the Industrial Revolution, the explosion of trade essentially concerned hardware (products). A new step now concerns the spread of service performing systems: exchanges concern not only hard tools or products, but are *extended* to ways and means of how to use (co-produce) them.

At first sight, the spread of the world service economy has an inborn mechanism for a more equilibrated worldwide development.

2.3.8. Material And Immaterial Values In The Service Economy - The Value of Education.
Many books and articles on the Service Economy (as well as on the "information" economy), talk about the idea that in the present economic system, we are faced increasingly with so-called "immaterial" goods and values [35].

This notion of "immaterial" comes from the observation that during the classical Industrial Revolution the main production had to do with material (hardware) goods and tools; whereas, in our present service information society, goods are very often "immaterial" (software), as for instance a piece of information or a computer programme (the support or transmission system is still "material").

In this type of analysis, there is also implicit or explicit reference to the ambition of presenting the Service Economy as less "materialistic", more open to "immaterial" values. Similarly, the word "quality" is used as an analogy to "immaterial" and is very often linked to the idea that a higher degree of education is the real and proper production factor.

All these analyses in fact maintain a dichotomy between tools and their utilization. Hammers, typewriters, chemical plants, rockets, radios are tools, material-tools, and they all need some form of utilization capabilities. No tool has ever been used without some kind of knowledge and culture, however low.

The question of services being "immaterial" can probably be considered more correctly in the following way:

- there has always been a combination of material and immaterial resources, in any type of economic activity. The fact is that during the classical Industrial Revolution, priority has been given (and in our view in a justified way), to the material side of the problem: let us produce things first and later find a way to use them, because the world is dominated by scarcity.

- In the new Service Economy, in which material instruments and qualitative conditions of utilizations are integrated as they have *always* been, the latter have become dominant simply because in the economics system they *now* cost more (money and efforts) than the simple production of tools. Therefore, there has been a shift towards the notion of the *function* of tools (which is an "immaterial" notion, describing utilization) from the previous priority given to their material existence.

To stress it again, the priority in the Service Economy is on functions where the primary interest is given to systems producing results. But it is equally obvious that these systems are heavily dependent on material tools even if they produce abstract products like communications.

One should therefore be careful not to use the word "immaterial" in such a way that it refers to a rather vague "idealistic" description of present economic development.

A "function" or a "system" is immaterial per se, as a machine tool is "material" per se. The intelligence needed in both cases may develop in different directions. More knowledge will go into the ServiceEeconomy as a continuation of the normal trend in progress throughout all phases of human history. Industrialization has a different knowledge intensity than traditional agriculture. The importance of knowledge per se is not new: even the man who invented the bow and arrow was an "intellectual".

Only once this point is clear are we better equipped to describe the higher and increasing levels of education, not as something new, but simply as something more appropriate in the present economic development.

The notion of "immaterial" values is fundamentally linked to the feeling that values are produced, which go beyond what is normally measured by current (industrial) economics. If one can talk in some cases of deducted values [36] (the case of the economic system overestimating the real increase of wealth), there are also many cases in which the results in terms of real wealth of modern technology are underestimated.

This takes us back to the problem of measuring results as against costs (monetarized costs) of production and of the absolute necessity of measuring value by some accepted indicators of personal and national wealth.

## 2.4. VALUE AND TIME IN THE SERVICE ECONOMY : THE NOTION OF UTILIZATION

2.4.1. The Cycle From Raw Materials To Products To Waste. The "life" of any product can be divided into five distinct phases: *design* and conception; *production*, involving a transformation of natural resources; *distribution* (transport and packaging, marketing and publicity); the useful life over a variable period of time (*the utilization period*); and the disposal of the discarded good (*waste disposal*). This whole process is referred to as The Product-Life [37].

The fast replacement of goods has been a persistent trend in economic history, and has gained momentum in our fashion-based consumer society (the syndrome of bigger-better-faster new products), as economists have become preoccupied with production optimization, economy of scale and fast depreciation and replacement. The success of this industrial production has been measured as the flux at the Point-of-Sale (expressed e.g. in the GNP), while the notion of the use of a product over time, the utilization, has been largely neglected.

However, it is precisely this *utilization period* which is the main variable in wealth creation! Who determines the length of the utilization period? A company can produce a plastic toy that breaks before it has ever been used and cannot be repaired, or a wooden toy that might last several generations, both with the same price tag and the same production and point-of-sale value. But how many of each will it sell year after year? Yet, the user has as much influence on the utilization period as the producer: identical goods such as automobiles, that are used in countries of different levels of development, will "last" an average of 5-10 years in "rich" countries, and up to 35 years in "poor" countries.

The Industrial Revolution has enabled us to get away from the times of scarcity, as expressed in the old English maxim:

> use it up,
> wear it out,
> make it do
> or do without.

An increasingly specialized production, first mainly in raw material sectors, such as cement and steel, and today increasingly in parts of the assembly sector, has led to highly efficient production systems. This efficiency has been achieved through increases in volume (economy of scale), a substitution of machines for labour (mechanization) and a specialization of the production process. However, this efficiency was focused exclusively on production and has often made interventions after the point-of-sale, i.e. during the utilization period, less efficient, or dependent on expensive special skills or specialized parts. When Henry Ford conceived the "Model T", one of the design parameters was utilization flexibility: any blacksmith had to be able to repair all major parts including axles. In contrast, todays cars depend for their maintenance and repair on product specific parts, tools and skills which are only available within dealer networks.

But even within the production process, the evolution has not been homogeneous. Let us glance at some basic figures: roughly three quarters of all industrial energy consumption is associated with the extraction or production of basic materials like steel and cement, while only one quarter is used in the transformation of materials into finished goods such as machines or buildings. The converse is true for labour, about three times as much being used in the conversion of materials to finished products as is required in the production of materials (see *Figure 6*).

The same logic of economy of scale means that the higher the entropy of the resources (uniformity and purity of materials), the higher the polarization of skills, the concentration of production and its vulnerability. Look at the World steel or cement industry.

Polarization of skills means a specialization towards both ends of the scale, i.e. into unskilled and highly specialized labour, both vulnerable to changes in demand. Only the French language has officially acknowledged this fact, by calling the unskilled workers "ouvriers specialises" (specialized workers).

> The most highly industrialized nation on earth is in danger of becoming a nation of industrial illiterates who do not know how to stop a running toilet, or identify anything on a car more complicated than the gas-tank cap,

observed Machinists' Union President W.W.Winpisinger (USA) some years ago.

Figure 6. Intensities of Labour and Energy inputs in the main production phases.

| INPUTS | BASE MATERIAL PHASE | MANUFAC- TURING PHASE | TOTAL INPUT INCORPORATED IN PRODUCT |
|--------|--------|--------|--------|
| LABOUR | 25% | 75% | 100% |
| ENERGY | 75% | 25% | 100% |

VIRGIN      PRIMARY
SUPPLY → BASE        → MANUFACTURING → PRODUCTS
           MATERIALS

Source: Stahel, Walter R. and Reday-Mulvey, Genevieve (1981) Jobs for Tomorrow, the Potential for Substituting Manpower for Energy, Vantage Press, New York, N.Y.

The increase in the size of companies has meant a concentration not only of production tools and power, but also of jobs: the Industrial Revolution is built upon the mobility of the worker. In the case of a reduction in the number of jobs available, this instantly results in pockets of concentrated unemployment in urban areas!

The dawn of the Service Economy and the slow disappearance of the notion of "free goods" such as air, water and cheap energy, have started to overrule the basic belief into the advantage of big production units applying extensively the principle of economy of scale. In fact, many small decentralized production units in areas such as beer brewing today are more profitable than big units, due to a much lower overhead structure, such as greatly reduced transport and marketing costs.

The same logic of the Industrial Revolution, applied to the regular occurrence of disasters involving industrial products such as airplanes or automobiles, has led to stricter product standards in design and manufacturing, rather than to *performance* standards of the utilization systems of which these products are part. Many of these product standards have today become the defensive fortresses of the Industrial Revolution, against either an optimization of the functioning of systems ("Why have speed limits now that we build cars that are safe at any speed?"), or against innovation leading to the technological updating of goods during their utilization period ("Old electrical goods are unsafe"). Many technical standards have thus today become obstacles to risk taking and innovation, and substitutes to vocational training and creativity! The search for technical perfection is sometimes no longer aimed at finding the best possible solution in a constantly changing time, but perfection has become an aim in itself, focussed on risk avoidance, on certainty.

2.4.2. The Utilization Period. The linear production-consumption system of the Industrial Revolution does not concern itself with the built-in environmental deterioration at both ends, linked to the depletion of natural resources through production (including the high energy and water consumption that goes with it), and the waste accumulation and disposal after the utilization period.

Short-life, incompatible goods and products characterized by the lack of economic repairability have meant not only that an ever increasing part of our income has been devoted to the replacement of products, thus maintaining, not adding to, our wealth, but also to the cost of disposal of a rapidly growing mountain of waste of increasing complexity and hazardousness: The fast-replacement system (*Figure 7*). In addition, the faster the production flow and thus the replacement volume, the bigger the surfaces needed for transport, distribution and waste treatment centers, adding significantly to the non-monetary losses of wealth, in assets such as wildlife, wilderness, even arable land.

However, there are alternatives to this fast-replacement system! Alternatives that would cut by half the use of raw materials and resources, and the amount of waste produced!

We can achieve this goal either through *long-life goods*, (e.g. extending the utilization period of products through design, as in the case of cars that are designed to last 20 years instead of 10 years, through the use of corrosion-resistant materials, appropriate assembly methods and periodic maintenance, (see *Figure 8*), or by doubling the utilization period of goods through *product-life extension* (*Figure 9*).

48

Figure 7. The fast-replacement system.

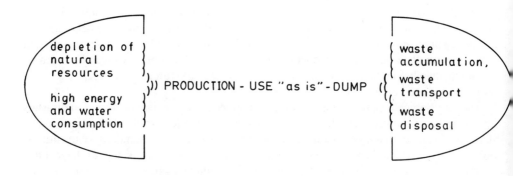

Source: Stahel, Walter R. (1986) "Product-life as a variable", Science and Public Policy no 4, London.

Figure 8. The slow-replacement system: long-life products.

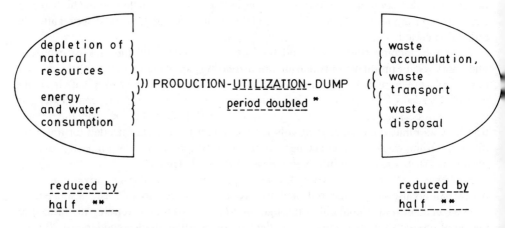

* in comparison to the fast replacement systems
** as *, per year of utilization

Source: Stahel, Walter R. (1986) "Product-life as a variable", Science and Public Policy no 4, London.

Figure 9. The self-replenishing system of product-life extension services.

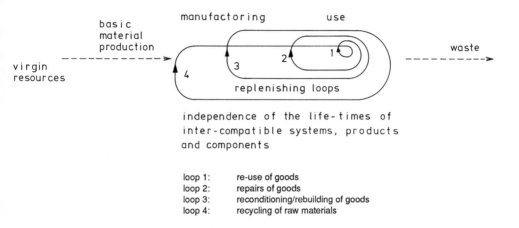

independence of the life-times of inter-compatible systems, products and components

| | |
|---|---|
| loop 1: | re-use of goods |
| loop 2: | repairs of goods |
| loop 3: | reconditioning/rebuilding of goods |
| loop 4: | recycling of raw materials |

Source: Stahel, Walter R. and Reday-Mulvey, Genevieve (1981) Jobs for Tomorrow, The Potential for Substituting Manpower for Energy, Vantage Press, New York, N.Y.

A sustainable or self-replenishing system based on product-life extension creates an economy based on a spiral-loop system that minimizes matter, energy-flow and environmental deterioration without restricting economic growth or social and technical progress. The "Four Rs" of product-life extension are (*Figure 9*):

REUSE (loop 1),
REPAIR (loop 2) and
RECONDITIONING combined with technological updating (loop 3) utilize used
    products or components as a source for new ones,
RECYCLING (loop 4) uses scrap as locally-available raw material.

A society relying on this self-replenishing economy is building on existing wealth and applying economics to optimize the total utilization period of goods. Financial and resource management is now aimed at reducing total long-term utilization costs, at reducing a country's dependence on imports of strategic materials, and at reducing waste dumps that can turn into time-bombs.

Not all of these activities of product-life extension have the same trade-off between labour and energy. But they all have in common the savings in resources, as shown in *Figure 10*.

50

Figure 10. Trade-offs between energy, labour and materials in various product-life extension (PLE) services.

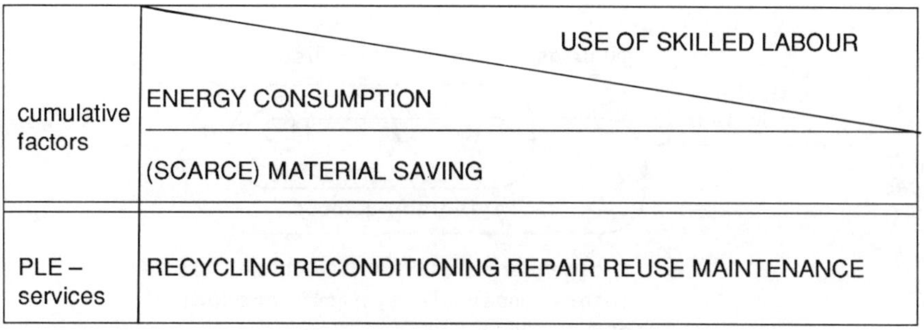

| cumulative factors | USE OF SKILLED LABOUR |
| | ENERGY CONSUMPTION |
| | (SCARCE) MATERIAL SAVING |
| PLE – services | RECYCLING RECONDITIONING REPAIR REUSE MAINTENANCE |

Source: Stahel, Walter R. (1984) "The Product-Life Factor", in Orr, Susan Grinton (ed.), An Inquiry into the Nature of Sustainable Societies: The Role of the Private Sector, HARC, The Woodlands, TX.

The economically most efficient activity in product-life extension is reconditioning, also called rehabilitation (of buildings) and remanufacturing or rebuilding (of machines). It restores a system or product to its original working condition; technological upgrading also adapts an existing system or product to the present state of the art of technology.

The effectiveness of the spiral-loop system is greatly enhanced by a strategy to keep the loops as small as possible: do not repair something that is not broken, do not recondition something that can be repaired, do not recycle a product that can be reconditioned. This inertia can in turn be applied to components, products and the systems themselves. In short, do the least possible intervention to the smallest possible unit only.

In terms of corporate strategy, the spiral-loop system has a strongly reduced vulnerability against supply and demand fluctuations, as it is based on the existing stock of goods the volume of which is vastly superior to the sales volume of new goods at any one time, good or bad.

Despite all these advantages, it would be wrong to assume that the existing manufacturing industry, "the children of the Industrial Revolution", will automatically take advantage of these new opportunities in the optimization of the utilization of goods. The need for skilled labour in product-life optimization may in itself limit the commercial potential, as qualified labour is difficult to find even in countries with high unemployment.

Long-life goods, as a manufacturer's more obvious choice, not only put the narrow thinking based on economy of scale and limited to manufacturing parameters, and the power that goes with it, on its head, it also seriously questions the validity of the Point-of-Sale strategy (and its short-term or zero warranty) in favour of new approaches, such as the long-term operational leasing (rental) of system utilization. This solution gives the producer the financial benefit of long-life utilization in exchange for the legal burden of long-life product liability. Operational or utilization leasing already exists for a variety of goods such as aircrafts, kidney-stone pulverization machines, computers, professional clothing, art-works and plants.

These new solutions imply a tertialization of industry (see also *Figure 5*), or in terms of the Service Economy, they imply that the manufacturer also becomes a fleet owner and manager.

Product-life extension activities are children of the Service Economy. They provide mostly very skilled and satisfying employment and are best carried out in comparatively small workshops, scattered throughout the country wherever there are items in need of re-manufacturing and repair and customers who need them. The "resources" for these activities are individual goods of little homogeneity which do not lend themselves to the standardized and centralized processes used in production. Profitability will depend on limiting interventions as far as possible, rather that in producing as much as possible. Marketing and transport costs are limited to local markets; growth can best be achieved through networking and franchising of know-how.

Compared to the production-oriented fast-replacement system of the Industrial Revolution, the utilization-oriented product-life extension activities of the Service Economy are a substitution of transformation and service activities for extractive industries and base material production, and thus a replacement of large-scale, capital-intensive factories by smaller-scale, labour and skill intensive, independent, locally integrated work units.

Today's unemployed are often poor, unskilled and not mobile. Product-life extension activities are labour-intensive and highly mobile, and are best undertaken where cheap labour is available, e.g. where the people who were replaced by machines are to be found, or alternatively, near the user and the goods he uses. These enterprises can be located in any rural or urban area with high unemployment, making product-life extension a doubly attractive proposition for job-creation.

The cost of extending the utilization period of goods varies with the technical complexity and the size of the goods. A reconditioned tractor Diesel engine costs 60 percent of a new one. The recovery for re-use of the first module of a space rocket results in savings of several million US dollars per take-off. A modernized and technically upgraded second-hand aircraft, equipped with new quiet and fuel economic engines, offers a dollar-per-seat price of 40-50% compared to a new aircraft. This is due to the cost structure in modern manufacturing, where manufacturing accounts for perhaps 25% of the sales price, and labour costs represent a small part only of these manufacturing costs. But product-life extension also exists in a non-monetarized form: some repairs, and even the reconditioning of certain products, can be done most cheaply by the owner/user himself, if he has access to the required tools, machines and skills. Do-it-yourself of, for example, housing and vehicles may be the only reconditioning poor people can afford, and thus is part of the non-monetarized wealth creation.

Market entry to product-life extension activities is facilitated by low capital requirements per workplace and the price advantage of reconditioned products over new ones. In the case of long-life products, the initial production costs will be slightly higher than the price of current short-life products, due to the use of higher quality raw materials. This price difference should, however, not be overestimated, as materials account for a minute part of the price of most products (about 1% in the case of a high technology jet engine). Commercial innovation such as selling the utilization of a good through e.g. operational leasing (rental) instead of selling the good itself can more than compensate the possible cost difference in materials.

In an economy focussed on the optimization of the utilization of goods and systems, the prevention of break-downs becomes a major preoccupation within the cost optimization over life-time. Preventive, periodic and routine maintenance services are then no longer a luxury but a money saving approach. In some cities, for example, 50 percent or more of the water that is treated and put into the distribution network is "unaccounted for": there are cases, not only in Third World Countries, where reconditioning and proper maintenance could provide as much additional water as expensive new facilities.

> 'Maintenance itself must be considered a development priority', says Michael
> Cohen [38] 'The creation of assets that are allowed to deteriorate represents
> a serious undermining of the development process' (and a loss of wealth, of
> course).

Many engineers have already realized that "producing" a bridge or a sewer system is important if there are few bridges or sewers. In a market near saturation, as is the case in most industrialized countries for e.g. infrastructures or consumer durables, the husbandry of resources through maintenance activities, the improvement of existing systems towards easier and cheaper utilization and their adaptation to changing utilization needs becomes the "new frontier", the new challenge. However, there are very few universities world-wide that train qualified O & M (operation and maintenance) engineers to a level of education comparable to production-oriented engineers.

A hidden advantage in this respect is that the optimization of the utilization of goods will itself promote innovation and technological progress. The owner of a good with a long life has an interest in its technological upgrading, i.e. in the replacement of components where a real innovation has taken place in favour of cheaper or enhanced utilization. And as he only has to replace a component, not the whole product as in a throw-away society, the consumer has plenty of money to buy innovative components. This will lead to new progress-oriented Research and Development, driven by a substantial number of economic actors: an acceleration of technological progress in "portable" components (compatible with products of different origins) will replace the fashion-driven R&D into throwaway goods that can be observed today in many sectors including cars and white goods.

2.4.3. Utilization-Oriented Innovation - Some Examples. There can be no doubt that utilization optimization will foster innovation and new approaches to traditional assumptions.

Many overspecialized production technologies suffer from the premises of the Industrial Revolution:

- manufacturing processes cannot cope with the slight tolerances found in recycled raw materials or re-used goods (such as glass bottles in bottling plants, recycled paper in newspaper printing machines, used banknotes in ATMs or cashpoints),
- the order of component assembly in the production of goods may be a fundamental obstacle in the disassembly for maintenance.

In both cases, therefore, existing manufacturing know-how is of limited use for the optimization of system utilization. New areas of technology that have so far been largely neglected need to be developed. They range from the conception and design of goods in functional modules, to mobile non-destructive testing equipment to measure changes of quality over time, to process technology for the remanufacturing of components and goods, to operation control components that protect goods against destructive abuse in utilization, and to methods of optimizing the service and product-life extension activities.

The highest added value in utilization optimization can be obtained by service activities related to the improvement or maintenance of components that are part of complex systems, such as railways and telecommunication systems, or by reconditioning goods where utilization value and economic value are wide apart, such as depreciated computer systems or cars that have been in a flood or a hailstorm.

By contrast, the lowest value added will normally result from the recycling of raw materials such as scrap steel or glass, or from product-life extension activities using manufacturing technology, such as the retreading of tires using high pressure and high temperatures.

Commercial and financial innovation will be needed to support technical innovation in a utilization-oriented economy. This includes a variety of subjects, such as the non-destructive collection of discarded goods, the creation of free markets for second-hand goods and spare parts, the fiscal equality of manufacturing activities and utilization-oriented service activities, and the selling not of goods but of their utilization through e.g long-term leasing without transfer of ownership.

Interestingly, the pioneers of research into product-life optimization, such as the Motor Insurance Repair Center in Thatcham, UK, have been motivated by financial savings in car repairs, not product-life extension or technical innovation. Yet they have come up with highly innovative techniques, such as "skin replacement panels", that greatly reduce waste in component exchange and repair costs compared to traditional techniques. Whereas hitherto production components had been used in repairs, the UK car industry has produced repair components for many years.

As with components, the processes used in manufacturing may not be appropriate to reconditioning. Take the retreading of tyres: the standard process requires high pressures and high temperatures, is relatively expensive and cannot be repeated, as it partly destroys the product's qualities. A novel process that uses vacuum in combination with lower temperatures allows repeated retreading and big savings: a truck tyre can be retreaded for a third of the cost of a new one!

In many cases, lessons from utilization optimization can be applied to enhance goods in manufacturing: users of software are the biggest innovators for new computer programmes;

some kitchen ovens and burners of heating systems are self-cleaning, thus reducing maintenance costs. More complex systems may use a "self-curing maintenance" design, such as a friction reducing system that injects more lubricant when the temperature rises in the critical area (this is part of a little known scientific domain called tribology, an interdisciplinary subject integrating friction, wear, corrosion and lubrification, that has started in Vienna 20 years ago).

Perhaps the strongest influence on the utilization optimization of components and goods could come from a new technology that is of little importance in the manufacturing of goods: in-situ monitoring of quality changes over long periods of time, and critical information that is available before things go wrong. The earlier a maintenance intervention can be done, the less damage and the less costs will be incurred. Equipment that detects faults in vital components such as pumps, elevators or fans and transmits the precise fault information to a control and intervention center before the system breaks down, as well as methods of non-destructive quality testing for e.g. cable-car ropes, bridges or aircraft parts, where a fault will normally lead to a disaster (and thus also end the utilization period) corresponds to an obvious need in a utilization-oriented system operation. Instruments to measure and record defects, deformations and hidden deteriorations accurately before a component such as a rail is worn beyond repair are required to make selective reconditioning feasible and avoid the product-life extension of unsafe components. Similarly, the destructive interference of users in the operation of goods may have to be prevented in order to safeguard the interests of the owner of a long-life good, e.g. through the attachment of RPM-governors to the engines of cars for hire!

One of the main sources of costs in today's repair works are spare-parts which are sold at a price that is out of proportion to the price of the total product, due to handling and storage costs, and dealers' profit margins. The US aircraft industry has developed the activated diffusion bonding technique which can for example bond new edges to the worn-out surfaces of turbine airfoils and thus eliminate the need for spares.

Existing processes in reconditioning, such as sand-blasting, can be improved to eliminate unwanted side-effects. Lockheed has developed an advanced system that uses frozen pellets of carbon dioxide - dry ice - to blast and clean metal surfaces. After striking the target surface, the volatile pellets quickly vaporize, and the vapor harmlessly dissipates. The process is low-cost, can clean complex machinery without the disassembly needed for sand-blasting, and can be used on anything from ships to electronic assemblies.

Utilization optimization activities are typical children of the Service Economy with regard to their orientation towards conditions of use rather than production. Their efficiency depends on factors such as the mobility of components. Immobile systems such as sewers or railway tracks are ideal candidates for mobile reconditioning units that can perform "in situ". Mobile goods such as ships, cars and aircrafts with easily exchangeable components are ideally suited to decentralized workshops which can be located according to prevailing needs, conditions and demand. Buildings and other immobile systems with exchangeable components require both on-site intervention and workshop activities. However, utilization optimization does not necessarily mean product-life extension. Components that become obsolescent by jumps in technology will best be recycled to recover the base materials, rather than reconditioned. Systems with a prototype character may not have a technical or production maturity that justifies an extensive utilization period, and goods damaged in fires or accidents may be in a state beyond repair.

At the other extreme, product-life extension activities can have a vital advantage in speed as compared to manufacturing. Who remembers today that all U.S. ships sunk by Japanese aircrafts at Pearl Harbor except for two, were refloated, overhauled and recommissioned within a short period of time? The building of new ships would have taken a multiple of the time and required a shipyard capacity that just was not there. Similarly, an old ship on a Swedish lake has been several times refloated and rebuilt on site over the last fifty years, because the transport (of a new ship) from the next shipyard to the lake is economically and with regard to the time involved not feasible.

However, an important contribution towards utilization optimization can be made by designing inter-compatible systems with distinct functional modules, separating clearly structural elements (the car chassis) from skin elements (the bodywork), wear and tear components (the engine) and control components (electronics). Standardization would further allow to use components on different goods, such as for example the standardized flight deck used on the new Boeing 757, 767-200 and 767-200ER airliners. Component standardization in design results not only in reduced complexity and cost of technical maintenance, but also in important savings in crew training and an increased flexibility in crew operation!

Thus, utilization optimization with the option to technically upgrade existing systems through the inclusion of new technology components as soon as they become available, would greatly enhance technical, commercial and economic innovation.

2.4.4. <u>Waste, Obsolescence And Fashion</u>. Waste in is many cases not a technical, but a mentality related phenomenon: There is only our unwillingness or inability to design goods for a utilization over long periods of time, through e.g. self-replenishing loops (see *Figure 9*), and to develop the necessary technologies and tools, or to implement existing ideas and technologies.

Obsolescence is the key issue to understand the complex relationship between the development of technologies and their economic applications. A tool or a production process can be obsolescent, even if it is still capable of performing its original function, but at costs which have become "uneconomical" in comparison with new tools or processes. It is therefore discarded even if it is not yet worn out.

A clear judgment on obsolescence, present and future, is therefore essential to evaluate the optimum life-cycle of products and processes, and it implies - once again - the complementary contribution of the engineer and of the economist (this latter considering not only the monetarized outcomes, but also the non-monetarized ones). The management of obsolescence is also linked to the problem of depreciation, where technical wear and tear considerations are often overruled by fiscal and financial thinking.

Four factors limit the optimization of the utilization period (and thus the product-life) of goods in different ways:
- technical disincentives, such as the non-availability of spares,
- economic disincentives, such as short depreciation periods,
- psychological obstacles within ourselves, such as fashion,
- scarcity through poverty.

Obsolescence through technical disincentives comes in many forms and for many reasons. At the design stage, many free options for ease of maintenance, such as functional modular distinction and out-of-sequence dismantling, are mostly ignored. This leads to the "Pars-pro-toto"-syndrome, where sealed-unit products such as hairdryers or radios would have to be destroyed in order to change even a minor component, and hence are thrown away. The same syndrome can occur in complex systems, such as satellites, when for instance the 50 cent switch to unfold the solar panels malfunctions, and a satellite worth 50 million U.S. dollars becomes a total loss.

This can be overcome by standardization and componentized design, as is the case with products by Motorola and JI Case, and by built-in repairability. Another common version of the pars-pro-toto-syndrome is the withdrawal of a key spare part by the manufacturer when introducing a new product, such as rubber seals for machines, or paper bags for vacuum cleaners. That leaves the consumer with the choice of either glueing his own bags from filter paper, or replacing the (perfectly working) vacuum cleaner.

Of course, there is also the technical obsolescence through jumps in technology. In most cases, this involves key components within a system, such as the jump from copper to glassfiber cables, or to telecom via satellite, and will lead to a gradual substitution of the new for the old technology. When jumps in technology occur in isolated products, such as the appearance of the electronic typewriter, parallel markets will normally develop: word processors will replace electric typewriters in the office, but manual and electric typewriters will continue to be used for a long time in small companies and at home.

Yet another type of technical obsolescence depends on the non-combination of ownership, utilization and technical expertise in one person or company. In the case of capital goods, such as production tools or railway equipment, this combination enables an extension of the utilization period, often in the owner's own workshops, as long as there is an economic incentive to keep the existing equipment. In the case of consumer goods, such as cars or refrigerators, the user is not a technical expert, and the utilization period of a product is normally terminated when nobody can be found to repair it! Commercial and technical creativity is needed to bridge this gap if utilization optimization is to take off for consumer goods.

Obsolescence through economic disincentives is possible through "economic confiscation", or profit and overhead structures, or taxation rules on depreciation, or the choice of materials in manufacturing. Replacement part prices of mass produced goods are prohibitive compared to the price of the over-all product: a car with a sticker price of $6,000 will cost about $26,000 in non-assembled spares. This price policy for spare parts, combined with the (fiscal) notion of residual value based on the original sales price minus annual depreciation sums (according to the economic rules of the Industrial Revolution) means that, when an old but perfectly well maintained car is involved in an accident, the insurance company can (in most countries) take possession of the vehicle against payment of a token sum (residual value) which bears no relation to the damages (repair costs) nor the *utilization* value of the old car. This trend is even strengthened by the "consumer friendly" actions of some governments, imposing a freeze on new car prices to fight inflation but without simultaneously regulating repair service costs. The result is often a criminal black market for selective spares supplied by car thieves.

Profit and overhead structures in many companies are designed to promote sales of new products rather than utilization optimization. A car dealer, for example, gets a mark-up of about 22% on a new car sale. It would be difficult for him to get the same "return-on-effort" on repairs or a rebuilt car. So why should he bother? The client will have to buy a new car, or refrigerator, or TV set.

Reduced depreciation periods are a popular method of increasing consumption and thus "economic growth", and result in many cases in an average utilization period far below even the design-life of goods. Since depreciation is often a state subsidy to business, the extended use of fully depreciated goods becomes an economic penalty for a profit-oriented company. Bottom line pressures will therefore push consumption, except if the connection between the time you use an equipment and the time you write it off can be broken.

The choice of materials in manufacturing is primarily influenced by commodity prices or considerations of speed in manufacturing, as product warranty periods are far below the effective utilization period. However, in order to optimize the utilization of components, the choice criteria of raw materials should also include topics such as relative failure modes of wear versus fatigue, or the maintenance costs of components made from different materials. For instance, the use of thin steel sheet and micro-coatings of paint in cars should also take into consideration the impact of impurities in recycled steel sheet, or of air pollution, on corrosion!

Psychological obstacles within ourselves are perhaps the most difficult ones to overcome. In consumer goods, the technology of a product often matters less to potential customers than its look and feel. Personal values have changed since the time of scarcity: properly maintained or repaired goods are no longer a sign of good husbandry, but of poverty and second-class status, with the exception of antiques. "I won't have you mending stockings in this house: Now throw them out!" says Willy in "Death of a Salesman" already in 1949.

Commonly, no distinction in values is made between "old" and "properly maintained" products, even by professionals. "It is worrying that, of the new work being commissioned, over a third is for rehabilitation of existing buildings. Rehab may be popular with the public, but most architects regard it as frustrating", said the RIBA-President (Royal Institute of British Architects) a few years ago.

Product-life extension activities require skilled manual work. But manual work and shopfloor have become dirty words, and there is a stigma on the young person who "has to take a manual job". Even in times of high unemployment good engineers are hard to find. The satisfaction of skilled manual work has become a non-subject. Yet utilization optimization depends on trained skilled labour. How can we convey the message of "old is resourceful"? In the industrialized economy where wealth is expressed in consumption, it will need a great deal of patience and education to de-monetarize beauty and distinction, and to persuade people that a sustainable nation that promotes utilization optimization as an economic policy is not a poor nation.

Fashion can, of course, be redefined in terms of components. This would mean keeping your class symbols technologically up to date, such as installing turbo-blowers or May fireball cylinder heads in your used car, rather than buying a new car equipped with, maybe, one of these innovations. The notion of caring can be transmitted through e.g. technical museums with old machinery in working order, the teaching of industrial archeology in schools, or the creation of playful self-help training in "industrial boy-scouts".

Obsolescence is perceived very differently by the "Fourth World": the 30 million Americans and 30 million Europeans who account for about 16% of total population and who are officially classified as poor. Minority groups are heavily overrepresented in this part of the population that still lives a time of scarcity-through-poverty that the consumer society has left far behind: A study published in France at the end of the "Golden Quarter Century", the time of unpreceeded economic growth after World War Two, revealed that 51% of the most inadequate apartments were occupied by people over 60 years of age, that it was the people from the lowest income brackets that lived in substandard conditions, and that the share of the net rent in total income is the highest for the lowest income group.

For these people living in the "Fourth World", cheapest product-life extension is a bare necessity, and quality standards and the notion of technical obsolescence or fashion is quite irrelevant. Quality of life standards based on production criteria rather than utilization value, such as "every apartment must have a tiled bathroom", or "heavily corroded cars are not allowed on the street", can effectively cut these people off from the only goods they can afford to meet their basic needs, such as shelter and transport, or force them to use unsafe equipment or illegal methods to get access to. Cheaper alternatives to new goods, such as product-life extension, will thus often extend existing markets, rather than limit production. For social insurance schemes, product-life extension can offer the opportunity to help a larger number of people with the same amount of money, e.g. by supplying handicapped people with rebuilt automobiles that have a high utilization value but a low price.

2.4.5. Coping With Time Duration And Uncertainty. The notion of value-over-time is one of the keys to understanding the Service Economy. The following *Figure 11* explains the fundamental difference between the use-value in an industrial society, and the utilization value in the service economy, using the example of a motorcar.

The real costs of utilization value have to take into account all costs involved. The following *Figure 12* shows the life-cycle costing, again for a motorcar, considering monetary costs only. Of course, to be even more precise, the costs of accidents, pollution, road wear, ill-health and so on should also be taken into consideration, as well as their variations over the lifetime of a stock of products or services.

For an automobile used over a period of 10 years, the costs incurred as a consequence of using the product during its lifetime are presented in *Figure 12*:

The utilization value approach of the Service Economy clashes most violently with the production value approach of the Industrial Revolution in the case of goods with a zero product-life. These include products such as nuclear power stations in the U.S. and Austria that were built but never started production, agricultural produce that is destroyed to maintain price levels, military equipment and spare parts that are scrapped due to overproduction, clearing of stocks or technological substitution. Another typical example of (built-in) zero product-life, linked to the shortcomings of centralized production, is publicity material that is distributed according to the "watercan" principle: most of it ends unread in waste paper baskets. However, it is economically "efficient" thanks to special postal rates which penalize a more sophisticated and less wasteful approach to information.

This last example illustrates the notion of "free waste" in production economics, as the community as a whole has to pick up the resulting exaggerated waste disposal costs. In many

Figure 11. Use-Value (in an industrial society) v. Utilization Value (in the post-industrial society): The example of an automobile.

| USE VALUE | = | • The car is *bought* to be *used* for a specific destination or purpose (for transportation, for holidays, for commuting, etc.)
• It may also be *bought* for personal satisfaction or other reasons (psychological, etc.) |

*BUT,*    Whatever the utility of the car, all such motivations to buy are elements which are resumed in the fact that a price is considered acceptable or not.

*SO,*    The *use value*, in traditional economic terms, *is finally included* and absorbed *in the* mechanism which determines the *exchange (added) value.*

The | UTILIZATION VALUE | is the utility gained from a stock of products or services for the *period or duration of their life time* whatever their destination, and *regardless of the fact that they are paid or not.*

Examples:
- An Automobile with which one can drive 200,000 miles in its lifetime has *twice the utilization value* of a car lasting 100,000 miles.
- A cotton bed-sheet which lasts through 50 washings, has *50 times more utilization value* than a disposable bed-sheet which is thrown away after one period of use. In fact, its value is even higher because an old cotton sheet has still a long life as a house-cloth, whereas a disposable, plastic impregnated cloth is much less suitable for secondary utilization.
- The housewife's domestic labour has a *utilization value* even if it is not paid for.
- The water of a polluted lake *has negative utilization value* for drinking or swimming.
- Many ancient roads and houses have an obvious utilization value even if they are completely amortized.
- Works of arts and literature have great cultural and educational utilization value in themselves (beside the value of the paper or other supports to transmit their message) even when the author no longer receives royalties.
- A destroyed city has *no utilization value,* even if by the very fact of being destroyed (by any natural or man-made catastrophe) it offers the possibility of producing – via reconstruction, anti-pollution equipment, etc. – a lot of "value added".

| THE UTILIZATION VALUE IS THE MEASURE OF REAL WEALTH AND WELFARE |

Source: Giarini, Orio (ed.) (1980) Dialogue on Wealth and Welfare, Pergamon Press, Oxford.

Figure 12. The real costs of utilization value (taking into consideration monetary costs only)

---

THEY ARE *ALL COSTS** INCURRED AS A CONSEQUENCE OF USING A STOCK OF PRODUCTS OR SERVICES *DURING THEIR LIFE-TIME*

For an automobile used during 10 year, they would be:

| | |
|---|---|
| Period (1) of preparation of the "stock of services" represented by a product | Costs of production |
| | Costs of use  – taxes paid for road infrastructure, etc. ... – gasoline, oil, etc. |
| Period (2) of actual utilization (utilization value) | Maintenance costs, including garage |
| | Repair costs and insurance |
| Period (3) of recycling the totally deteriorated – unusable – "stock of services" | Costs of disposal and recycling |

*Whereas*, the shorter the utilization period (2), *the greater* the global costs of preparation (1) to face accelerated substitution, and *the greater* the recycling and disposal costs (2) as a result of accelerated waste.

*In a period of no environmental limitations and of increasing returns of technology, the gains in production costs (1) can more than compensate the loss of utilization value of period (2) and the additional costs of period (3). It is a period of net real value increase due to the industrial revolution.*

*In a period of environmental limitations and of diminishing returns of technology gains in production costs (1) are not sufficient to prevent a net loss of real (utilization) value.*

---

\* Of course, to be even more precise, also the costs of accidents, pollution, road wear, health effect, etcetera, should be taken into consideration, and their variation with the lifetime of a stock of products, or services.

Source: Giarini, Orio (ed.) (1980) Dialogue on Wealth and Welfare, Pergamon Press, Oxford.

cases, short product-life also means a loss of wealth in terms of reduced national heritage (historic buildings, art-works) and increased environmental costs.

The cost of the non-durability of goods due to the choice of cheap materials in manufacturing can be estimated. A study commissioned by U.S. Congress in 1977 has estimated the annual losses caused by corrosion in industrialized countries to be equivalent to 4.2 percent of GNP! A more recent study on the cost of structural failures through fractures has come to a similar order of magnitude for the economic loss incurred.

Market saturation and its twin brother purchase power are factors that strongly influence the utilization period (or "economic durability" in OECD terms): economic growth can only be achieved by higher production volumes. In saturated markets, this can only be done by shortening the utilization period of products, thus speeding up replacement. This phenomenon, often called affluent society or conspicuous consumption, is really planned waste production. *Figure 13* shows the levels of saturation for some typical consumer durables in France in 1985, according to social classes and income levels (including the non-active part of the population that largely forms the "Fourth World").

Nevertheless, even in saturated markets for average clients, commercial innovation based on "selective reconditioning" - price before beauty - can be successful. One example for many is "Rent-A-Wreck", a U.S. company that hires out cars that are around ten years old and look it. They are mechanically sound and clean, though they may sport a dent or two. Daily charges in 1981 were $15 to 21, while Avis shiny, new models cost up to $64 a day. In 1982, Rent-A-Wreck sold for the first time old cars that had became uneconomical to operate, and run into a major tax problem. The cars fetched prices that were higher than what the company had paid for ten years earlier (whereas depreciation is the main cost factor in new car rental). While depreciation (equal consumption) is tax deductible, capital gain (in this case equal husbandry) is heavily taxed: the logic of the Industrial Revolution is still with us!

The Service Economy might help us to reconsider this fundamental choice: either we become "Parisian" in a fast moving, fashion-driven environment where products have to be new and smart (corresponding to Erich Fromm's "to have"), or we strive towards Erich Fromm's "to be" with products that are intelligent, lasting and adaptable to changes over time.

Flexibility and adaptability can be achieved through design, such as the plug-in compatibility of components in many electronic goods. Adaptability can also come through innovative product-life extension approaches, such as the transformation of a VLCC-tanker into a life-stock carrier; or the development of new technologies, such as plastic resin injections into components made out of wood or concrete in order to improve their original performance (strength, impermeability); or through product-innovation based on high quality waste as raw material, such as cutting sandals from used tyres, or cutting decommissioned railroad ties (sleepers) into oak wood panelling.

Periodic maintenance is one way to control system-inherent uncertainty: The U.S. Navy uses SLEP (Service Life Extension Program), a complete overhaul and upgrading procedure lasting 2 years, to extend the life of its major vessels, including nuclear-powered aircraft carriers, by 10 to 15 years. However, it is crucial to realize that the maintenance of a complex system has to be equally or even more sophisticated than its manufacturing! The NASA

62

Figure 13. Penetration rates in the market for durable household goods, France, 1985.

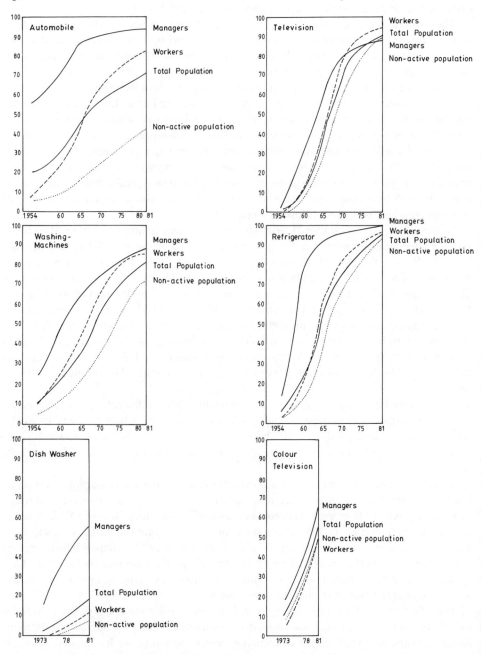

Source: Consommation no 1 (1985) Enquetes de conjoncture aupres des menages, Paris.

space-shuttle programme, which had finally put to rest the erroneous notion that reconditioning activities combined with reusable goods are associated with second-class technology or less-than-best solutions, has shown that such approaches will provide fresh technological and R&D impetus! Tragically, the need for highest skills and judgement in maintenance and "routine" rebuilding operations has been greatly underestimated, leading to many maintenance problems and finally probably to the explosion of "Challenger".

Another approach of coping with uncertainty over long utilization periods is the "cascading" of goods and materials. Cascading combined with periodic reconditioning is common with most fleet managers including railway companies: the original performance of, for example, a locomotive is maintained over a very long period of time.The theoretically increasing risk of a break-down, and its consequences for the railway system, are managed by gradually reducing the intensity of utilization for the locomotive over time, in tasks of decreasing importance of system operation: from express trains to goods trains to standby duty and finally to service on the shunting yard.

The same approach could considerable increase the utilization value of hybrid materials, such as oil or timber, that can be used for different applications at different levels of performance: the same tree could consecutively be used as structural timber, planks, chip- or fibreboard, and fuel. Alternatively, it could be transformed into paper, recycled paper (even multiple cycles), cardboard, home insulation panels and fuel.These options are normally wasted, however, in order either to facilitate the transport to the site of production (wood chips), for lack of caring and ideas (burning old timber in house demolition), or because of the need for physical survival (cooking in poor countries).

All these considerations put once more in evidence the fact that the Service Economy is about a new way to consider the problem of wealth production. They emphasize the shift in priority from producing "hard ware" to the new priority of optimizing the functioning (or operation) of systems. And the "performance" of a system has to be measured by reference to the optimum product-life of goods (products and services).In this process, an economic dream has to be at least partially abandoned: the "certainty" provided by the method of measuring the value of goods only at their "point-of-sale". Measuring the value of systems in a time duration, which is influenced by many factors, implies the adoption of methods which include and accept "uncertainty". But because, after all, uncertainty is an unavoidable part of real life, it is more rational as well as more realistic to admit this and to try to cope with it, rather than strive for theoretical schemes which, in search of certainty, end up by looking less and less rational.

## 2.5. THE SOCIAL STRATEGY IN THE SERVICE ECONOMY.

2.5.1. Employment And Productive Occupation. If we go back to the Domesday Book, written in 1086 in England, we find that "service" was not a job: it was a stage in people's lives. A third of all English households seem to have contained servants, who were mostly younger than 25, the average age of marriage. These servants, from the age of ten onwards, might thus have spent almost half their lives working for little more than their keep, in someone else's family, until they got married and set up a household of their own [39].

Thus, before the industrial age, everyone was bound to those above them by ties of service, often unpaid, and to their peers by ties of community and mutual support.

> The household was a place of production and work. Its work was linked into the work of the local village community. People provided the necessities of life for themselves and their families. Money, therefore, played a smaller part in their lives than it does in ours. Most of the work was unpaid. [40]

The economists of the Industrial Revolution then correctly (for their time) realized that not all labour was productive in terms of developing the wealth of nations. Accordingly, they distinguished between productive and unproductive labour. "Labour" was defined to produce "three kinds of utilities: utilities fixed and embodied in outward objects; utilities fixed and embodied in human beings (e.g education); utilities not fixed or embodied in any object, e.g a pleasure given, a pain averted" [41]. Only the first was accepted as productive labour, essentially linked to the idea that wealth must be susceptible of accumulation: therefore material wealth that can be sold (i.e monetarized) and that is embodied in material objects.

> The skill of an artisan is accounted wealth, only as being the means of acquiring wealth in a material sense... . A country would hardly be said to be richer, however precious a possession it might have in the genius, the virtues, or the accomplishments of its inhabitants; unless indeed these were looked upon as marketable articles, by which it could attract the material wealth of other countries. [41]

This shows how far economics is de facto identified with the study of the industrialization/ manufacturing process.

All other labour, however useful, was classed as unproductive!

> By unproductive labour will be understood labour which does not terminate in the creation of material wealth, does not render the community, and the world at large, richer in material products. [41]

And from this it followed that the more material wealth labour produces, the more valuable it is: specialization became a way to higher material wealth, despite the obvious dangers that were highlighted as early as 1835 by De Tocqueville in "Liberalism":

> When a workman is increasingly and exclusively engaged in the fabrication of one thing, he ultimately does his work with singular dexterity; but at the same time he loses the general faculty of applying his mind to the direction of the work. He every day becomes more adroit and less industrious; so that it may be said of him that in proportion as the workman improves the man is degraded.

While this degradation was not a major problem in the beginning of the Industrial Revolution, its effects are today hitting many of the highly paid specialists working in the "engines" of the Industrial Revolution, such as the coal and steel industries, as shown in the employment figures of the energy industry in the United Kingdom (*Figure 14*).

Figure 14. UK energy employment 1960-85.

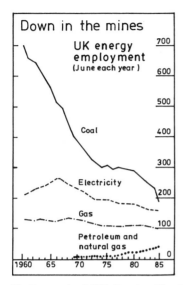

Source: The Economist (1985), London, Nov 9.


And in order to make specialization worthwhile, labour had to be concentrated, i.e. the industrial town was born. In 1800, three quarters of all English people lived in villages of between 50 and 500, surrounded by green fields. Today, a third of the British population lives in one of the country's seven great urban sprawls which between them cover less than 3% of the land area.

But paid employment in industrialized society has become more than simply a source of income for many people. Monetarized occupation for the accumulation of material wealth gives us a sense of identity, a social role, a new "family", an opportunity to meet people, ultimately the sense in life. This also means that the "unproductive labour" of surgeons and teachers is not accounted in terms of their actual results to develop health or culture: their economic utility for the Industrial Revolution is quantified by their prescriptions for medicine or the consumption of pencils and of learning tools (the objects representing the embodiment of wealth).

However, enterprises have not only to create the objects of wealth, but also reduce the costs in doing so. *Figure 15* shows that rationalization or mechanization is the obvious alternative for producing accumulated material wealth if labour gets more "expensive" or less attractive (monetary and non-monetary costs) than machines. Skills *in themselves* have no value.

The traditional solution for the labour that was substituted by machines has been mobility, in order to find a buyer of one's specialization somewhere else. But the smaller the specific labour market gets, and the smarter the machines become, the less valid the notion of labour mobility is, resulting in resignation and concentrated pockets of (urban) unemployment.

Figure 15. The enterprise as the focus point.

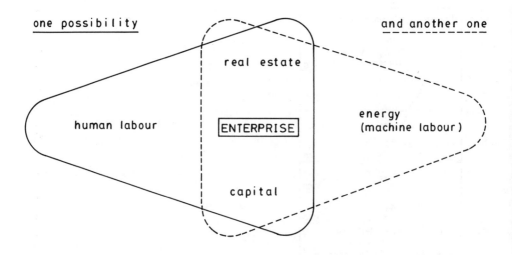

Source: Perutz, Peter and Stahel, Walter R. (1980) Arbeitslosigkeit - Beschaftigung - Beruf, Neue Berufe und Innovation, Beitrage des Instituts fur Zukunftsforschung no 11, Minerva Publikationen, Munchen.

Karl Popper once mentioned that he did not have much of an opinion of economics in general because the essence of every science and discipline is to identify and tackle priorities first. He thinks that the key priority for economics is the employment problem, but current economics does not seem to propose adequate solutions to this problem. In addition there is the inadequacy of economic theory in proposing an hypothesis to solve unemployment in a better way.

An impolite economist of the Industrial Revolution might have replied to Sir Karl that he was shooting from an offside position, being part of unproductive labour himself. Nevertheless, even if he might have felt that there was some truth in Sir Karl Popper's words, economic theory tells him that "material" wealth has to be produced, not "unproductive" jobs!

Both opinions are correct in their context. The key feature of the Industrial Revolution has been to produce tools and products in a monetarized environment for customers lacking those products. The more efficient this process was, the more people could buy the needed goods, and the more people were needed to produce them. Industry thus absorbed a great quantity of labour coming from the agricultural sector, and started to shed some labour to the tertiary sector that was growing for reasons of the complexification of the productive system.

However, once the markets for many goods started to be conditioned by factors closely linked to the environment and the functioning of services, the Industrial Revolution had outperformed itself: material wealth "production", although essential, is no longer the long term priority in quantitative terms to stimulate the wealth of nations. It has become clear that "unproductive" labour is probably the key to redefining productive activity in the new general economic conditions.

At present, the service sectors and its "unproductive" labour are already employing more than 50% of the active population of industrialized countries, and increasing returns of technology have become apparent in services that are likely to produce an accelerated growth in the productivity of service functions. In addition, non-monetarized aspects of labour appear to contribute in an essential way to the production of wealth.

To come back to Sir Karl Popper, provided we get richer in material wealth through efficient production, why have this obsession about employment?

Labour is not a commodity,

says the constitution of the International Labour Office (ILO). Even worse, manpower is the most perishable of all resources, as unused skills are easily lost or outdated by new techniques, and the mental motivation needed for work, once lost, may never fully be recovered. Whereas most resources such as oil and ores do not deteriorate when left another fifty years in their natural state, we cannot waste labour and deprive people (including women, handicapped and old people who want to contribute) of meaningful work for long periods of time!

Services focused on system optimization and on maintaining the wealth we have, such as labour and skills - even if "unproductive" or non-monetarized - have today become a priority over the production optimization that characterized the Industrial Revolution.

In a Service Economy, the value of the non-remunerated activity of the boy-scout who picks up discarded bottles in order to preserve the environment, and takes the bottles to a shop to have them refilled, is as productive as the monetarized activity of the bottles' manufacturer.

Are jobs in the Service Economy, non-monetarized or remunerated, *lacking sex appeal*?

The underlying principle of many service jobs is "caring" and "sharing", which are soft words relating to activities without "visible" results: once a sick person has recovered, the sickness and the healing process (or service) are no longer visible.

Caring also implies an awareness and motivation *over time*: servicing and repairing the same car regularly, or cooking the family food every day, is a periodic work that leaves no traces (i.e. is invisible) and is only too often taken for granted. The fact that the car keeps running is credited to the engineer who designed it, at least in industrialized countries, rather than to the anonymous mechanic in a garage who services it carefully. In the long run, this tends to influence negatively the food quality as well as the quality of the car service, and thus its operation.

In contrast, people involved in manufacturing the "bigger-better-faster" new products are involved in a linear process, of which the assembly line is the logical expression. The end product is new, fashionable and allows every worker to identify himself with this "progress" from raw material to finished goods. How long the product is going to last, or how big the satisfaction of the user will be, is unknown and of less importance in this linear world.

Some researchers qualify the periodical (or cyclical) process as female, and the linear process as male work, again referring to the Industrial Revolution that separated the men from their home and families and their predominantly caring philosophy. One could of course also qualify the two activities as predominantly product-oriented in the case of the linear production, and as predominantly activity-oriented in the case of the cyclical services. This then implies that in a Service Economy, the client (and that is all of us) has to learn primarily to appreciate and praise the *work* done, rather than to admire the *product* at the point-of-sale! Or to put it still differently: services need people skills, large scale manufacturing needs technological capabilities.

### 2.5.2. The New Risk Takers In Work : Women, The Younger And The Elder.

Even at the height of the Industrial Revolution, only a minority of the total population was "making a living in productive labour", or having a full-time waged job, i.e. passing through the inner tube of the "cylinder of success" (see *Figure 16*). Most other people, however, are not lazy lay-abouts, but hard working in the non-monetarized sector in a productive and useful way: housewives, schoolchildren, mountain farmers, nuns. Others do not have the opportunity of joining the inner tube of success, due to physical or mental handicaps, often acquired while working for a living or fighting for their country, i.e. through no fault of their own. Still others are expelled from the tube because of age, even if valid physically and mentally, or because of other discriminations.

In a Service Economy which extends the notion of productive value both to service and to non-monetarized activities, and the notion of wealth to the total assets of the community rather than its industrial monetarized activity only, social acceptance and recognition for the people involved in these "unproductive" activities should become the norm. The present discussion about women working at home, for example, can be solved by monetarizing their activity, or by giving monetarized and non-monetarized work the same value. The economic theory of the Service Economy will help to give more social recognition to useful non-monetarized activities.

A Service Economy focussing on an increase in total assets through the optimization of the utilization period of goods and the optimization of systems operation will depend on the supply of fast, cheap, reliable and flexible services. This may sound trivial, but today's lack of these performances is at the roots of the present widespread discontent of customers with a variety of services such as repairs, health, maintenance and mail delivery in remote areas: At the beginning of this century, it was not uncommon in big towns to have up to twelve mail deliveries per day, compared to one today. Similarly, the provision of public transport to rural populations that have no cars has continually declined over the last 40 years. In many of these cases, the missing service productivity is due to the exclusive notion of industrial "productive" employment, making full time jobs, specialization and exclusive work for one employer a must for any employee aged over 40 years of age in order to qualify for maximum social security and retirement with an old age pension at the "legal" age.

The new risk takers in work are already exploring a new strategy to increase their personal wealth: seeking part-time jobs for several employers or self-employment, and combining state social security (which depends after all on the total real wealth produced by a community) with the possibility of a longer period of active and enriching occupation. The choice for flexible schedules and part-time jobs should not be confused with an imposed general reduction of full-time employment or of weekly working hours; flexible organization is a necessity for economic success in many service activities!

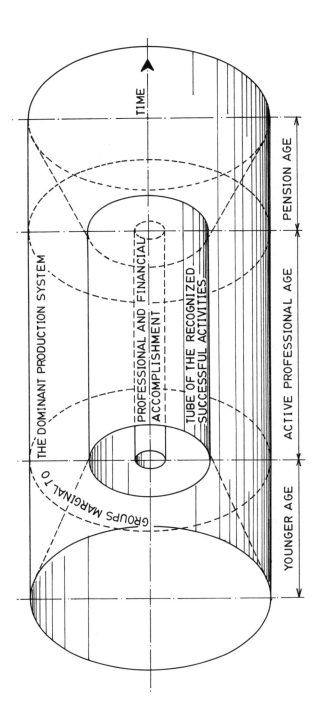

THE DOMINANT PRODUCTION SYSTEM

TIME

GROUPS MARGINAL TO

PROFESSIONAL AND FINANCIAL ACCOMPLISHMENT

TUBE OF THE RECOGNIZED SUCCESSFUL ACTIVITIES

YOUNGER AGE

ACTIVE PROFESSIONAL AGE

PENSION AGE

Figure 16. The life-tube, with its inner cylinder of success.

Source: Perutz, Peter and Stahel, Walter R. (1980) Arbeitslosigkeit - Beschäftigung - Beruf, Minerva Publikationen, München.

The British Post Office, in order to increase the efficiency of its operation, has introduced part-time work for its sorting and delivery services. The vast majority of new part-timers have been women. Not many men see a job sorting letters for four or five hours in the evening as "real" work, nor do they yet see the advantages of this type of work for complementing non-monetarized activities such as child rearing.

Part-time jobs in the Industrial Revolution were linked to an insufficient protection of the workers and to work instability, and are disliked by trade unions for these reasons. However, the protection of consumers as well as of workers is normally guaranteed today (even if it can be still be improved!) by government law, thanks partly to the efficiency of union action in the past. Yet the stability of employment required for the blue-collar worker will be giving way to the flexibility of the "service-collar" individual. This is one of the basic issues confronting the survival of the labour unions in the future.

The persistently high unemployment since the late 60's in industrialized countries, the widening gap between high and low earners, i.e in Britain and West Germany, rising illiteracy, mass redundancies in big corporations such as the car industry, have all led to an increase in the Fourth World, i.e. poverty within the industrialized countries, that includes about 15% of the total population, since the 70's.

The situation in the Less Developed Countries is not better. The Third World is plagued by massive unemployment, balance of payment problems and budget deficits, stunted economic growth and high inflation. According to a report by the International Labour Office, legions of misfits arc now growing up in developing countries: over 200 million 12 to 17 year old out of school, of which 137 million are in Asia, 45 million in Africa and 19 million in Latin America. These teenagers have had either no schooling whatsoever, or have dropped out of school before finishing the minimum educational level, to become functionally illiterate persons. The majority of this vast army of disadvantaged youth live in rural and poor urban areas. Girls are more severely affected by the educational and training handicap than boys.

The clear lessons we have to draw from these developments are:
- big corporations in manufacturing and services will no longer provide the jobs for most of the young people leaving school in the future. These corporations will compete in a global market dominated by the highly efficient production of "commodity" or staple goods, such as motorcars or international airline services, where economy of scale continues to be the key factor;
- small companies and self-employed people, in a local and innovative market place, will grow in both manufacturing and service activities where adaptation to local conditions or caring for specific needs are dominant, as well as in small volume world markets for high-tech products;
- the individual, as opposed to the enterprise in the industrial age, will move into the center of attention (see *Figure 17*). Many individuals will actively choose their work between the corporate world of big business with its own "demonstrative or conspicuous wealth", and the small local enterprise where the place or work is the center of pride and credibility, and the people are its primary assets.

The global Service Economy is the playing field of this new work strategy.

Figure 17. The individual as the focus point.

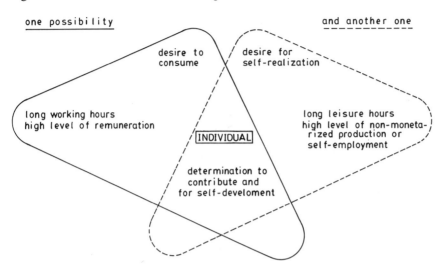

Source: Perutz, Peter and Stahel, Walter R. (1980) Arbeitslosigkeit - Beschaftigung - Beruf, Minerva Publikationen, Munchen.

In terms of social classes and productive activities, part-time jobs are vital to reintegrate those pushed into a marginal position by the Industrial Revolution: the younger, the older, and women.

Part-time employment leaves open the option of continuous education which is vital to employment flexibility as highlighted by De Tocqueville in 1835. Young people in higher education systems should similarly have a practical activity in their studies, adding higher education to increasing job experience in a part-time world.

For women, part-time activities are an opportunity to combine their traditional role in the home with education and employment. People who have reached the age of retirement have been considered a burden by the Industrial Revolution, while the Service Economy considers them an asset, a treasure of wealth and of productive experience. Part-time jobs, adapted to the needs of the elderly, might become a key issue to mobilize this hidden wealth.

The new risk takers in the service economy have to overcome a double handicap: many of the young and women have no previous work experience, and they first have to create themselves the infrastructure (educational and social) appropriate to their activities.

New forms of employment and work organization are appearing (*Figures 18A, 18B and 18C*) :

- In the UK, the number of co-operatives registered has gone up from about 500 in 1980 to 1,000 in 1985;
- Management buy-outs of companies become everyday news;
- In the UK, the number of people who are self-employed increased by nearly a third between 1979 and 1984, while the number of people employed by someone else

72

## Figure 18: Changing job patterns in Great-Britain.

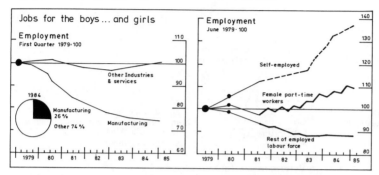

## Britain's changing jobs

|  | thousands | | | |
|---|---|---|---|---|
|  | June, 1978 | March, 1985 | Absolute change | % change |
| Agriculture, forestry & fishing | 378 | 321 | − 57 | − 15.1 |
| Energy & water | 708 | 608 | − 100 | − 14.1 |
| Other mineral & ore extraction | 1.156 | 780 | − 376 | − 32.5 |
| Metal goods, engineering & vehicles | 3.314 | 2.553 | − 761 | − 23.0 |
| Other manufacturing industries | 2.711 | 2.034 | − 677 | − 25.0 |
| Construction | 1.177 | 942 | − 235 | − 20.0 |
| Distribution, hotels, catering, repairs | 3.951 | 4.239 | + 288 | + 7.3 |
| Transport & communication | 1.428 | 1.263 | − 165 | − 11.6 |
| Banking, finance, insurance | 1.496 | 1.926 | + 430 | + 28.7 |
| Other services | 5.804 | 6.009 | + 205 | + 3.5 |
| Self-employed | 1.843 | 2.527 | + 684 | + 37.1 |
| All | 23.966 | 23.202 | − 764 | − 3.2 |

Source: Department of Employment

THE ECONOMIST OCTOBER 5, 1985

dropped by 8%. One in ten of all those at work is now self-employed, the highest proportion since 1921. And 40% of the self-employed had, in 1983, already become employers themselves;
- Companies increasingly employ part-time workers, consultants and contract labour in order to reduce overhead costs, labour hassles and to improve productivity.

New entrepreneurs become active in the Service Economy: Cities and towns are increasingly involved in economic development and employment creation, both as coordinators of national policies - which they tailor to suit local conditions and requirements - and in cooperation with other local partners, as independent promoters of autonomous strategies and specific measures.

> Not so long ago, mayors played the role of magistrates and leading citizens.
> Today, they are tending to become entrepreneurs!

recently commented a speaker at an OECD conference on Local Employment Initiatives (LEIs).

New tools are needed in Local Employment Initiatives [42], such as business incubators or industrial parks, i.e. multi-tenant buildings where a collection of small businesses share services including technical assistance and business advice. They are only one job-creation tool among several, but they offer the encouragement of shared effort and the chance to compare notes and learn from the others' experience. They develop from inside the community on a sensible economic scale, i.e. very small. The Small Business Administration in the US has found that 70-80% of the companies formed in incubators survive the first three years, compared to only 30% of those set up in the big cold world outside.

Commercial tools that incorporate social and innovative actions tailored to the informal and co-operative work environment of the small business sector start to appear:
- franchising is an existing possibility,
- ethical franchising between small companies is an alternative suggested in the UK by ITDG, London,
- joint R & D financing, or licensing of R & D results to small businesses working in a local market (sharing knowledge),
- sharing clients through marketing networks,
- sharing knowledge through executive secondment,
- innovation transfer: big companies, worried by sluggish innovation, are buying stakes in small firms, through e.g. venture capital. Entrepreneurs who are primarily explorers encourage this, because it is useful to have partners with deep pockets when competition heats up.

Women's role in risk taking is rapidly increasing. In the USA, the Bureau of Labor Statistics indicated that between 1972 and 1984, the number of women starting an enterprise increased by 87%, and that women were responsible for almost 50% of the 2,420,000 new enterprises created in this period.

Similar trends are reported in Sweden, with an annual growth rate for self-employed women of 8.7% between 1972 and 1982, and in the UK with growth of 6.3% per annum.

However, in most countries, the potential for women's economic development seems greater than that currently being achieved. Most businesses created by women are concentrated in traditional areas such as food, services, fashion and child care. Nevertheless, areas such as high-technology and finance are being entered as well as the gathering, processing and distribution of information [43]. In West Germany, 95% of the part-time workers are women.

The role of elder people, including a rapidly increasing number of middle managers that are pushed into early retirement at the age of 50 or 55, mainly by big corporations, could become crucial in the expansion of part-time and self-employment, as most new jobs are created by small companies (80% of new jobs in the U.S. are created by firms with less than 100 employees); and in traditional areas of technology (according to two Stanford researchers, U.S. jobs related to new technology are expected to increase 46% by 1995, yet they will still account for only six percent of all new jobs created in the next ten years [44]. In addition, most new jobs are in the "tertiary" sector: in the U.S., services, which employ 75% all nonfarm workers, have contributed some 2.1 million new jobs in the first nine months of 1985, 40% of them were in the sector of personal services such as those for business and health care. In the same time span the factory sector has given up 337,000 jobs.

How is the Service Economy going to deal with the dangers for these new risk takers?

In many cases, experiences are available from the past: operation around the clock has always existed in the mainstream economy when technical reasons demanded it, e.g. shift work in the steel industry where a continuous operation is a necessity. Shops that stay open 24 hours a day through the introduction of flexible work patterns have been common in areas such as New York, especially in the case of small owner/ manager operations; but not in Europe. Job-sharing in service industries is very similar to the shift work in the steel industry, where several workers share the same workplace and tools. The employees get the additional freedom to organize their own worktime within self-imposed limits, taking into account general organizational constraints.

Who will organize and protect the new self-workers, or part-time workers with a flexible schedule or working as casual contract labour? Employment agencies normally keep their labour force in a status of self-employed, depriving them of the social security which is mandatory for salaried employees. This situation needs to be looked at carefully.

Estimates in the UK in 1984 have shown contract labour increases of 40% of man hours supplied in one year. This development affects industries from construction and lorry driving to office work and nursing.

Is this a new objective for the (trade) unions? However, will the self-employed want to trade their flexibility against more constraints and more security? Practical acceptable solutions have to be negotiated case by case. Some examples already exist, such as Numast, the UK Merchant Navy Officers' Association, with a subsidiary that acts as employment agency providing shipowners with contract labour. Some employment agencies, such as Manpower, are themselves the employers of the men and women on their books. And some socially advanced organizations and government offices employing consultants have established their own registers in order to send tender offers directly to small businesses that might be interested rather than to publish a "call for tenders" in the legal state publications which are only read by the lawyers of large corporations.

**2.5.3.** <u>Negative Income Tax And Social Allocations</u>. Despite these obvious signs on the horizon, governments stubbornly push concepts of the Industrial Revolution which often favour cheap capital for investments rather than labour subsidies, or punish pro-work attitudes of the unemployed instead of promoting creative occupation.

One of the reasons for this is that governments during the Industrial Revolution went through a similar evolution of centralization and economy of scale as industry, and are today facing the same problems as many industries: Government is generally large-scale, centralized and cautious, while small enterprises are local and entrepreneurial in their attitude. Relationships between the two can never be easy. However, local employment initiatives based on activities satisfying local needs and using local resources will be best placed to promote regional development and economic growth in a bottom-up approach. Examples of this are the promotion of local employment initiatives (LEIs) by OECD and the Commission of the European Communities in industrialized countries, and the labour-intensive Special Public Works Programmes (SPWP) launched by ILO with financial aid from UNDP and various countries in the Third World. The latter, however, translate often into a redistribution of political power, and thus raise immediate objection from central government.

Similarly, the present anti-work attitude by governments in dealing with unemployment insurance is based on central instruments to control the unemployed and prevent abuses: no dole money for people who work, or refuse workfare for doing boring jobs. A pro-creation attitude that is pushing people to employ their skills and talents in the monetary or non-monetary sectors of the economy (own work, self-employment, community do-it-yourself) needs a decentralized, tailor-made approach for which civil servants have not been trained.

In the UK, for example, only 10% of the people who have become self-employed in 1984 did so through the government's enterprise allowance scheme.

High unemployment may be the major driving force: manual workers in particular feel better if they can say they are self-employed, rather than unemployed. Among the 273,000 newly self-employed in the UK, the majority said (during a labour force survey), that they had previously been unemployed or economically inactive (e.g housewives and retired). Manual workers accounted for 31% of those who switched from unemployment to self-employment, but only 16% of those moving from employment to self-employment! France, a successful example of top-down policy which can be applied in a decentralized way, promotes bottom-up initiatives and leaves all options open to the individual. Here, the concept is one of paying a newly unemployed person a lumpsum corresponding to the capitalized amount of one year's unemployment benefit, if he decides to start his own business.

The state government has also become involved in social security as a protection of the waged workers and their dependents who become unfit for work through illness, accidents or old age. Again, the same problem is encountered of control to prevent abuses, and of applying a central policy to a variety of problems.

A further crucial issue is the implication of the system of part-time employment and re-valorization of non-monetarized work in terms of fiscal policies. Whereas in the first area, government can be stimulated to play a progressive role, in the second area, it is normal to expect a very conservative reaction. It is here therefore that a lot of research and proposals to adapt fiscal policies to the mounting reality of part-time work and of non-monetarized jobs has to be done. Part of this great issue is the problem of accepting the fact of the underground economy, of its beneficial aspects, up to the point at which the underground economy has nothing to do with criminal activities. The problem in dealing with the "underground" economy is to preserve and even stimulate its creative and productive aspects.

All these state interventions lead to the question of importance of the state as an income provider, and its efficiency in this role.

> In the five big countries of Western Europe today, more than half of all adults depend upon governments for all or part of their weekly income: e.g. wages for civil servants, pensions for the old, dole money for the unemployed. This suggests that as many as three-quarters of all families in Britain, France, Italy, Sweden and West Germany have at least one member whose main income comes from national or local government and state agencies. Even in free enterprise America, 42% of all adults are financially dependent on public money.
>
> However, whereas in 1951, the biggest single public employer in every country was the armed forces, today, the soldiers, sailors and airmen are outnumbered by armies of nurses and teachers: 40-50% of all public workers are in health, education and other social services. [45]

If the nation-state has become the number one source of income, then its attitude in distributing this income becomes crucial: does it encourage risk taking? Is it done in an efficient way?

Does its structure correspond to the needs of the people? Are there any alternatives to the present highly complex system?

One such alternative, the universal, unconditional basic income [46] paid by the state to each individual citizen, is very simple. A basic income would provide each individual with a form of material independence never previously enjoyed in the Industrial Revolution, except by property holders. Women would no longer depend on men for subsistence, nor workers on employers for wages, nor unemployed on a state office for their social benefits. The shock that today goes with any change in a family's situation, such as the bread-earner dying or becoming unemployed, often linked to a long wait before receiving any social benefits, would be dampened.

A basic universal income would unify and simplify the immensely complex tax and benefits system. At present, the state distributes more in tax allowances than in social security benefits, but few people understand or recognize this. Under the basic income scheme, all income from all sources would be taxed, and everyone would pay according to their age and health. The basic income scheme would thus abolish both the poverty trap, under which at present many low earners lose income from benefits, by increasing their earnings; and the unemployment trap, which makes it unprofitable for people to return to work.

Above all, a basic universal income would encourage risk taking and innovation by individuals. Absolute poverty is an inhibitor to the risk–taking and activity creation that is the main chance for women, youth and the elderly to get access to wealth creation, in productive or unproductive activities, in terms of monetarized material wealth or non-monetarized activities. Education and training can be integrated with employment at the choice of the individual, not the needs of the employer. Work motivation would obviously also gain a new importance as the unmotivated would probably prefer to work for themselves. Technological change would be easier, as workers would have fewer incentives to protect jobs for jobs' sake, since their basic incomes and their personal dignity would be guaranteed through the basic income scheme.

Arguments against the basic income scheme focus mainly on costs and work incentives. Some experts have worked out revenue neutral schemes using current figures, keeping basic incomes near the present supplementary benefit levels and considering tax relief and income tax allowances [47]. Some people would certainly change from formal employment to self-employment or self-servicing activities, e.g. taking the optimization of the utilization period of the goods around them in their own hands, rather than to rely on expensive expert service. This possible increase in the "informal" economy would still increase overall wealth as measured in assets and system operation, even if it does not qualify for the Industrial Revolution's measures limited to paid employment resulting in products that are sold. Socially useful non-monetarized activities would equally be encouraged by a basic income scheme, such as looking after and caring for one's own parents rather than locking them up in an old people's home. Various forms of co-operatives would be enabled, and could be established by workers pooling their basic incomes during the time it takes to become commercially viable.

The debate on the basic income is now open and is presented in several forms, including the "negative income tax" by Milton Friedman. In fact, the proliferation of many sorts of benefits, insurance schemes and allocations brings this perspective constantly closer to reality and will probably derive with time from two major motivations and necessities:
- the coordination of what already exists, and
- the perspective to incentivate a risk prone society taking care of the minimum survival needs (and avoiding the negative incentives or moral hazard effects of the speculative behaviour of individuals specialized in accumulating privileges from an excessive number of sources).

2.5.4. The "Four Pillar" Strategy For The Elder. The notion of the "Fourth Pillar", or creative pillar, of social security is derived from the Swiss system :
- the first pillar, the mandatory state insurance, guarantees a basic income in case of death, invalidity and old age,
- the second pillar of social insurance, mandatory for all employed people, voluntary for the self-employed, covers the same risks as the first pillar, but is based on a return-on-paid-premiums approach,
- the third pillar consists of individual savings and investments,
- the fourth pillar is a scheme that enables the elderly to continue a productive activity, part-time and under favourable conditions with regard to education, taxation and work quality.

Today, the Fourth Pillar is mainly relevant to the age structure that is found in highly "developed" countries where the proportion of the active population is diminishing with

78

Figure 19. Age pyramids for different countries, 1985.

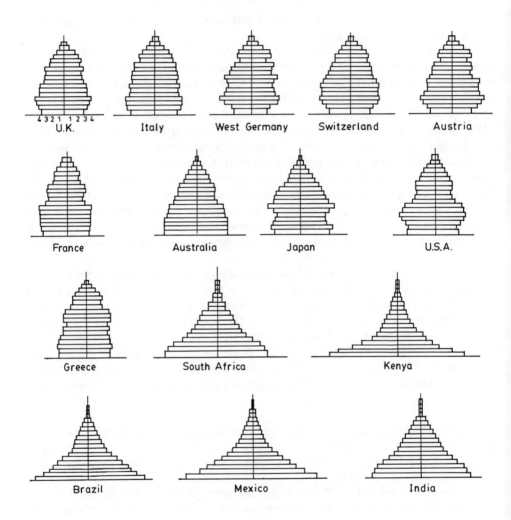

4 3 2 1  1 2 3 4
U.K.    Italy    West Germany    Switzerland    Austria

France    Australia    Japan    U.S.A.

Greece    South Africa    Kenya

Brazil    Mexico    India

Source: Long Range Planning, 1985

Figure 20. Forecast for the age pyramid of the population of the Federal Republic of Germany: 1985, 2000, 2030.

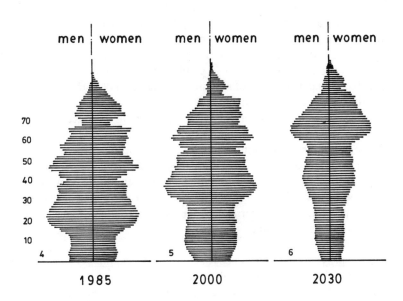

regard to the "pension age" population. In such conditions, the real class struggle might become a struggle between age groups.

Nevertheless can the Fourth Pillar also be applied in Third World countries, bearing in mind that their present huge reservoir of very young people will, in 30 to 40 years from now, create in these countries the situation that exists in Europe today?

The diagrams in *Figure 19* highlight the present radical but transitory difference of the human resources as assets in a country's development. If we pick Western Germany as a typical example of an industrialized country, and study the expected changes over the next fifty years, assuming that the mortality rate due to heart and circulatory diseases will decrease by 50% till the year 2000, the age pyramid develops as shown in *Figure 20*.

The key issue for Europe must therefore be to develop productive work attitudes and policies for the elderly, abolishing the system of salaried retirement in favour of a system of basic guaranteed income. The challenge of the Service Economy as part of the solution to this problem is to promote qualitative work, productive occupations and part-time activities acceptable to the elderly. In this way, a societal "grand design" can be proposed by stimulating the continued integration of the whole population into the active world of work, thus reversing the mechanism of the Industrial Revolution which has favoured many forms of segregation. How can we stimulate the development of an economic system in which the positive potentials of all age groups can be stimulated to engage in "productive" activities (in the largest possible scale)?

The notion of state guaranteed social security is linked to the restrictive notion of value inherited from the Industrial Revolution, underestimating the value of non-material assets such as personal skills.

Most of the people retiring today will drop from full employment into full unemployment from day D to day D+1, in the same way that school-leavers are supposed to start full employment within day 1 or their active life. Yet part-time employment and methods of transition from employment to self-employment can be developed for the elderly of today. And the need of the service economy for qualified interventions on a local level, for skill teaching and learning through experience, combined with access to "knowledge banks" similar to data banks, e.g. in the case of system maintenance, involving components that are no longer available, could be the matchmaker in this situation.

This will be a major but temporary task over the coming years, as the majority of the younger people involved in today's economy will probably no longer spend most of their active life under the illusion of lifetime employment with big corporations, followed by retirement. Corporations are also learning to rely on sub-contractors for hardware, and consultants for software requirements, activities where flexibility and general knowledge combined with permanent education, is as important as the perfection of a single specialization. Within this perspective, the "permanent education" programmes have to be revised to encompass the whole life of people.

2.5.5. <u>Selling Security Or Means To Face Risks And Uncertainties</u>. The Industrial Revolution developed a set of priorities based on the material production of wealth, economy of scale and the mobility of the worker. In exchange, the worker was offered material security in his old age, specialization in his employment and a salary at market rates.

In the transition period from the Industrial to the Service Economy, it turns out that many of these securities cannot be cashed in. Material security in old age is threatened by inflation and an upside down age pyramid, specialization can mean an impossibility in finding a new job in a changing work environment, and salary at market rates in a global market often means that somebody somewhere, man or machine, is going to undercut your livelihood.

The social strategy of the Service Economy could be to provide as many people as possible with the means and capabilities of facing risks and uncertainties in order to survive by relying on their skills and knowledge. Service activities often face less international competition because they have to be performed where the need is, such as hairdressing, local transport and repair work. Service activities have a high mobility: whereas a specialized worker in the automobile industry could not go to a nearby town and find the same job, or start on his own, a health worker or a car mechanic can do this. The independence of tools and the relation of knowledge to market needs and products also make it easier to pass knowledge from one person to another. Skills and information activities that the Industrial Revolution condemned as unproductive labour can be shared between several people without anyone losing, unlike material goods. But to teach these is a slow process of learning. The example of the Swiss watch industry is telling: there are plenty of watchmakers out of work who were formerly employed in factories in the Swiss Jura region, yet there are very few and mostly very old real craftsmen left in the same region who can build a watch from a simple sketch into a working timepiece on their own.

The influence of this development is, however, not limited to the industrialized countries. In Third World countries, even if the reasons are different, a similar dependence has developed. The Green Revolution has made many a peasant farmer, in a formerly non-monetarized world, dependent on the purchase of chemicals, fossil fuels and expensive machinery he did not need before, in order to exploit new methods of intensive planting of cash crops for export. When the prices on the foreign markets collapse, he cannot sell his production locally, as city dwellers at home are too poor to buy the beef and dairy products produced for export. The Service Economy enables the regaining of space to manoeuvre, as well as flexibility.

The society of the post industrial service revolution is therefore developing in the following direction:

- The big centralized corporations that rely on economy of scale, global marketing and mass-production of "commodity goods" such as cars, standardized microchips, aircrafts, or of "commodity services" such as long-distance air transport, international banking and shipping, will increasingly produce an interconnected world network. Their activities rely on huge market volumes for staple needs that are standard the world over; their production is capital-intensive and robotized, the production tools will have a high flexibility to guarantee a long product-life in order to depreciate investments over long periods of time, compatible with technological obsolescence. At the same time, they will accentuate every possibility of flexibility, and go as far as the electronics and the robot revolution will allow in customizing production and reducing storage constraints (e.g. just-in-time production),
- Flexibility and an overlap of boundaries will characterize medium and small local businesses and crafts which manufacture specialized goods adapted to local needs, or customized goods for small volume World markets. These businesses offer services that range from adapting mass-produced goods to local conditions, maintaining and updating existing systems and goods in operation, to labour-intensive community-based services in health, education and banking based on original solutions. In this sector, workforce management will also rely on workforce participation and involvement.

The two parties in this economy are partners among peers. They both contain high-tech and low-tech activities and demand high skills, they both contribute to the wealth of nations and they need each other as complements in order to offer efficient systems operation.

The complexity and sophistication of work that can better be done on a local level depends strongly on the environment: what is feasible in an industrialized country will not necessarily work in a less developed country, and vice versa.

A report on the import of commercial vehicles in Third World countries concludes that a degree of local skill can be tapped in trades such as welding, sheet metal work or electrical circuits, even in the least developed countries. It is worth remembering that for every $100 equivalent of local content that can be added, $100 less has to be bought in, so the net balance is improved by $200.

What this global, networking, service society has in common is reliance on the knowledge worker. In fact, one of the reasons for the change in large corporations today is organizations' failure to adapt to the new workforce of knowledge people. This had led to a reluctance on the part of the brightest, to join big corporations, and to the sale of hundreds of divisions of big corporations, such as General Electric Co., in order to "gold-collar" workers cum managers. Others have set up their own garage operation, rather than submit to corporate pressure. A well-known example of this phenomenon is Steve Wozniak, a onetime employee of Hewlett-Packard Co. Wozniak approached management with his ideas to build what today is knows as a personal computer, only to be told that this was not what he was hired for (i.e. calculators), and to stick to his knitting. As we know, Steve Wozniak went off with Steve Jobs to start their garage operation in Silicon Valley which later became known under the name of Apple Computers Co.

However, is this process really radically new?

> As an inventor-entrepreneur, Edison presided over the process of technologi-
> cal change from problem identification to innovation and technology trans-
> fer. Creative fulfillment, however, came to him mostly from the inventive act,
> not from the other phases of technological development. He counted his
> patents more than his money, at least until his later years, when he began to
> look to industrialists like Henry Ford as status models. Edison flourished as
> an inventor-entrepreneur in the late 1870's and early eighties, the period
> when he was presiding over the invention and introduction of his system of
> electric lighting. His historical peers were other inventor-entrepreneurs, such
> men as Robert Fulton, Samuel Morse, and Cyrus Hall McCormick, who, like
> himself, did not rest until companies (usually those they established) were
> manufacturing their inventions. Edison formed a number of companies to
> organize his invention and the introduction of the lighting system: a company
> for research and development, others for manufacturing components, and
> another to preside over the operation of the system. In each case, he allied
> himself with men whose interests and capabilities complemented his own.
> Persons with legal and financial experience, for instance, compensated for his
> lack of experience and special aptitude for the complexities of organization
> and financing. Despite their presence, however, it was Edison, as inventor-
> entrepreneur, who pulled most of the strings of the complex system. [48]

Perhaps the more interesting distinction between the founders of Apple Computers and Edison is this: while in Edison's days innovation was mainly linked to optimizing produc-tion, which allowed Edison to stay in control of his innovation, the founders of Apple Computers quickly found out that in today's Service Economy, innovation is linked much more closely to marketing and selling the product.

Steve Jobs and Steve Wozniak have both left their brainchild Apple Computers after the initial success period, unlike Edison.

Another feature of the Service Economy is a less distinct frontier between "production" and "services". In fact, any employed person turned self-employed has generally gone through a de-specialization that corresponds to an up-skilling. Present statistics once more cannot cope with these subtle changes.

Many of the new micro businesses are thus statistically featured under retail, or distribution.

A fairly typical example is small-scale innovative catering:

- pizza delivered to your home: a new entrepreneur will bake pizzas on request, and deliver them at the requested time to the purchaser at his or her home or office address,
- party buffets: a new entrepreneur will prepare elaborate "nouvelle cuisine" hot and cold dishes for parties at home or at the office, given a few days notice, will deliver them including china, glasses and cutlery, will serve your guests and take everything back at the end of the meal.

In both cases, this corresponds to a substitution of a service such as a restaurant, for a traditional DIY activity (cooking). However, unlike the restaurant, there is a dis-economy of scale (very little fixed investment and thus a high volume flexibility, combined with a high mobility) which makes it possible to cope with a large variety of menus and volume without a high entrepreneurial risk.

In both cases, there is a de-specialization but not a de-skilling compared to the restaurant: the new entrepreneur has to be an excellent cook, and a good delivery driver, and a fairly good marketeer and salesman. However, he does not need a very large clientele that will regularly come back if his service is good. In fact, he has higher overall skills than a chef or a taxi driver, which he offers in a multifunction business. His financial advantage thus stems from a "packaged product" where the cost is cheaper than the sum of the individual parts purchased in the market place.

Now where is one going to put him statistically? in catering? in retail business? in distribution? There is no statistical class of new multifunctional entrepreneurs, which would allow us to keep track of them.

The higher the percentage of people in self-employment, or in multiple part-time activities (which corresponds to the skills needed in self-employment), the less important will be the need for social interventions to develop special "Fourth Pillar" schemes.

In fact, to misquote Napoleon:

> any knowledge worker, and this includes most self-employed people, already has his Fourth Pillar-baton in his professional knapsack.

And at this stage, facing the risks of one's profession, having the qualification and the liberty to do it, one has already bought an excellent asset in security. One which is both the Fourth Pillar and the necessary precondition of the existence of the other three.

Notes Chapter 2

(for notes nos. 1 and 2, see end of Chapter 1)
3.  for the notion of Dowry and Patrimony, see Giarini, Orio (ed.) (1980) Dialogue on Wealth and Welfare, Pergamon Press, Oxford, pp. 168-248.
4.  Zimmermann, Erich (1933, 1951) World Resources and Industry, Harper & Broth, New York, N.Y.
5.  in his Essay on the Principle of Population.
6.  Kahane, Ernest (1979) Parmentier ou la Dignite de la Pomme, Essais sur la Faim, A.Blanchard, Paris.
7.  Campbell, R.H. and Skinner, A.G. (1982) Adam Smith, Croom Helm, London.
8.  Heilbronner, R. (1971) Les Grands Economists, Seuil, Paris pp. 46-48.
9.  one of the best books on the history of the Industrial Revolution is: Landes, David S. (1972) The Unbound Prometheus, Cambridge University Press, Cambridge.
10. evaluation made by Ivan Illich in a paper on Shadow Work, presented at a conference at the University of Kassel, September 1980.
11. see Giarini, Orio (ed.) (1984) Cycles, Value and Employment, Pergamon Press, Oxford; also Mensch, G. (1977) Das Technologische Patt, Fischer Verlag, Frankfurt.
12. as in the case of Marchetti, C. (1980) "Society as a Learning System: Discovery, and Innovation Cycles Revisited", Technological Forecasting and Social Change, 18, pp. 267-282.
13. Meadows, D. (1972) The Limits to Growth, Universe Books, New York, N.Y.
14. see Leveson, Irving, Hudson Institute Strategy Group, New York "The Service Economy in Economic Development", paper presented at the Graduate Institute of European Studies, University of Geneva, April 16, 1985.
15. see Fourastier, Jean (1958) Le Grand Espoir du XXe siecle, Gallimard, Paris; also Clark, Colin (1960) Les Conditions du Progres Economique (The Conditions of Economic Progress), PUF, Paris; also Bell, Daniel (1973) The Coming of the Post-Industrial Society, Basil Books, New York, N.Y.
16. see Enthoven, Alain (Stanford University) "The HMOs", lecture presented in Paris, April 23, 1985, at the Institut la Boetie; also Zigler, Martin (1985) "The Changing Face of Health Care Delivery", in Emphasis, by Tillighast Actuaries, Atlanta, Georgia.
17. the definition of the service economy as a networking system has been presented also by Leveson, Irvin (1985) The Networking Economy, Hudson Institute Papers, New York, N.Y.; the same orientation is taken in a recent book by Bressand, Albert and Distler, Catherine (1985) Le Prochain Monde (Resopolis), Paris.
18. see Berliner, Baruch (1982) Limits of Insurability of Risks, Prentice Hall, Inc. Eaglewood Cliffs, N.J.
19. Knight, Frank (1921, 1971) Risk, Uncertainty and Profit, University of Chicago Press, Chicago, Ill.
20. as 19.

21. see Arrow, Kenneth (1978) "Risk Allocation and Information", The Geneva Papers on Risk and Insurance no 8, Geneva, pp. 519 and bibliography.
22. see Furstenberg, George von (ed.) (1979) Social Security versus Private Savings, Ballinger Publishing Company, Cambridge, Mass.
23. see SIGMA Bulletin, Swiss Reinsurance Company, Zurich (yearly).
24. see Forrester, Jay (1975) Counter-Intuitive Behaviour in Social Sciences (collected papers), Wright-Allen Press, Cambridge, Mass.
25. George, A. (1979) "Les Pertes Informatiques", The Geneva Papers on Risk and Insurance no 13, Geneva.
26. The Energy Outlook (1985) Etudes et Dossiers no. 93, The Geneva Association, Geneva.
27. see Hailey, Arthur (1985) Strong Medicine, Pan Books, London.
28. The European Communities, Brussels (1985) Directive on Product Liability.
29. see Kunreuther, H. (ed.) (1986) Transportation, Storage and Disposal of Hazardous Materials, papers from a conference at IIASA, Laxenburg /Vienna, Wharton School, University of Pennsylvania, Philadelphia, Penn.
30. see Baglini, Norman (1976) Risk Management in International Corporations, Risk Studies Foundation, New York, N.Y.
31. among other references: Stiglitz, Joseph (1983) Annual Lecture of the Geneva Association, The Geneva Papers on Risk and Insurance no 26, Geneva.
32. see Tobias, Andrew (1982) The Invisible Bankers, Pocket Books, New York, N.Y.
33. there is a delicate economic and social trade-off problem here: a high level of compensation for unemployment might be socially desirable. But it is also socially desirable not to use the working taxpayer's money beyond a certain level which might favour nonmotivated others to be supported without real need.
34. Stiglitz, Joseph (1983) The Pure Theory of Moral Hazard, The Geneva Papers on Risk and Insurance no 26, Geneva.
35. see Nussbaumer, Jacques (1984) Les Services, Economica, Paris.
36. Giarini, Orio and Louberge, Henri (1978) The Diminishing Returns of Technology, Pergamon Press, Oxford.
37. Stahel, Walter R. (1984) "The Product-Life Factor", in Orr, Susan Grinton (ed.) An Inquiry into the Nature of Sustainable Societies: The Role of the Private Sector, HARC, The Woodlands, TX.
38. statement by Michael Cohen, Division Chief, Water Supply and Urban Development Department, The World Bank, Washinton, DC.
39. see Laslett, Peter (1987) The World we have lost, Methuen on the Domesday Book.
40. see Robertson, James (1985) Future Work; jobs, self-employment and leisure after the industrial age, Gower Publishing Co., London.
41. Mill, John Stuart (1968 reprint) Principles of Political Economy, Routledge and Kegan, London

42. see also the Newsletter of the co-operative action programme on Local Initiatives for Employment Creation, OECD, Paris.
43. see in particular the initiative "Women's World Banking", launched by Michaela Walsh in New York, USA, with a record of successful initiatives in Africa and Asia.
44. New Scientist, May 10, 1984.
45. Rose, Richard (1985) Public Employment in Western Nations, Cambridge University Press; summarized in The Economist, November 16, 1985.
46. Jordan, Bill (1986) "Basic Incomes and Hidden Economic Potential", Science and Public Policy no 4, London.
47. see the work of the Basic Income Research Group in London.
48. from Hugues, Thomas P. (1983) Network of Power, John Hopkins University Press, Baltimore, Maryland, and London.

(for notes nos. 49 to 85, see end of Chapters 3 and 4)

# Chapter 3: Producing the Wealth of Nations; the Risk Takers and the Supply-Side of the Economy. The Dynamics of Disequilibrium

## 3.1. PRODUCING

3.1.1. <u>Life As An Activity In Production</u>. Standard economic theory assumes a situation of general equilibrium between supply or production and demand or consumption. In fact, this equilibrium, or situation of symmetry, is a key reference because it provides a monetarized price through the act of exchange between goods and services produced (offered) and consumed. The fact of providing a measurement yardstick has been considered of key importance. During the Industrial Revolution, this assumption was of practical use.

In real life, beyond the moment when exchange transactions take place, the activities concerning production on the one side and consumption on the other are totally asymmetric in time: we can only consume what actually exists; but every production process, until completed, represents at best a probability of something which might exist in the future.

The notion of "production" has to be taken here in a very broad sense: we can produce a meal, a song, a book, a theory or an idea, a house, a good feeling. We produce tools, culture and we even produce ourselves and our personality. Not all these production processes are necessarily done consciously, based on rational or even explicit decisions.

Many, even most production decisions or activities are the consequence of cultural or environmental inertias; but they are all *projects* which presuppose a future outcome and thus will always be more or less uncertain: there is never certainty. In fact, we always live with a multitude of projects, be it going out to dinner tonight, or writing a book, or buying a new car, or learning a new language, or taking or avoiding some initiative in terms of our future career or in terms of winning a friend. Determination of character, environmental conditions of human or non-human hazards all contribute to the outcome of our "productive" endeavours. Our decisions (or lack of decision), individually and collectively, constantly propose a partly unknown future. Some decisions have greater inertias than others. Often, such inertias are evident from the beginning. When an automobile industry was implanted in Detroit or in Turin, a great inertia was created which has constantly "planned" the future of these cities. By producing his operas, Mozart has been rather determinant in influencing the musical culture for more than two hundred years after his death. Planning is about understanding inertias combined with determination and hazard.

In going back to our old friends Adam and Eve, taken as a symbol which can be found in many religions or myths, we find that they have been sent down to earth from heaven in order to produce in a world of scarcity. And their descendants, up to the present time have produced civilizations, philosophies, material goods and technologies in ever increasing quantity and of a more and more diversified quality.

Production, any sort of production, from writing a poem to making money or inventing a new business, always starts with a dream. And, by definition, once a dream is fulfilled, it has stopped being a dream. Achievement is the moment when the former dream is realized and can be "consumed". The time is then ripe for other dreams.

No enterprise is built with dreams alone and none without.

This is the typical and essential ambiguity that having dreams without any attempt to make them come at least partially true is no way to successfully develop our personality or a civilization. Dreams allow us to define goals, and goals are the targets which stimulate the strategies of survival and development.

It is often said that "we must produce first in order to consume". In reality, at the individual as well as at the social level, consumption comes first. It is because we can consume what has been produced that we can plan and act to produce what we (as individual or as society) shall probably consume tomorrow. During the first years or even the first decade of our life as individuals, we are net consumers of immaterial and material goods, but also start to produce at least references for human contacts and emotions. The agricultural society was able to transform itself into an industrial society because of the future project concerning a richer material world of tomorrow. In the same way, the accumulated wealth and knowledge of past productions have made it possible for us to consume, at least in the Western World, in a better way than before the Industrial Revolution. We thus have a margin to reconsider our chances of improving all sorts of productions (material and spiritual) on which will depend the capacity of the new world to create a new civilization with our contribution.

We always live in the present, but in a present which is continuously moving through time where our decisions, particularly with regard to our projects to produce, make the present inevitably and very closely linked both to our near and to our more distant future.

Planning [41] does not make this future certain. If the future were certain it would be predetermined at present with no possibility of choice. However, choices which modify the environment and our development in the long term may be restricted in time and space, but nevertheless do exist.

3.1.2. The Conditions Of Supply: Uncertainty And Risk. Any decision or act leading to any sort of production is inevitably done in a condition of uncertainty and risk. Of course, there are often situations of excessive levels of uncertainty, which make it practically impossible to take any decision because either the goal or the way to reach it, remains essentially indeterminate or because there are risks which could be totally destructive. But, in fact, good economic analysis of risk evaluation and comparison is, or should be, the best tool to eliminate, or at least to do our best to control, unmanageable and unsustainable situations.

The true issue is that the choice, in real life, is not between risky and safe situations, but between different degrees of risks and of possible outcomes. Living in a totally clean environment without a single microbe or virus can be considered a desirable situation, where we would be capable of avoiding any infection. But an excessive preoccupation in this direction will put us at a much greater risk if, by accident or by unforeseen and unforeseeable circumstance, our body should encounter a virus, having lost any capability to fight it. Total social security that guarantees to all citizens a definitive and certain relief against all sorts of social or physical ills (bad health, accidents, unemployment, retirement) through a collective organization, might look appropriate at first sight but would in fact undermine the capacity of the collective organization to really fulfil its role. What if, in a difficult economic situation, the State itself goes bankrupt, extreme inflation or deflation destroy the value of the assets and the functioning of the economy itself? The certainty of not having an accident in an automobile can only be achieved by not using any automobiles. However, we still do it because we have so well integrated the automobile into our culture that we finally accepted the high level of risk it implies as if it were of the same type of risk that we face by the very simple fact of walking and living.

Even those activities which are said to provide security, like insurance companies or industrial manufacturers producing safety equipment, are in fact _not_ selling security but the tools to manage uncertainty and risks of all sorts. Insurance does not help to avoid hazards, it helps to control their consequences. The choice again is not between security and uncertainty but between different degrees of risk. Our economic and human choices, in all fields, are a tradeoff between different forms of risks, between the costs and goals of our action.

As a boy, Einstein did not know he was going to be _The_ Einstein nor did Mozart know he would one day write operas which a century later would be better known than those of Joseph Haydn. History always tells us of events, such as the scientific discoveries of Einstein, the geographical discoveries of Christopher Columbus, the artistic achievements of artists, the invention of television or of air transport, _after_ they have happened. The more important these events are the more unpredictable they are. Hermann Kahn, in his book "The Year 2000" published twenty years ago [42], wrote about the difficulty of predicting important issues: He made a list of those events of our century which were _impossible_ to predict at the beginning of the century. They are: the Russian-Japanese War, the "belle epoque", the Mexican (1910) and Chinese (1911) Revolutions, the First World War, the fall of the Ottoman Empire and of the Austrian Empire, the Russian Revolution, the emergence of the United Nations, the great crises of 1929, the growth of fascism and nazism, the major discoveries in science, the development of communism, the decolonization movement, the nuclear bomb, the boom of the consumption society.

History is misleading us if we have the impression that through the study of great events of the past, and because we know something about them _ex-post_, we can predict similar events in the future.

There are of course possibilities to limit uncertainty, but the best we can do is in fact to understand the possibility of major risks such as nuclear war and the necessity to reduce the probability of such an event taking place, i.e. to avoid a nuclear holocaust. We need a strategy to face the great risks and to control uncertainties. And we must also be aware that many important events and probably the determinant ones which will shape the world 100 years from now, are essentially unpredictable. It is this unpredictability which is the precondition for our world culture to make a quantum leap towards creating a better world striving for a higher level of consensus on our goals around the planet. When this is achieved we shall have reached a higher level of civilization.

Coming back to the economic entrepreneur in our society, we find the uncertainty and risks of any activity implicit in every endeavour:

- Any advanced technological company that invests money in research and the development of new products must have the ability to spread its investments over a number of products and research avenues in order to increase the probability of having at least one positive result from time to time to compensate for all the risks taken. In the chemical industry of the 1960's it was normal to expect that only one out of ten projects had a chance to succeed. This successful one thus had to carry the costs of an average of nine failures. In some pharmaceutical sectors, the spread is much thinner: one success out of dozens or even hundreds of experiments. The real game in modern technology has been the capability of taking as many different risks as necessary in order to put the odds of having one good success on ones' side. This is the reasoning behind the many concentrations in the area of research.
- The success of a new product can be guessed by market studies: they are at best, good approximations. There can be positive surprises as in the case of the French high-speed train (TGV) where the traffic between Paris and Lyon today is 30% higher than the most optimistic forecasts had predicted. There are many other cases in which the market reaction has been much lower than even moderate predictions. And as the speed of the modern economy constantly increases the number of products and services, it is clear that the struggle against uncertainty has become a key issue: mastering the different degrees and levels of uncertainty is the real challenge today.
- Similarly, insurance companies have to ask premiums based on the forecast of a distribution of damages over a future period of time. Historic figures can lead to approximate forecasts, but variations can again be substantial, particularly when the systems at risk are of increasing complexity and vulnerability.

Yet another trend has to be taken into consideration in all these cases: Whereas, by comparison with the pre-industrial world, products, tools, machines, systems and qualifications tend to change all the time, the organization of new systems and the development of radically new technologies is increasingly slow. It can take a decade or longer to develop a fundamental discovery until it becomes economically significant. Constant change does not mean that change is very rapid: When the price of oil started to increase rapidly in 1973, it took almost a decade for the consumption of oil to react and diminish. Changes in habits, but above all adaptation in production processes and distribution systems, take a long time. The evaluation of cultural and technical inertias are therefore a fundamental part of uncertainty management in the modern economy. In the primitive industrial revolution, one could speak of instant elasticities of production and demand in relation to price. In many technologically advanced sectors modern economic life has introduced inertias that exclude rapid change and adaptation to an abrupt increase or decrease in price as happens in a very simple market. It is very often specialization itself which is at the roots of this increased rigidity. One of the great priorities of present and future technologies is precisely to cope with and to reduce all sorts of rigidities.

The price that a product or a service can achieve in the market is not a precise element of reference, but one of the uncertainties in managing the production system. In the same way, writing a book or a song always implicitly means to deliver oneself to the uncertainty of the success that this endeavour might achieve.

What is thus happening in the modern world and in the modern economy is that we are more *consciously* confronted with risk and uncertainty. The fact that we are beginning to live in a period in which hopefully we need less theories and ideologies to promise us a more certain world free of risk may be a sign that, after all, we are making progress. We may even be at the beginning of a new period of real cultural and economic revolution.

3.1.3. Risk And Responsibility. Recognizing risk and recognizing uncertainty is strongly linked to a profound evolution that is going on in the Western World at the present time with regard to the notion of responsibility.

After all, if the dominant ideology is promising or "scientifically" justifying a situation of complete control of reality with an almost total elimination of risk and uncertainty, the feeling and notion of responsibility cannot but decline. In a world regulated by deterministic laws, where the future has no surprise, the notion of personal and even of collective responsibility fades out. Why take responsibility for something if it is going to happen anyway?

The notion of responsibility in the Industrial Revolution has at the best been limited to a specialized performance. In the last ten to twenty years, however, a great change has taken place: we can very clearly notice the transition from the classical Industrial Revolution to a Service Economy in attitudes and responses to the notion of responsibility.

In the course of the industrial revolution, it was important and sufficient to do one's own job reasonably well (when this was the case). In the Service Economy, it does not suffice to perform a specific activity, but it is vital that this performance really yields useful results.

A case in point was the problem that the Nestle company had in selling its powder milk in Africa. Nestle was accused of not making it clear enough that this powder milk had to be mixed with clean water in regions where this was not part of the normal attitude. In addition, it was accused of destroying the natural habit of breast feeding in favour of powder milk. Twenty years ago, the attitude of Nestle on this point was typical of institutions related to the Industrial Revolution, whether "capitalist" or "socialist". The priority was to produce something useful (and the need for powder milk in many developing countries has always been obvious); the conditions of utilization and its possible negative effects were something that the consumers had to account for. The manufacturer's responsibility was limited to selling a good product and did not include the fact that the utilization value of his product derived essentially from the way it was actually used. It was not Nestle's fault to have to face the criticism of having indirectly provoked the death of babies. What was at stake during those years was a profound transition from the notion of economic value linked to the mere existence of products (e.g. powder milk) to the notion of utilization value, i.e. the effective way of using products in a useful way (the powder milk with the proper water quality).

This notion of responsibility, that products and activities have to produce useful *results*, has spread in recent years in many fields especially in the United States. The pharmaceutical industry is in a particularly sensitive situation: the risk of selling a product which might produce related negative effects, in the short or the long run, hangs like a Damocles sword over the whole sector. It does not matter how many products have been useful in the past: one faulty new product can cause a lot of harm to the public (see the case of Thalidomide) and consequently also destroy the company. Therefore, the problem of the right choice in adequate economic and social terms becomes dramatic, especially when considering how many people could possibly not have been saved because they were *not* allowed to take a medicine considered not to be tested sufficiently [43]. One side of a risk has to be weighed against another side: one group of people's interest against those of another group.

Another case in point is the spread of cases of malpractice in the United States, with some cases spilling over to Europe: Doctors are held responsible for having made a wrong diagnosis or a wrong treatment. Their responsibility might be obvious in cases of clear negligence on their part, but the problem becomes difficult when the notion of responsibility is extended to the idea of compensating the victims, regardless of fault; the risks of a medical doctor, a lawyer or any other expert or manager is defined in a way which considers him objectively (or strictly) liable for any harm which results from his activity, whether he has been acting negligently or *not* [44].

This is an example of a passionate debate which is actually going on, particularly in the Western industrialized countries, and where the problem is ultimately to find the right balance between different types of conflicting risks and responsibilities which exist in any human endeavour and activity.

It is obvious that uncertainty also concerns the results of the functioning of a system. What makes the discussion of this subject, and of possible solutions, sometime difficult, is the old-fashioned view that the degree of certainty of the result is higher if more science and technology is involved. Due to the fact that we are in a better condition today to manage risk and uncertainty, and because all human and economic activities are expanding and taking different degrees and more complex levels of uncertainty, the contrary is probably the case. A particularly uncertain world is that of medicine, where in addition to the uncertainties involved in scientific analyses and the medical treatment of each patient, evidence exists that one third of all patients react to placebos. This shows the importance of the psychological attitudes of patients, which add to the uncertainty of medical treatments [45].

Today we are living through the hard transition from a situation in which a doctor or any other expert is perceived as an intermediary with a level of "superior" knowledge (close to god's in some cases...) to a situation where the expert is viewed as a kind of broker of uncertainty. We only need to be very ill to understand how difficult it is to accept situations of utter uncertainty. However, beyond that, in normal life, it is obviously safer in the long run to be more conscious of the real dimension of uncertainty. It is by recognizing risks and uncertainties, that we improve our attitudes and knowledge to live with them more efficiently and even exploit them as challenges. Of course we need experts more than ever, but as professional *risk* managers in their own field, not as salesmen of certainty.

Advancing in the modern Service Economy and society and understanding the explosion in the real world of all the problems related to the definition of responsibility, is an indication of a tentative step forward in considering that economic value is attached to the performance of systems (including experts) and that this performance is linked to a certain degree of risk and uncertainty. It is such an acknowledgement which will make us more responsible.

3.1.4. <u>The Supply In Classical Economics</u>. Economists as well as the man in the street recognize that our world, despite having a great dowry and patrimony in terms of natural resources and human culture, is still essentially dominated by a situation of scarcity as one of the major components of social life.

Most economists, up to the end of the last century, have been "supply-siders". This means that they always considered it a priority for economic activity to stimulate production. The idea was that in a world of scarcity all production would have been consumed sooner or later. This concept was formulated in the "law" of Jean-Baptiste Say. From Adam Smith to Ricardo, and up to Karl Marx, the notion of value itself was then closely related to the notion of production. The price, the reference quantifiable yardstick, was given by the sale of.the product. The money from the sale was then used to pay the salaries of the workers and/or the interest of capital. In this redistribution of the money received by selling a product, Karl Marx saw the seed of a class struggle, the result of which was that the remuneration of the capital absorbed more than its due and reduced the remuneration of the labour force to a minimum subsistence level. Marx did not foresee that even the capitalists would have an interest in transforming the middle and lower classes into consumers once the technology would be advanced enough to initiate a great new period of mass-production and consumption.

It is important also to underline that all classical economists were supply-side oriented, whether politically linked to the conservative side or to the left wing. This was consistent with common sense at their time.

However, what had not been obvious to most classical economists was the process of monetarization linked to the process of industrialization, as described in *paragraph 2.1.3.*. This latter means that it was not enough to say that, because of scarcity, all production would one day be distributed for consumption, as could be said in an agricultural society which was hardly monetarized and where in fact non-monetarized production for self-consumption or for non-monetarized distribution was by far the most important economic characteristic.

The growth of the monetarization of the economy parallel to its industrialization also meant that a growing share of economic production and of consumption had, in order to be used and exchanged, to rely on the availability of money in the production, exchange and distribution mechanism. If a good was available only in a monetarized form (i.e. if money was the only way to have access to it), it could only reach a buyer with the corresponding purchasing power in a monetary form.

Yet another key phenomenon was also underestimated or not taken into account adequately during the period dominated by classical economics, up to 1900: the development of technology. Science was celebrated essentially in a cultural and ideological form! There is limited evidence that the power of new technologies to stimulate an enormous increase in supply capabilities was really perceived as such, and in all its power, before the first decades of our century. The misunderstanding and underestimation of the growth potential of supply capabilities has also been at the origin of most cyclical crises, as shown in the next chapter.

The upsurge of the great industrial expansion at the beginning of our century, which quickly accelerated after World War Two, led to the unique development of new science-based technologies and the subsequent belief that supply was something adaptable at will. The faith in science and technology, as a new magic, culminated in the belief that no more limits were to be expected from the supply-side, since in the sixties there were more people working in laboratories and in new technologies than ever before since the beginning of humanity. The last period of the classical Industrial Revolution exploded like an enormous firework and expanded the possibilities of production to such an extent that the problem of supply the assumption that the key question was to face scarcity in our economic world faded away. In this situation of extreme elasticity of production, the bottleneck in economic terms had, from the beginning of this century and in particular from the 1930's to the 1970's been the problem of regulating and stimulating consumption and demand.

After this parenthesis of 40 to 60 years we have to consider the great importance of evaluating and stimulating production in the Service Economy. The new importance of the supply-side is not an exclusive one, as we will see, but refers to a process in which both production and consumption (supply and demand) constitute essential elements of economic development and evolution, but which take place in different time dimensions and meet only once, at the exchange moment (or point-of-sale).

### 3.1.5. The Prosumer, The Services Supply (Externalizing Process, Self-Service, Spin-Offs).

In order to understand the cycles in the Industrial Revolution up to the present Service Economy, where the supply is emerging as one of the key issues, it is essential to highlight the difference between the notion of supply in the Industrial Revolution and in the Service economy.

*Paragraph 2.3.* described the service production system as a complex system integrating tools and services aimed at providing results or an economic value defined in terms of actual utilization.

Another important aspect in the definition of utilization value has to be underlined: the contribution of the consumer himself as part of the production system. Alvin Toffler has coined the word "prosumer" [46] to describe this situation.

A "producer" following his "product" passed the point-of-sale and into the utilization by the customer inevitably also encounters situations in which he needs the active collaboration of the user who conditions the possibilities of generating usable results. The user or consumer thus becomes himself a condition for making the "production" work.

There are two aspects to the "prosumer": a monetarized and a non—monetarized one:

At the industrial production or manufacturing level, the maintenance or quality control team using a machine delivered by a manufacturer is a clear case of integrating production and service functions. Similarly, the private customer who uses a personal computer and is investing money to learn how to use it, is in fact a "prosumer" and an essential element of "production" in terms of utilization value.

The notion of "prosumer" extends also to the qualitative and non-monetarized aspects of producing utilization value: the good maintenance of a room, of a hospital, of a tourist sight, of a washing machine, are all qualitative non-monetarized features which condition the efficient functioning of the *monetarized* products of reference. Good and careful handling (and even kind behaviour) has an impact on the smooth functioning of systems, and therefore also on their operating costs.

Self-service is yet another sector in which the prosumer contributes to produce an economic value (of utilization) by providing his *free* activity, as a substitute for the *paid* activity at the level of the delivery systems. Picking up our dishes at the counter of a self-service restaurant is an economic activity (unpaid, non-monetarized), which substitutes for the paid service of a waiter. The same is true for all self-service shops or manufacturing units. We experience in these cases the integration of monetarized and non-monetarized activities with the aim to maximize total economic value (utilization value) delivered against a minimum of costs and efforts (monetarized or not).

The Service Economy is a process in which there is a constant trade-off between internalized and externalized processes and activities in an economic institution, not only in their monetarized but also in their non-monetarized version. The services of a lawyer, a medical doctor, or an insurance activity can be integrated within a company producing goods. Alternatively, a bank or insurance company might internalize the production and printing of its brochures (a manufacturing activity) within its organization. Or, the services of lawyers or medical doctors and the printing of brochures can be done in each case quite separately by independent organizations or individuals. One of the key considerations in these externalizing or internalizing, or spin-off and spin-in processes is linked to their capability of availing themselves of non-monetarized contributions (better qualitative performances, 24-hour service, free-willing contributions).

There are no general rules to determine if externalizing processes should prevail over internalizing processes or vice-versa. These spin-offs and internalizing processes are not new in the production system. What is new is their dimension, the great flexibility which they must preserve and the necessity to adapt increasingly to conditions of utilizations, which, by definition, can be unforeseeable. The prosumer is therefore at the center of a great new trend towards more flexibility which counters the growth in rigidity which was typical of the 1960's.

## 3.2. CYCLES IN PRODUCTION

3.2.1. Crises And Deflation In The Industrial Revolution. The history of the Industrial Revolution has been punctuated by a series of crises and cycles of different duration [47].

The major crises have been characterized by increased unemployment and deflation. It is only since 1973 that unemployment has grown together with inflation. A slight deflationary trend has been a characteristic of the whole Industrial Revolution in the great majority of those countries which have contributed to this development since 1750. As put in evidence in a book by Landes [48], a kilo of bread cost twenty to thirty percent less at the end of the last century than it had cost at the end of the Napoleonic wars, eighty years earlier. This is true for most parts of Europe.

The general trend of declining prices and the accelerated decline in prices during the downward periods of the great cycles are both a clear indication of oversupply. This oversupply was in great part due to the dynamic development of technology which was making production increasingly efficient and therefore supply more elastic. It was not until after the 1920's and 1930's that the necessity was recognized to absorb the increasing amount of supply by allowing demand the possibility to grow (by stimulating the purchasing power of demand). This was not only a technical or theoretical step, it was as much a societal, historical and partly an ideological one.

Landes, one of the best writers on economic history, has clearly put in evidence that the pace of the development of technology, and in particular of technology based on scientific discoveries after the middle of last century, had increased the potential and the productivity of supply to an extent which had never been experienced in past history. However, it was extremely difficult to recognize the weight of this phenomenon and its amplitude. On the ideological side, the falling prices and the increase in unemployment were explained by Marx as an aspect of social life to keep the working population at the subsistence level in terms of a fierce class struggle: the conclusion for Karl Marx was then to support the poorer majority of the population in this struggle. He did not see that the explosion of productive possibilities on the supply side was shifting the interests of entrepreneurs towards a mass-consumption society where it was essential not to let the majority of workers starve but on the contrary to put them in a condition to buy at least an automobile and a refrigerator.

It is difficult today to imagine a period of deflation and unemployment as was the case recurringly throughout the Industrial Revolution. It is also difficult, under the given cultural conditions, to perceive that the actual advancements of technological development were in fact underestimated for the greatest part of the Industrial Revolution. This derived in part from confusing the very favourable ideological attitudes during the 19th century towards the notion of science which accompanied positivism and scientism, with the difficulty of seeing the big gap that existed between these ideological attitudes and the putting into practice of more technologies, derived from scientific knowledge or otherwise. A careful reading of the history of technology in the 19th century, as well as the history of the life of major scientists and engineers, shows how big this cultural gap was.

Even Karl Marx in "The Capital" is clearly mistaking science and technology when describing the wonders of new weaving machines and of spinning frames as proof of the conquest of science in his time. These were conquests of engineers and of technologists and had very little to do with true advancements in scientific knowledge. David Landes [49] makes the problem very clear by describing the example of the great development in the production of steel in England and its extension on the continent. After having recognized that a lot of coal and iron ore was available in the Ruhr, an initiative was taken in order to start a new coal and steel industry in this part of Germany. The production system of steel was developed, taking into account the English experience. However, whenever the iron ore was heated in the same way as in England, the production of iron ore fell continuously. There was a night watchman called Gilchrist in these ironworks, who had a cousin of the same name who used to come and play cards with him. This second Gilchrist was a kind of "marginal" individual. He spent all his time on devising chemical experiments, which at that time was considered as the activity of a philosopher or an artist. (The cultural link between scientific research in physics and chemistry and its possible technological applications had not yet been made). Gilchrist, the watchman, was worried about losing his job because of the continuous failure to produce iron from the local iron ore. When told about this, his cousin asked for a piece of iron ore (it was the so called "minette"), and compared it with the iron ore used in England. He found that the German ore contained a high degree of phosphorous, which modified the chemical reactions during the cooking of the raw material. This phosphorous had to be neutralized and separated. In this way, not only could he help to get the production of iron started, but he also initiated a new industry, which still exists today, using phosphorous particularly in the field of fertilizers.

It was therefore a family coincidence based on the encounter of a night watchman and his "marginal" cousin, that brought about the start of the Industrial Revolution in Germany, by bridging the gap between scientific advancements and technological applications. In similar ways, many other possibilities were recognized rather than discovered. It took, for instance, almost one century to commercialize the knowledge that some silver salts were sensitive to light: the discovery at the basis of the development of the photographic industry. Many decades were lost not in research and development but simply because of the maturation need in Western culture to learn how to put scientific knowledge into practice.

All this explains why supply and productivity in production have increased in a way which revealed the low level of perception and understanding by economists, industrialists or scientists. Things were happening very often by chance. Only after the 1920's did research and development become professionalized inside industry, or outside, as described in *paragraph 2.1*.

From the 1930's onwards (and particularly since World War Two which had given the final touch to the definitive professionalization of all activities in scientific research and technological development), the delays in utilizing new inventions and discoveries have been essentially of a *technical* nature. Whereas during the 19th century, they had been essentially of a *cultural* nature.

The main characteristic of the whole Industrial Revolution has thus been a period of economic development during which deflation was the main problem. The paradox of this time has been the great *elasticity* of supply, capable of producing much more than society was ready to ask for. This has been accompanied by an economic theory, the basic assumption of which was the fundamental rigidity in supply.

After so many experiences in deflation, it was inevitable that, slowly but surely, the idea of considering supply as the major economic problem, lost a large part of its credibility. Demand then started to come to the forefront of economic analyses and of economic policies.

3.2.2. The Great Expansion Of The Industrial Revolution And The Role Of Demand.
Increased possibilities of consumption, i.e. increased capacity of purchasing (or demand) had in fact already forced action to stimulate economic development during the last century. During the 1870's gold inflow to Europe stimulated demand and therefore production. A large new economic cycle with little inflation [50] started for five to six years, stimulated also by the new developments in railroad transport. Today, we would say that gold played a Keynesian role by expanding demand.

Alfred Marshall, as a typical economist at the end of the last century gave more attention to the role of demand in the economic system in his "Principles of Economics" [51]. He pointed out that demand could quickly shift from one product to another, whereas production was conditioned by a greater inertia. We can decide to drink a beer instead of wine today, but switching production from beer to wine takes many years.

We note today that increasing inertia does condition demand when passing from the Industrial to the Service Economy, and particularly so when consumption is integrated in a pattern of utilization which cannot be changed quickly. When the price of oil went up in 1973 and the following years, it took almost a decade to modify significantly the pattern of demand. In the contemporary economy, supply and demand (production and consumption) need to be considered from the point of view of their rigidities or elasticities *in time* (which means how many months or years does it take to modify in practice a production or a consumption pattern or system). Instant elasticity due to sudden price modifications is probably a minor part of modern economic transactions. A precise and important research topic for economists would be to verify for *all* economic activities the relative rigidities or elasticities *in time* or their inertia.

Alfred Marshall thus opened the door in 1890 to a closer attention to demand; through this door then passed the new establishments of economists who were to dominate the economic scene from the 1920's up to the 1970's, i.e. for half a century.

But this cultural movement also started a deep ideological and analytical change in the notion of economic value itself. Whereas in classical economics, value is linked to the production side and the contributions of labour and capital to the supply of wealth, John Hicks formulated in 1939 the basis for the new notion of value linked to the demand side [52]. Hicks spoke of a "subjective notion of value" which was more closely attached to the idea that value in fact depends on psychological and subjective attitudes towards what we wish to purchase or buy: demand defines what is of value to the consumer which either accepts to buy at a given price or to discard it. The ideological significance of this theory relies on its vigorous affirmation of the social function of the freedom to choose and to consume. A few years ago, Milton Friedman wrote a very successful book titled "Free to Choose" [53], largely in the tradition promoted by John Hicks.

An ideological element in this debate is rooted in the fact that Karl Marx had built his economic and political theory largely on the basis of the notion of value as developed by the great tradition of the classical Industrial Revolution, i.e. concerned essentially with supply. As a consistent part of that tradition had thus been captured by Marxism, John Hicks could only reaffirm the values of liberalism (in the European sense of the word), by laying the foundations of the new economics of *demand*.

However the real advance of economic theory and its practical applications after the 1930's comes from Keynesian theory. Keynes founded his well-known economic theory on the management of demand, in order to stimulate the best utilization of all resources and in particular with the elimination of unemployment as its main objective.

The situation of a great elasticity of supply together with a constant overproduction in periods of crisis (producing deflation) were the reference conditions which enabled the stimulation of mechanisms to increase demand instead of diminishing supply. This demand could be increased by state interventions investing money into new activities and thus distributing salaries and purchasing power, as long as the economy was not in an inflationary state. John Maynard Keynes is credited with having defined this situation as well as the measures of intervention (by deficit spending) to compensate the amount of money which was diverted from the economic circuit, to buy available goods.

Whereas Adam Smith had made it clear that saving money was a virtue, John Keynes added another dimension to this virtue: spending in some cases more than what had been saved can have the virtuous effect of absorbing unemployment and avoiding *deflation* provided of course there is sufficient elasticity of supply. At a theoretical level, "Keynesian-ism" stands for many measures which were taken in several parts of the world and under different ideological covers. The pragmatic President Roosevelt of the USA admitted that "Keynesian" measures worked, despite the fact that he could not really understand the theories of Keynes. Equally "Keynesian" was the programme to build highways in Germany which contributed to the elimination of unemployment at the time of the Third Reich.

The social consequences of "Keynesianism" were welcomed by the trade unions as the economic stimulation of the purchasing power of the masses coincided with the unions' aim to defend the interest of the worker per se. But it was also a good deal for the capitalists: the increasing purchasing power was a guarantee that any new industrial venture, any new product proposed to the market, had a better chance of being bought.

Henry Ford had already been Keynesian "ante litteram" earlier in the 20th century. Producing automobiles in a more standardized way was a good thing, but the increased production could only be sustained by an increased number of people capable of buying these expensive products. It was recognized that in the economic system, both at a practical and theoretical level, demand had to be organized in a monetarized form and stimulated up to the level of full employment, in order to absorb the production or supply.

This development at all levels of demand and consumption was made possible by the quantitative and qualitative jump of supply benefitting from traditional technological developments and from the new possibility of exploiting scientific knowledge as a basis for new technologies, as emphasized before. The greatest period of economic growth in human history started right after World War Two and lasted for a quarter of a century (what we called the "Golden Quarter-Century" earlier on) at an unprecedented rate. It greatly profited from the full professionalization of technological development largely based on scientific knowledge and the destruction of traditional social barriers against increased consumption. Any forecast made in 1945 about the performance of the economy during the following 25 years would have been considered completely mad if it had foreseen what later happened in reality. Mass-production and mass-consumption have been the last triumphant period of the classical Industrial Revolution, up to 1970.

Another major event in the history of economics after the 1930's has been the use of defence expenditures as a practical "Keynesian" tool to stimulate the economy. Today, between one and two billion dollars are spent every day on armaments in the world, and it is obvious that this type of consumption (or "demand") is of great political as well as economic significance. Although some of the economists capable of exercising influence on the Reagan administration claim to be "supply-siders", many of the economic measures taken have had a clear Keynesian flavour. Perhaps the most obvious example to stimulate high technology development and consumption for the purpose of defence has been the so called "Star Wars Programme". The American "supply-siders" are in fact following the ideological line derived from John Hicks: they essentially favour the idea of greater economic freedom, or "Laisser-faire", through which a greater degree of liberty to choose and consume as well as reduced State intervention should better stimulate the development of supply. These American supply-siders are still far from an objective analysis of the conditions of production typical of the new Service Economy. They have neither recognized the possibility of diminishing returns to technology, nor the nature of the change to a Service Economy.

3.2.2. The New Supply Bottlenecks Of The 70's And Inflation : Quantitative And Qualitative Rigidities. Several phenomena converge to contribute to the conditions of the rigidity of supply in the present economic situation. These conditions are of a quantitative, qualitative and social nature.

Firstly, quantitative conditions are linked to a situation of diminishing returns of technology in various sectors. Despite new technologies in the field of telecommunications and electronics developing higher levels of productivity and new jobs, we are a far cry from the classical situation of the Industrial Revolution, when technology not only opened new possibilities of development in virgin areas (such as the chemical industry), but also gave great impulses through the whole spectrum of industrial production. The iron and steel industry, the textile industry and the mining industry which in the past have been the engines of important phases of the Industrial Revolution, are today facing great problems of quantitative re-adaptation and adjustment. In the last twenty years there has been a net decrease in the total number of "industrial" jobs available in Europe and in the United States.

Secondly, the transition from the Industrial Revolution to the Service Economy is at the origin of an even more significant rigidity in supply, which however also opens the door for new challenges and possibilities. If eighty percent of the costs of making any product available to the buyer depend on the functioning of services and systems, then the old schemes of stimulating industrial production in order to develop the economy are over-whelmed by the weight of these services. Furthermore, if services are perceived as barriers to the continuous diffusion of industrialization during this phase of the new economic development, then we are in a difficult situation, for psychological rather than real reasons. Our main problem today is to concentrate and develop the service functions through which 80 percent of the wealth production and utilization really take shape, albeit without forgetting the twenty percent of the costs linked to the manufacturing process. Considering that tomatoes as well as computers only have a (utilization) value if and when they reach the final customer who needs them and knows how to use them, the challenge must be to stimulate productivity and improve these service functions which are the dominant parts in quantitative terms of our present economic reality.

Therefore, if the transition from the industrial society to the Service Economy creates many new barriers and rigidities to supply, considered in the traditional sense, it also clearly defines the space and the battlefield where efforts can be developed for creating wealth under the new conditions of the Service Economy.

Thirdly, general political and social conditions, including fiscal regulations and the degree of State interventions at the various levels of productive activities are an additional element of rigidity in supply. This last argument is the favourite of the American School of "supply-siders". Of course, there are many social and political conditions which increase the rigidities that hinder the various possibilities to develop productive activities. However, during the periods of the great technological advancements in the Industrial Revolution, these innovations always had the power to overcome social or political limitations. The growth of social security systems for old age, accidents and ill health for instance has had the effect of increasing demand in a situation of high elasticity of supply. If, therefore, such social achievements start to be considered today as not always economically justified, it is precisely because supply has no longer the expected flexibility in terms of technological production capabilities.

In the coming decades, the key issue for economic activity will be to improve the use of available resources of any kind (from materials to knowledge, from monetarized to non-monetarized activities), in order to control and reduce scarcity. But the world over, the reduction of scarcity and the increase of wealth depend today much more on the proper functioning and the constant improvement of service functions than on a simple increase of production. Producing meat or potatoes is not sufficient if there are no adequate storage, conservation and distribution systems; if crops are not adequately protected against pests and animals; if delivery is not guaranteed while the produce can still be sold and used. The paradox of a world producing in some areas a large surplus of agricultural produce and food, while other parts of the same world are experiencing real famines, is a formidable challenge to the service economy: the elimination of such disequilibria is clearly linked to the battle to increase the productivity and efficiency of service activities (transport costs and organization, among others).

The persistence of inflation in the monetarized world shows a lack of adequate perception of the fact that in the new Service Economy, the key attention has to be focused on the *systems* of production and of *access* to economic goods, where the consumer is part of the game and becomes a "prosumer".

The experiences in managing demand over the last fifty years have been a tremendous step forward in our capability to control the economy: whenever we will be in a situation of deflation again (a real one), we should have no hesitations in re-using Keynesian tools in order to put things straight and to avoid the waste in management which we have experienced in the first 150 years of the Industrial Revolution. But with these weapons of economic management at hand, the priority for the time being would seem to be to concentrate our efforts on the rigidities of supply. A supply which has little in common with the traditional definition of supply in classical economics (from Adam Smith to Karl Marx), or with the Modern American "supply-siders". Of course, several points brought forward by these old and new schools should still be given attention; however, the key issue is to recognize the predominant reality of the Service Economy in re-evaluating the importance of supply and in reopening the path of progress for the wealth of nations, and by including the contributions of productive non-monetarized activities.

Defining the Service Economy and identifying its new goal for wealth creation and development also means to distinguish among the new risks and uncertainties those which represent a real challenge and an opportunity for progress. Our inability to change perceptions and our continued attachment to the old ideas of the Industrial Revolution lead us to consider risk and uncertainty as threats, whereas, in fact, there is a growing realm for seeking and seizing opportunities.

## 3.3. THE ROLE OF DEMAND

3.3.1. <u>Supply And Demand In A Static "Perfect" Equilibrium</u>. The act of selling or buying goods always takes place at a given instant moment in time, at which a price is agreed and paid. The general economic system is considered by standard economics to be based on a "General Equilibrium" which represents the various transactions taking place in the overall economic system. Prices agreed for transactions represent the equilibrium point between supply and demand. This price, as already underlined, is extremely important because it is taken as the yardstick for measuring the real value of the goods transacted (the exchange value), and because it is the base of measurement for either the notion of supply (added value) in classical economics or of the subjective, demand-based notion of value in neoclassical economics.

Price thus represents a situation in which equilibrium is self-evident: an equilibrium where supply is by definition equal to demand. The reference to time and equilibrium in this context is equivalent to the one that dominated Newtonian science in the 18th and 19th century in Europe: the equilibrium between supply and demand is clearly analogous to the Newtonian equilibrium of our solar system. The planets, the sun and the moons of the various planets find themselves in a situation of "instant" equilibrium, which can be reproduced by e.g. photography. The whole reality is then contained in an instant moment of time from which considerations relative to real time or time-durations are excluded. This is in fact the application of "Cartesianism", which supposes that reality can be discovered by segmenting or isolating each part of any event or phenomenon in discrete (separate) units of time and space. As has been noted by Clark [54], this notion of instant time is the complement of the notion of universal time which is the realm of metaphysics or religion. This is the dichotomy already mentioned in *Chapter 2*. The historical value of equilibrium theory in economics based on a monetarized price system is linked to the fact that one of the essential features of the Industrial Revolution has been the monetarization of the economy as a tool for solving the logistic problems in exploiting ever higher levels of technology. However, giving a universal significance to the notion of price equilibrium and a kind of definitive scientific validity (based on the definition of science before Einstein) is much more a matter of belief or even ideology than one of truly scientific attitude.

The notion of equilibrium is not really a concept or an explanation, but rather a tautology ("something that is right because it is right"), to which has been attached the value or the role of an axiom (those basic self-evident truths used by mathematics for developing subsequent logical deductions). Understanding this notion of equilibrium, where supply is equal to demand, is essential because it explains why economic theory has from the beginning always tended to be one-sided: it is an oxymoron that the notion of economic equilibrium as the key preoccupation of classical economists in reducing scarcity or of neoclassical economists in defining the behaviour of consumers, has favoured attitudes such as: "if supply and demand are by necessity equal, once we have clearly understood one part of the equation, we have also, by definition, defined the other side". This has been a tricky simplification: it had induced classical economists not to understand, for 150 years, that demand had to be expanded to cope with deflationary economic crisis, and later has helped neoclassical economists concerned essentially with demand mechanisms, not to get to grips with the problems of the present rigidities of supply over the last decades.

The notion of general equilibrium in an instant moment of time is also linked to the ambition of the 19th century to find certainty. For a positivistic or a scientific culture, certainty is equated with scientific evidence: if we have not yet reached a perfect equilibrium, or if we have not yet a complete certainty of a given situation, it is simply a matter of time: sooner or later, according to the ideology, we will reach perfect certainty.

The theory of perfect, instant (fundamentally timeless) equilibrium (which is in reality only "certain" because of a tautology) has thus become the basic reference for thought and analysis confronting a reality which is condemned to be looked at as a world of "contingent" imperfections. But imperfections and disequilibria are not "contingent", they are connotations of development, of a dynamic reality.

Over the last couple of decades, the imperfections of general equlibrium have been closely scrutinized by a large number of economists: the notions of incomplete and of asymmetric information [55] have entered the jargon of economic theory and analysis, as a recognition of the many obstacles in achieving a perfect equilibrium. But these notions are still used as if a perfect equilibrium could ever be achieved. The scientists' and positivists' utopia is still there to suggest that we can increase the level of information on the market functioning to such a point that a perfect equilibrium will one day be achieved. This reasoning simply shows that the notions of time of the pre-Einstein era, the idea of isolating instant moments of time outside reality, is still with us. Uncertainty and *dis*equilibrium become the reference reality if we accept real time. Introducing the notion of real time into the economics of supply and demand (service based production and consumption in modern terms) is a radical alternative to the view of the economic process based on timeless (instant) equilibrium. Accepting time-duration, i.e. real time, implies that any decision to produce is inevitably taken in a situation of (greater or smaller) uncertainty with regard to the moment of time when the product will be available and presented to the market. In this dynamic view of the economic process, it is recognized that any decision to produce is taken *ex-ante* of the traditional moment of the economic equilibrium, and that any price definition is always *ex-post* of it.

The moment when the price is fixed in the market is only a *part*, a sub-system of a wider economic system. In the succession of decisions over time, from production to distribution to the Point-of-Sale and further to utilization based activities and the recycling or elimination of waste, the market function of fixing a price is an important element in the process, but it is one element only of a *greater* economic system. And in this greater economic system, uncertainty is not an element of "imperfection", but a given *fact,* containing incompressible elements of risk. Any economic activity or endeavour is based on some unknown and uncertain factors or possibilities, simply because their objective lies in the future.

Once we have accepted the dimension of real time, we may try to make a future event as probable as possible, but we cannot control it to absolute certainty because we cannot control future time, except by eliminating life. In nature as well as in the economic system, many competitive and often redundant production processes are continuously being proposed, of which only a part will reach the point-of-sale and/or the moment of utilization. The successful modern technologies are only a small part of all technologies in which money has been invested but which have nevertheless failed. One successful product on the market allows the possibility of compensation in a strategy based on many initiatives, a great part of which will fail. It is at this point that the role of demand, distinct in time from production, acquires a dimension and an importance which makes it an essential element of the economic system, or of any living system.

3.3.2. <u>Demand As A Selection Mechanism</u>. In economic and in biological reality, an enormous number of uncertain productions are constantly taking place before being *selected* by demand. There is a great difference between an equilibrium process (of supply and demand), and a process in which demand has not an equilibrium but a *selection function*.

A similar attitude has been taken by Karl Popper in his refutation of induction and his defense of empiricism.

> There is no induction: we never argue *from* facts *to* theories, unless by the way of refutation or "falsification". This view of science can be selective, as Darwinian. By contrast, theories of method which assert that we proceed by induction which stress verification (rather than falsification) are typically Lamarckian: they stress *instruction* by the environment, rather than *selection* by the environment. [56]

Current neoclassical demand-based economics sees demand as giving instructions to the economy on how to do things: in this way, a fundamentally deterministic philosophy still shows how it permeates social sciences and economics in particular. By contrast, even if a process of selection can provide some hints and information as to the way it will work, it will always be a simple hypothesis as it normally is in practice, which will only be verified empirically *later*, by facts. But at the same time, a zone of uncertainty will always be preserved because of the fundamental impossibility of forecasting a fully predictable environment if real time, evolution and dynamics are accepted as connotations of real life.

It must be stressed and repeated again that we are now in a dynamic situation in which a static, equilibrium theory of economics cannot help to solve our major problems. Our hypothesis is that of a situation in which economic equilibrium theories are too incomplete to be really efficient; they therefore have to incorporate more problems and less incomplete hypotheses. This precludes the possibility to simply go back to the older economic thinking by stressing the importance of supply. Time dimension gives a much wider sense to the production function than it had in classical economics, and it also underlines the essential complementary role of demand. "Disequilibrium" theory requires a proper in-depth understanding *of both,* demand and supply, *at different levels*.

Whereas priority in economic theories could swing in the past from supply to demand and be considered individually and separately as workable instruments, we now not only need to reconsider the importance of the supply-side, but also the fact that the *selection function* of demand is an absolute necessity, a complement to the production function. By analogy to the quotation of Karl Popper, we could say that an economic system has to produce on the basis of a hypothesis (and maybe even of dreams or any other process stimulating action and initiative): this is the first essential step. But the demand process must also be as efficient as possible in its selective function (including criteria of how to best use material and human resources and societal values).

All this of course does not mean that demand is totally unpredictable when taking production decisions, but even the best market research studies done in the modern economy always have an incompressible level of approximation. We must admit that there is no certainty, but that of course any approximation is better than no approximation at all. We have to *live with* an inevitable degree of uncertainty, which in itself provides the margin for improvements, modifications, new ideas and progress.

The selection function of demand is essential although it can sometimes seem difficult. Production without control by selection can proliferate to a point of being self-destructive for the whole system: cancer is a biological form of uncontrolled self-production with inefficient selection. Demand is efficient because it can select: the deterministic philosophy which has as aspiration to perfectly define demand in advance, to pre-regulate production, is unnatural and can only be inefficient and an element of destruction of material and human resources. The deterministic pretension can only survive through its "imperfections": the greater the imperfections, the better it is.

Demand has to decide over time if in fact available productions are useful. Sometimes, after a first feverish success (like computer games for instance), it may fade out very quickly. In other cases, the fact that this selection mechanism exists guarantees the striving for a better quality of production. Mozart has produced his operas among hundreds of other contemporary composers. He was the essential pre-condition, but then demand has selected him and still does, every time we listen to his music e.g. on the radio or in concert.

In the new Service Economy, where the utilization value implies taking into account real time, demand fulfills an essential complementary role to production. It is no longer a matter of concentrating either on the supply or on the demand-side, as within the framework of general equilibrium theory, but on the economy as a whole. Accepting uncertainty means that we come closer to reality.

## 3.4. EQUILIBRIUM VS NON-EQUILIBRIUM

### 3.4.1. Economics Between Certainty And Uncertainty, Between Static And Real Time : The Reference To The Paradigms Of Natural Science. Economic thinking is still very largely related to traditional Cartesian (and Newtonian) concepts of science. (1)

(1) To the point where a Nobel prizewinner like Prigogine now sees a possibility for a "new alliance" between human and natural sciences. These are no longer different in kind: they are simply more or less indeterminate. As to Weisskopf, he defines the Heisenbergian Paradigm in the following way: "The Heisenberg's principle of uncertainty (or indeterminacy) implies that in microphysics influence of the observer on the position and velocity of particles makes it impossible to ascertain both, their position and velocity, together. Thus, the bases of precise predictions are destroyed". This leads to a different view of reality: "There is no complete causal determination of the future on the basis of available knowledge of the present. It means that every... measurement... creates... a unique, not fully predictable situation". The conclusion was drawn that "we cannot observe the course of nature without disturbing it". Niels Bohr has stated that "man is at once an actor and a spectator in the drama of existence", and Max Born compared the situation to a "football game where the act of watching... applauding or hissing has an influence... on the players and thus on what is watched".

Man is a finite and conditioned being. He is conditioned by his anatomy, physiology, life history, social environment, and innumerable other factors. The position of the scientist is not different; he is also a person subject to such conditions. He cannot step outside himself. His cognitive horizon is limited by his conditioning. Within the limits of these conditions man is free, and he can transcend then within limits by his consciousness. However, this knowledge, scientific or otherwise, contains these conditions as (often silent) assumptions. The reality he recognizes is true reality under the conditions of his existence. He thinks and knows, but the "he" is a conditioned being.

This ontological analysis contains ideas similar to the indeterminacy principle in physics and could be called the philosophical Heisenbergian paradigm. It is more than an accidental coincidence that in two such disparate fields similar ideas were developed. They are rooted in the spirit of the times. The new ambience in metaphysics, physics, and politics is one of uncertainty. If pushed to its ultimate conclusion, the Newtonian model elevates man as the objective, detached, "scientific" observer to the level of an omniscient deity who can foresee the future. In contrast, the Heisenbergian model demotes man to a participant who cannot extricate himself from the reality he wants to analyze. This new world view exposes the helplessness and uncertainty which is inherent in the human situation and which was repressed and denied in Newtonian thought.

It is the recognition that "action is the setting in motion of a new beginning with uncertain outcome", which makes "action" both real and possible.

It has been rather surprising to note during recent decades that while "social" scientists of all kinds, economists in particular, have been chasing after an "objective" image of their "science", and have often implied that social sciences would in this way come one day to bear comparison with the "more scientific" natural sciences, the latter have in the meantime moved away from the traditional Cartesian-Newtonian paradigm. (2)

(2) W. Weisskopf states very clearly that "The Newtonian paradigm, used in classical and neoclassical economics, interpreted the economy according to the pattern developed in classical physics and mechanics, and in analogy to the planetary system and to a clockwork: a closed, autonomous system, ruled by endogenous, mutually interdependent factors of a highly selective nature, self-regulating and moving toward a determinate, predictable point of equilibrium. The Newtonian paradigm, in line with eighteenth century thinking, represents economic events as a reality independent of the observer. The observing subject is supposed to be detached from the observed object, but he can grasp this object with his reason. An objective reality, subject to natural laws, is comprehensible to and knowable by human reason. The idea of natural law was the intermediate link between subject and object which, despite their mutual independence, united them through "scientific" understanding.

Thus separate subjects, objects, natural law, and reason formed a quaternal unitary configuration. The natural laws were laws of causation, interpreted as causae efficientes, not causae finales; as moving forces, not aspirations and motivations; not only in non-human nature but also in the realm of human existence. The goal of this pattern of thought was to predict future events and to arrive at determinate solutions in all dimensions of reality. If all variables, all cause-and-effect relations were known, we could understand and predict the events in the universe, in society, and all human action. The basic conviction of most scientists was and to a large extent still is that despite temporary ignorance, ineluctable laws determine all events and actions. No place was left for freedom, choice, uncertainty, and mystery. This pattern of thought was used in classical and neoclassical economics as the foundation of equilibrium models: it was supplemented by fictitious assumptions, such as perfect knowledge and perfect forecasting, and through elimination of time and change by the ceteris paribus clause. This paradigm, as applied in economics, was connected with a belief in the beneficiality, justice and fairness of the free market and industrial system".

The Cartesian mechanism of thinking, although effective and influential in situations where industrialization is the top priority and the best tool for organizing wealth and welfare, has raised a series of methodological and practical problems. Isolating monetarized economic factors is a method that is today showing more and more weaknesses. In order to clarify this point, consideration will first be given to the way the notion of science is often perceived in economics.

It was customary in the nineteenth century to believe that the Cartesian or Newtonian method of scientific research consists first in defining a situation or a problem clearly, identifying and measuring all its constituents, as if the said situation or problem could be fully determined (or at least assuming that anything left out had no appreciable influence on the system under observation). In this way, a water molecule can be isolated and studied. In this way, Newton gave a clear view of celestial mechanics. In this way, the economist hoped to provide scientifically framed and determined "models" of reality. In practice, this is often still the simple, even trivial method used and still conceived in accordance with the underlying assumption that the reality examined is for the most part "objective". This view presupposes simple systems and, as an essential corollary, the divisibility of time and space.

It has been clear in the natural sciences for many decades that even if a multitude of realities exist which we can profitably research in the "Cartesian" way, when we get down to basic issues (such as: What is matter?), and to issues related to "objectivity" (if such a thing exists), we find ourselves in extremely complex and even indeterminate systems.

(Indeterminate is used in the sense of Heisenberg. The whole controversy, started by Einstein with his "probabilistic" reality, is an important reference for this point.).

If what has been said here is only partially acceptable, it nevertheless follows that it may benefit economics to question some basic assumptions, especially the notion of value, on which economics itself is founded, as well as its historical and cultural determinants with reference to the notions of time and space.

In the Cartesian-Newtonian universe, time is either infinite or specific: one can isolate a moment in time. One can statically examine "reality" as if it were a picture, freezing all movement. The equlibrium of Newton's universe is like the equilibrium of the supply/ demand curves of the economists: at a given moment in time (instant time) the situation is such and such. Simple, definable forces determine equlibrium situations, and each state or situation can be isolated.

Under such conditions, the relative behaviour of phenomena in time and space tends to disappear, or to be represented in a static framework, eliminating duration or real time.

Today, the notion of uncertainty has become a "fact of life", linked to specific perceptions or a particular business cycle. Furthermore, ever since Einstein had to admit implicitly against his will and deep moral conviction that God "plays with dice", there has been a constantly growing volume of literature dealing with fundamentals concerning the nature of science and the structure of knowledge. Basic notions such as relative time/space, the indetermination of systems, the historical relativity of axioms, and uncertainty are increasing all through the natural and social sciences spectrum of research [57].

Contrary to what happened in the past century, during which science was considered to be equivalent to a more efficient way of attaining "universal" truth and, as such, a competitor to religion , it is now generally accepted that science is a method of "falsifying" (in Karl Popper's terminology) all theories, hypotheses and facts. In other words, there is no such thing as "universal" scientific truth, but only a limited operational validity in time and space of any scientific law or theory (which means that "it works").

Our culture, by and large, is not yet used to looking at science in this way. It is very revealing to find the survival of the "universal objectivity" notion of science even in recent literature. A brilliant example is "The Sleepwalkers" by Arthur Koestler, in which science and religion are treated as complementary ways of reaching universal truth. In our opinion, underlying these attitudes to truth and science is the notion of time/space. If time/space is considered to be something that can be isolated in a given moment or place, this "abstract" moment (like Newton's notion of the universal equilibrium) can logically be considered to be of "universal value" [58]. But this pretension to "universal" logic breaks down when mathematics tells us that there are no more "universal", unchangeable (Godsend) axioms.

108

Economics itself has developed for more than a century on the basis of this cultural background of a "static", Newtonian notion of time/space, which goes hand in hand with the assumption of certainty that still dominates today's thinking.

The notion of uncertainty has also started to make some important inroads in economic thinking. A major breakthrough will come with the adaptation of economics to the notions of real space/time dimensions, which implies taking into account real and relative duration: This process has already virtually begun. It calls in the first place for the definition and acceptance of a new notion of value [59].

In general terms, it should be recalled that life itself, real life, is based on uncertainty. Risk and uncertainty characterize life not by choice, but as a condition if only because life is real time, and risk and uncertainty are connotations of real time. The corollary is that:

> future events - for the Heisenbergian paradigm - are the result of unpredictable human actions and reactions, ...if the Newtonian paradigm on the one side enthrones man as a potentially omniscient, detached observer of an independent objective reality, ...at the same time nature, society and man are subject to inexorable "natural" laws which determine unequivocally man's future and fate. [60]

We insist that during the classical Industrial Revolution such principles have been rather efficient. But our present century has witnessed the degradation of their consequences, including the undermining of the notion of responsibility and freedom of action.

Ten years ago, Rene Passet [61], a French economist, wrote that economics has until now been concerned with "dead things". He starts his analysis by drawing attention to the correspondence between economic thinking during the past two centuries and changes in the notion of science [62]. Dead and living things are opposites analogous to static and real time being opposites. The transition from one to the other is a transition from utopian certainty to the challenge of real uncertainty, from essentially deterministic thinking to the possibility of building real responsibility and freedom, taking advantage of a largely indeterminate world.

Of course, too much uncertainty leads to impotence, which is precisely the reason why its origin must be understood whenever possible (as in the case of understanding that the present rigidities of economic supply are conditioned by the diminishing returns of technology). But in the end, the problem is how to live better, i.e. to learn how to face risks better.

A new synthesis (which we hope will soon take place) between the advancement made in economics and the various social sciences, and in the basic thinking underlying the advancement of natural sciences, is of vital importance.

3.4.2. From Newton To Prigogine : Equilibrium As A Goal Or "Attractor" In A Far From Equilibrium System.

> Today, wherever we look, we find evolution, diversification and instabilities. A fundamental re-conceptualization of science is going on... . The artificial may be deterministic and reversible. The natural contains essential elements of randomness and irreversibility. This leads to a new vision of matter that is

no longer passive, as described in the mechanical world view, but associated with spontaneous activity. This change is so deep that I believe we can really speak about a new dialogue on man with nature... .

We are more and more numerous to think that fundamental laws of nature are irreversible and stochastic; that the deterministic and reversible roles are applicable only in limiting situations... .

Today, our interest is shifting to known equilibrium systems, interacting with a surrounding through the entropy flow... . The thermodynamical point of view is one of interaction, we could say a holistic one... . Dynamical systems have no way to forget perturbations... . In thermodynamics, perturbations may be forgotten. In the thermodynamic description including dissipation we have attractors.

Without attractors, our world would be chaotic. No general rules would ever have been formulated. Every system would pose a problem apart. We can now also understand in quite general terms what happens when we drive a system far from equilibrium. The attractor which dominated the behaviour of the system near equilibrium may become unstable, as a result of the flow of matter and energy which we direct at the system. Non-equilibrium becomes a source of order; new types of attractors, more complicated ones, may appear and give to the system remarkable and new space-times properties.
I like to say that at equilibrium, matter is blind; far from equilibrium it may begin to see... . [63]

These quotations come from Ilya Prigogine [63]. He is at the forefront of the research and debate which is finding a profound echo in many sectors of natural and social sciences. Books from different horizons are multiplying in the world which all go in similar directions: the acceptance of the notion of uncertainty, of disequilibrium, of real time considered in its duration, not as imperfections of our scientific knowledge, in whatever field, but as the very connotations of the dynamics of life and of evolution [64].

A fundamental philosophical aspect of all these trends is the constantly growing interest in indeterminism, visible in major publications such as the recent updating of the famous book by Karl Popper on "The Logic of Scientific Discovery". His last three volumes ("Realism and the Game of Science", "The Open Universe: an Argument for Indeterminism", "Quantum Theory and the Schism in Physics"), published in 1983 [65], constitute a recent exhaustive "post script" to this fundamental work.

Given this background, economics will hardly be capable of maintaining the notion of general equilibrium as the basic reference for a general theory applied to our contemporary world for a long time. At best, the notion of equilibrium, in practice, might be identified with the notion of "attractor" (3).

(3) The notion of attractor indicates the direction in which a system moves towards a focalization point (or points); the notion of equilibrium is often seen as a goal, not necessarily achieved, but it is this function (i.e. the fact of being a goal, a direction or a focalization point), which gives practical relevance to the notion of equilibrium in economics. In this sense, one could also underline the fact that present economic theory is *incomplete* with regard to present economic problems, where many phenomena, which are still considered outside the realm of economics will have to be included in a larger general theory. Some evolution is in the air, such as expressed in an article of Hirshleifer of 1979, analyzing uncertainty, putting in evidence that the equilibrium system itself is always certain, and that uncertainties have to be considered as *exogenous* elements to the economic system itself. This sounds like a last desperate defense; it is however possible and probable that the notion of equilibrium (or rather the motivations which are presently behind this notion) can be preserved if defined as "attractor" within a more global economic system, which is accepted as uncertain and includes in its general theory a larger number of elements in time and space.

Attractors then are points of reference, indicators of directions (possible, probable or even improbable), in a real time dimension. By carefully reading the writings of many contemporary economists, one can easily find that, under the formal definition of the general equilibrium theory, goals, objectives and possible directions are described. But the real issue in accepting the idea that systems are essentially in a far-from-equilibrium situation is the better identification of the dynamics of economic progress and evolution: the dynamics of real time. If disequilibria, and the acceptance of the fact that every judgment is at best the expression of a probability, then accepting and managing uncertainty becomes the key issue.

Our ignorance and our imperfect information are a state of disequilibrium, a condition of life and of evolution. Our growing ignorance, determined by the growth of our knowledge which increases the number of unanswered questions, is the best indicator that we participate in the flow of life. Experience tells us that each time we have the feeling of having *completely* mastered and understood a problem, it is often because the object or the situation of reference no longer exists: we are just at the edge of discovering that our confidence in our capacity to "totally" understand is at least partly misplaced. Normal life is not so different from the process of scientific thinking: hypotheses are emitted and tested; they may work for a while until at some point in time, something does not fit into the picture anymore. We then have to re-adapt, re-think and re-formulate our ideas, our understanding or our theories in a broader or different framework.

In the words of Ilya Prigogine [66]:

> The views of evolutionary changes as a dialogue between "randomness" and "deterministic selection" is at least as old as Darwin; but in the views developed here, the randomness results partly from the ignorance of the actors concerning the system as a whole, a lack of knowledge which allows the exploration of new ideas that give rise to creative reorganization.

Ignorance is there to be continuously challenged and reduced, but its very existence allows us to discover and to create; in short, to develop ourselves.

## 3.5. ACCOUNTING FOR VALUE IN THE SERVICE ECONOMY

**3.5.1. <u>Measuring Value In The Industrial Revolution : The Monetarized Flow</u>.** We have put in evidence the fact that price is the reference yardstick to organize a measurement system capable of quantifying economic phenomena and results, within the framework of the industrial process.

Price is given by exchange, and the money obtained through each transaction is then used to remunerate all those who have contributed to the production of the goods or services. Labour is paid wages or salaries, capital (representing an accumulation of labour in terms of tools made available for production, e.g. a plant, a machine, a system, a level of knowledge, a managerial capacity) gets interests. Each contribution to the various steps of transforming raw materials into usable products or usable functions represents a "value added". Adam Smith built his notion of value on this idea of "value added" and considered it equivalent to the "exchange value". *Figure 21* resumes these notions.

Figure 21. The classical economic concept of value in the industrial society: The example of an automobile.

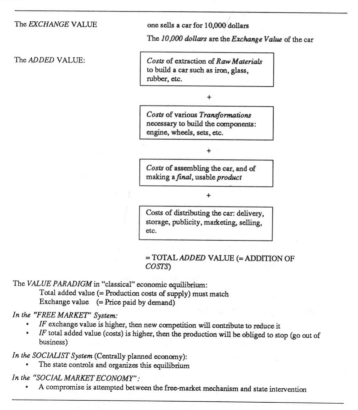

The *EXCHANGE* VALUE     one sells a car for 10,000 dollars

The *10,000 dollars* are the *Exchange Value* of the car

The *ADDED* VALUE:

*Costs* of extraction of *Raw Materials* to build a car such as iron, glass, rubber, etc.

\+

*Costs* of various *Transformations* necessary to build the components: engine, wheels, sets, etc.

\+

*Costs* of assembling the car, and of making a *final*, usable *product*

\+

Costs of distributing the car: delivery, storage, publicity, marketing, selling, etc.

= TOTAL *ADDED* VALUE (= ADDITION OF *COSTS*)

The *VALUE PARADIGM* in "classical" economic equilibrium:
    Total added value (= Production costs of supply) must match
    Exchange value   (= Price paid by demand)

*In the "FREE MARKET" System:*
- *IF* exchange value is higher, then new competition will contribute to reduce it
- *IF* total added value (costs) is higher, then the production will be obliged to stop (go out of business)

*In the SOCIALIST System* (Centrally planned economy):
- The state controls and organizes this equilibrium

*In the "SOCIAL MARKET ECONOMY":*
- A compromise is attempted between the free-market mechanism and state intervention

Source: Giarini, Orio (ed.) (1980) Dialogue on Wealth and Welfare, Pergamon Press, Oxford.

But the notion of value added has not just remained historically a basis for economic theory. In recent decades it has become a reference for the fiscal system through the introduction of value added taxes.

It is essential to understand that the measurement of value added in economics refers to the measurement of a flow. Although reference is made to the selling price (which could give the impression that it is the measurement of a result), the reference to the cost of the production factors is conceptually linked to the measurement of what contributes to the production of wealth, and not to the measurement of wealth itself. This can best be explained as a bath-tub with two taps, as shown in *Figure 22*.

Figure 22. The bath-tub of economic wealth.

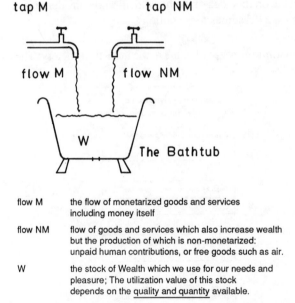

| flow M | the flow of monetarized goods and services including money itself |
|---|---|
| flow NM | flow of goods and services which also increase wealth but the production of which is non-monetarized: unpaid human contributions, or free goods such as air. |
| W | the stock of Wealth which we use for our needs and pleasure; The utilization value of this stock depends on the quality and quantity available. |

The bathtub contains a certain amount of water $W$ representing a stock of wealth which we use for our needs and pleasure. This stock of water $W$ is fed by two taps:
- the tap $M$ represents the flow of monetarized production, which pours additional wealth into our stock $W$,
- the tap $NM$ symbolizes the flow of goods and services which also increase our wealth, but the production of which is non-monetarized. It refers for instance to free, unpaid human contributions, or free goods like air.

When reading about economic indicators, many problems arise in our mind from the lack of distinction between what relates to our stock of wealth $W$ (monetarized or not), and what refers to the flows $F$ (monetarized or non-monetarized). The value added in economics is essentially a measurement of the *monetarized flow*. It measures how much monetarized production is passing the tap $M$ to increase the stock of wealth $W$. The underlying assumption rooted in the Industrial Revolution is that any addition represents an equivalent increase of the stock $W$.

The reason for choosing the monetarized flow $FM$ instead of the stock of wealth $W$ as the measurement reference is that the (statistical) measurement of the flow is easier to do. The measurement of the stock, in contrast, appears much more complex because all sorts of non-monetarized productions that inevitably intervene may not be noticed and because, in the case of the sale of a part of our stock, a definite reference value to refer to the loss in stock or wealth may not be available.

However, the fundamental assumption of this reasoning still is that the production of the monetarized flow $FM$ is equivalent to an increase in wealth $W$ !

Over the last ten to twenty years, we have perceived the emergence of a new type of problem linked to environmental and ecological constraints, which strongly suggest that the monetarized flow is not always an addition to wealth: the monetarized flow contains a non-negligible part of pollution which does not add to, but destroys wealth [67].

The measurement of growth as expressed in the Gross National Product is precisely and only the measurement of such a monetarized flow at the macro-economic, national level. It excludes the standard accounting practice used by all industrial companies and individuals: an accounting of total assets or stock available, and total liabilities incurred (the Balance Sheet), of which the analysis of the flow of activity performed during a given period of time (the Statement of Income and Expenses) is an integral part. At the micro-economic level, it is a matter of common knowledge and common-sense that the differential in total value of assets (e.g. stock) does not necessarily coincide with the volume of activity performed over a given period of time: the accounting of assets is a process which puts in evidence the accumulation of an activity during a longer period of time, rather than simply to know if the monetarized flow during this same period has increased or decreased (remaining always bigger than O!).

During the classical Industrial Revolution, it could be assumed that the amount of monetarized flow largely corresponded to increases in the stock of wealth. In the Service Economy, this is no longer true: the real level of wealth (i.e. the stock) depending also on non-monetarized contributions and deducted values. Value added coincided largely with the real utilization value and as such became the primary indicator of the growing wealth. The notion of utilization value itself refers to the assets (stock) and the way it is used, in contrast to the notion of added value referring to the flow of monetarized production.

The measurement of such stock can of course only be approximate and will be partly subjective: this means that the decision of what has value then partly becomes a matter for political consensus, similar to the estimated "goodwill" in the Balance Sheets of a company. The future choice may well be between a system of flow measurement which is quantitatively precise but is increasingly loosing its significance, and systems of asset measurements which might be less precise but will be more relevant to the real world. The quantification of non-monetarized wealth elements can be achieved by adequate indicators. This is a crucial topic, as any method of asset accounting would also enable a better definition of riches and poverty, and thus avoid the perpetuation from a higher level of wealth than officially recorded, as the non-monetarized contributions to the wealth of one country may be higher than the one of another country [68].

3.5.2. <u>Old And New Shortcomings : Wealth And Riches, The Paradox Of Relative Prices, The Deducted Value, The Non-Accounted Value</u>. Classical economists, and in particular Ricardo, were well aware that the accounting of economic wealth that they were elaborating was not really comprehensive of the real level of wealth of an individual or a country. A clear distinction was made between the notion of riches on the one side and of wealth on the other [69]. There was even an implicit admission that an increase in wealth could eventually not correspond to an increase in riches.

However, these considerations remained secondary because the main problem during the Industrial Revolution was to identify the most dynamic system of increasing the wealth of nations, i.e. the industrialization process, and to concentrate on its development. Inconveniences and discrepancies between wealth and riches were considered as of minor importance. The writings in classical economics and some of the later commentators [70] were a consequence of the fact that the first formalization of economic theory was a description of the industrialization process: the priority was to measure a flow of goods and the value added, whether supply or demand-based, was quite adequate for this purpose.

In the Service Economy, when the industrialization process per se is no longer identified as the prime mover to increase the wealth of nations, the problem is quite different and the contradiction between wealth and riches becomes much more important.

The divergence of the notion of riches versus the notion of wealth corresponds to what can be called the development of the deducted values in the modern economy. The increase of these deducted values stems from the increasingly higher allocation of economic resources to activities which do not add to the real level of wealth (or of riches), but which are in fact absorbed by the rising costs of the functioning of the economic system.

Let us look at an example: in many households, the level of wealth is strongly increased by the introduction of washing machines, other electrical appliances and new tools that make home work easier. But with the increased level of wealth comes an increase in the amount of waste produced at home, which, during the 1960's, has led the research centers of companies producing household appliances to develop new machines to get rid of kitchen waste. In a traditional sense a waste shredder (or a waste compactor) machine adds to wealth, whereas in reality, it is just coping with the increased nuisance at one place in the system (the private house) and creating a system breakdown at another location (the sewage or waste treatment plant). In addition, we have not become richer by having a machine to destroy garbage, compared to when we had no garbage in need of disposal. But in the economics of the Industrial Revolution, our wealth has increased.

There are many other examples around us to witness the evolution since the 1960's: air and water pollution are clear situations of diminishing real wealth (or of diminishing riches): if money is invested to de-pollute water or to develop alternative solutions such as bottled water, special reservoirs for drinking water, or swimming pools next to a polluted seashore, we have again "catch 22" situations where investments are necessary to compensate for riches lost through e.g. pollution: these investments are not net added value to our wealth!

The growing discrepancies between levels of wealth and riches (or the contradiction between economically accounted wealth and real wealth) are strongly suggesting the need to refer increasingly to stock, i.e. variations in real wealth, as a substitute for the measurement of production flows (the bath-tub example). Furthermore, there is also a problem of matching real added values against deducted values: a concept of thinking in terms of systems and measuring the real results will have to replace the simple analysis of the costs of an isolated activity.

The notion of deducted value implies the need to take into consideration the notion of negative value. In economic analysis, this is already a step forward, considering that the negative side of economic activities has so far often simply been non-accounted for in many cases. Diminishing increases of an economic situation have in fact to be distinguished against a net negative process. Measuring wealth through flows that do not fill a bath-tub, or even worse, are shut off, exclude the notion of negative flows. Only by looking at the stock can positive *and* negative variations be measured and can decision be taken if the flows produce values added or values deducted.

We should also consider that the present accounting system is even inadequate, in the positive sense, to measure many increases in the real wealth. This phenomenon is linked to some paradoxes related to the notion of relative prices.

Relative prices and their changes are one of the major indicators to verify if a new technology or a new production system has really been efficient in a given sector. When there is a great advancement in a new sector, the costs of products do not only diminish per se, but their price also strongly diminishes related to other products offered in the market: ten years ago, the price of a small calculator was the equivalent of 500 kilos of bread; it is now less than 10 kilos. This means that the relative prices of pocket calculators have strongly diminished, in terms of bread.

At the level of the individual, the substitution of a rare and expensive product (as, for instance, calculating machines thirty years ago) for a cheap product greatly increases his riches, but can diminish his wealth. The fact that we can buy products today, such as pocket calculators, which twenty or thirty years ago we could not afford to buy for private use, is an indicator that we are much richer today, in real terms. But in terms of the monetarized wealth at our disposal, any person who could afford such a machine twenty or thirty years ago was considered to be much richer than we are today, when we need little money to buy it.

At the macro-economic level, this phenomenon might be less contradictory. If, today, the price of pocket calculators is 1/10 of what it was ten years ago, and if, instead of selling ten calculators ten years ago, it is possible to sell 1.000 today, we have increased the sales value ten fold in terms of money. But the real wealth of people has increased much more: some of the revenues and profits generated through the expansion of the pocket calculator market can be used for buying those goods which have remained expensive, i.e. the relative price of which has remained high.

In terms of measuring our real wealth, the mere fact of knowing if and how much the world has grown richer is much less obvious to evaluate than we normally think. While on one side we have become poorer over the last ten years because we must pay *more* for previously free goods or services, such as uncontaminated drinking water or swimming in non-polluted water, we have, on the other side, become richer by having pocket calculators and video cassettes available for the equivalent of a few hours of salaried work. And we can afford to see high quality operas and plays that were reserved for Kings and Emperors at the time of Moliere.

Trying to measure the value added and to consider the mechanism of relative prices therefore leads to conclusions, in terms of evaluating increases in wealth, that are much more complex than expected at first. The easy way out is to measure the levels of real wealth available (its utilization value) with approximate indicators. The complication linked to the "Industrial Revolution accounting" is nicely described by the paradox of hell and heaven, linked to the notion of scarcity. Heaven, being probably blessed by an infinite stock of goods and services of all sorts (material and spiritual), does not know scarcity, economics and the economy therefore do not exist: there are no prices and there is no money because everything is available without any restrictions or work: heaven must be something very different from earth, but also a place of zero GNP. Hell as the opposite of heaven, is a place which consumes a lot of energy to maintain its image and its assumed activities. It therefore probably needs to develop a huge value added which nobody has ever tried to measure: GNP must be very high.

On our earth, the maximum possible achievement in the fight against scarcity is to achieve abundance in as many sectors as possible. But human and economic development is also linked to the identification and fight against *new* scarcities. Scarcity is finally a connotation of the disequilibrium system in which human endeavour is embedded: it is the sine-qua-non condition for the search of fulfillment.

3.5.3. The Bath-tub System : Measuring Results Through Indicators. One of the major paradoxes in value accounting and defining the development of wealth is that an increase in real wealth corresponds in some cases to increase costs for pollution control (e.g. investments for waste disposal and for environmental purposes which are clearly a deducted value type of cost), while on the other side, many real increase in value are under-rated. For instance, GNP growth figures published each year by governments indicate that the economy has grown by so many percent. However a large part of this growth is in fact absorbed by factors which do not necessarily add to our wealth, whereas other factors that represent net increases in our well-being are not, or only inadequately, taken into account.

Going back to the paradox of hell and heaven, we may still be reluctant to reconquer paradise as we are in a strange way more at ease with hell.

Referring to the example of the bath-tub in *paragraph 3.5.1.*, it seems important to define a level of the wealth of nations in terms of stock, its increase, its depletion, its use, its conservation and its diversification. The measurements of value added are important for the organization of the industrially productive system, which is an important sub-system of the whole economic system. But it is only partially relevant in measuring, targeting and organizing the wealth of nations.

These measurements can be made using indicators which have been developed in many sectors and for many purposes over the past four decades. Yet these indicators need the reference to a general economic theory that gives them the status and the relevance of instruments fulfilling a doubly fundamental role: organizing and creating consensus (around their definition), and being efficient for the general development of riches, of the real wealth of nations.

Furthermore, the transition to an economic system and theory going beyond the traditional notion of economic (added) value requires the acceptance of a certain degree of uncertainty as far as the measurements are concerned. This uncertainty is linked to the fact that the very question of what wealth should be includes the definition of some goals and expectations: the definition of a level of wealth is relative to the evolution of time and history.

Another element of uncertainty in the notion of real wealth and welfare is linked to the fact that many riches are conditioned by climatic conditions: countries with cold climates will always need to develop more sophisticated heating systems than countries with a milder climate. In the former case, more monetarized activities have to be developed in order to provide artificial, man-made sources of heat that can be stockpiled for winter. In milder areas, less provisions are needed and expenses incurred for heating. Who is the poorer and who is the richer here: he who *needs* to spend a lot of money on heating or he who has no need of heating?

We should never forget the paradox of hell and heaven: less scarcity leads quite naturally to less economic monetarized wealth.

However, where the constraints are harder, the stimulus to avoid hell in order to survive is probably greater: many potentially poorer people have in the past become more industrious and richer than those who lived in a more blessed environment. This is true for individuals in all parts of the world as well as for nations. But it is a historical process and it can be reversed. Furthermore, not all advantages are necessarily on the same side: where life is exuberant and easy, it is so not only for the human species, but possibly also for competing biological beings like viruses.

This whole domain is hard to define: indicators of the level of wealth, of health, of happiness, of knowledge and of the availability of material tools and means are concepts that are somewhat uncertain and changing. The notion of value added is apparently much simpler and has the attraction of having been proposed and used as an instrument of universal management, as a standard that can be applied everywhere.

The wisest way to proceed, in science as in other activities including economic ones, is it not to start always by using the simplest system?

The problem is that the universal validity of the concept of value added is essentially a measurement of an industrial production process. The establishment of a sound statistical basis for the measurement of the stock of wealth and its variation by an adequate choice of indicators which may be different in different parts of the world (but do not exclude a minimum level of homogeneity to allow comparisons), is not necessarily more complicated than the measurement of value added [71].

After all, there are already plenty of economic indicators in use which are redefined periodically, such as the consumer price indices that serve as a base for the determination of the level of inflation in many countries. These indices contain a number of well-weighted elements entering into the composition of the index.

They are by definition not identical in all countries as they reflect the evolving structure of consumption.

Why not define the real level of wealth or of riches in a similar way and allow the definition of wealth to vary in the same way as the definition of the typical consumption pattern vary in each country?

In the mature Service Economy this type of index might be politically more appealing, especially if it succeeds in closing the gap between the measurements of GNP which do not reflect the reality of real wealth variations, and the perceptions of the individuals, the "prosumers", who already experience in practice what it means to become richer in contemporary economic conditions.

## 3.6. THE PROBLEM OF DEMARCATION IN ECONOMICS

3.6.1. Opening Up The Boundaries Of Economics : Beyond Production (Services), Beyond Time (Uncertainty, Risk), Beyond Monetarization (The Environment); Complexity And Uncertainty. In the introduction to his "Principles of Economics", Alfred Marshall [72] wrote:

> Economics is a study of mankind in the ordinary business of life; it examines that part of individually social action, which is most closely connected with the attainment and with the use of the material requisites of well-being. Thus it is on the one side a study of wealth; and on the other and more important side, a part of the study of men...; the two great forming agencies of the world's history have been the religions and the economy. Here and there, the ardor of the military or artistic spirit have been for a while predominant: but religions and economic influence have nowhere been displaced from the front rank even for a time: and they have nearly always been more important than all others put together. The religions' motifs are more intense than economic, but their direct action seldom extends over so large a part of life.

Alfred Marshall's definition of economics is thus a very broad one. His interest in economics relates to his perception that it is the single most important activity of human beings and societies. Religion is of equal importance, but only on moral grounds. War making and the arts maybe important, but are secondary.

This introduction conveys the feeling that economics is all embracing, and that even for a moralist like Alfred Marshall, it opens the door to a materialistic view of life which had been present at different degrees, in most of the thinking of the 19th century. Alfred Marshall recognizes in one of the appendices of the same book the great importance of Adam Smith as a founder of economics as a discipline or science, in view of his definition of value. However, as the notion of value is based on the process of industrialization (a monetarized process), the methods of economics, and finally of classical (and neo-classical) economics, do not consider the wide definition of society as proposed by Alfred Marshall, but consider only the most important development taking place within society, i.e. the industrialization process in a monetarized form.

Once the industrialization process takes account of the new Service Economy as a priority for the economic development of society, we are coming closer to the vision of Alfred Marshall.

But there remains a fundamental problem of the demarcation of economics as such.

The positive affect of the notion of specialization introduced in a systematic way by Descartes in his "discours sur la methode" was to be an antidote against the tendency to rely too much on generalists' knowledge: too much thin widespread knowledge can and often does lead to superficiality and inefficiency [73]. With the growing volume of knowledge and given the limitations of the human brain, specialization not only of tools, but of sciences and disciplines, is essential. The growth of new disciplines has been outstanding in recent decades and new ones are still emerging, such as astrophysics and molecular biology.

The necessary strategy for each discipline to become credible and useful and to increase general knowledge, is to have a clear idea of its goals and of the methods it will use to study and analyze them. What really happens in this process is a setting up of demarcations between what a discipline is and is not doing.

When, in 1776, economics was officially born as a specific discipline, as a brainchild of Adam Smith, the identification of the industrialization process as the key for general economic development corresponded to the identification of the main goal. And the method of analyses was provided by the notion of value added (exchange value, based on a price derived from an equilibrium system).

Even if this problem of demarcation was not always clearly expressed in the writings of classical economists, the deepening of the process of the industrial revolution and the development of the monetarization process of economic activities have progressively made the demarcation lines of economics more apparent and clearer. In the process, the discipline of economics itself has become richer and richer, has expanded human knowledge of economic phenomena, and has started a great struggle against the situation of ignorance on economic matters. *Within* the demarcation lines of this increasingly defined discipline or science of economics, many key changes of a theoretical nature have taken place during the last 200 years. Switching the reference of the notion of value from the supply to the demand side is an example of such a change that took place *within* the boundaries of economic thinking, within the demarcation line of what constitutes economics with respect to other sorts of societal analyses put forward by, for instance, sociology and anthropology.

The demarcation problem is a wide one and concerns all disciplines. And as for technologies, the methods derived from within the demarcation lines encounter situations of diminishing returns when problems arise which cannot easily be solved, respecting the traditional demarcation lines. In economics, as long as the dominant activity was the industrialization process, major switches could take place within the paradigm of a notion of value (monetarized and static). But the change from an industrially dominated economic system to a service dominated one is a process where the existing demarcation lines of economics will have to open up.

The opening-up of the existing demarcation of economics will be guided by the service economy as a major reference and the notion of time as the reference for value measured over the period of utilization. Furthermore, the demarcation lines will have to give up the paradigm of certainty; the notion of uncertainty is the key reference of any human activity considering real time. The notion of risk itself, which has been treated much more by sociologists than by economists during the whole history of the Industrial Revolution, is becoming the key reference of the new Service Economy in the way previously described [74].

In addition, the traditional demarcation lines of economics will also have to open up to the contribution of non-monetarized activities (human activities and contributions by the environment), which are increasingly integrated in any monetarized activity. To summarize, a notion of value, a notion of utilization value, is at stake. This is the message we have tried to transmit in the previous paragraphs.

Finally, the demarcation lines will have to open up when the present linear production process is substituted in the service economy by a highly interrelated and increasingly complex system, the value of which will be measured in terms of the results of its functioning. As we have already stressed, economic value will then be less related to the existence of a tool or of a product and increasingly to the functioning of a complex system.

On the question of complexity, it is obvious today that the functioning of an air transport system is much more complex than the transport by horse drawn carriages which was dominant up to the middle of last century. This trend towards ever greater complexity has led us to consider the notion of systems and of their capacity to produce results as one key feature of the Service Economy.

In economic history, complexity has grown both vertically and horizontally: more specialization (a vertical process) leads to the creation of more functions to make the specialized products useful, and to more communication networks to guarantee organizational functioning as the system becomes more complex (processes of horizontal complexity) [75].

3.6.2. <u>Restructuring New Boundaries For Action</u>. Before giving up all the advantages of a specialized tool clearly operating within specific demarcation lines, one must be sure that the gains to be achieved are higher than what might be lost in a period of troubled adaptation.

Many economists react to this issue by interpreting all the problems which attack the demarcation lines of economics in a way which either keeps them out or tries to make them fit within standard economics. For instance, many problems linked to what we have called "deducted values" appear to be treated as problems of internalization of costs: it is argued that a freely available good such as water, which becomes polluted and therefore scarce, enters the normal monetarized priced economic system and is treated like any other traditional scarce resource. This is one way of looking at the problem. But one can counter-argue that the process which reduced a free resource to scarcity started when this resource had not yet a price and was still unpolluted, i.e. when it was still completely non-monetarized. Recognizing its value ex-ante, when the "free" resource is still outside the market, is an obvious necessity; for it is normally internalized only ex-post, once the real level of wealth has already diminished (and has not been accounted as such).

The theory of "ghost prices" affirms that many non-monetarized activities are conducted with implicit (ghost) prices: the famous text-book of Paul Samuelson goes even as far as saying that economics is about all sorts of resources (including the non-monetarized ones). However, the accounting of values, at the end of the day, does not take into account the contributions of all resources but reflects the traditional conditions measuring flows of monetarized production only, and thus lets the discrepancy grow between wealth and riches (of real global wealth).

In a previous chapter, it was shown how Hirshleifer tackles the problem of uncertainties by simply stating that once something has been internalized in an economic system, within its traditional boundary demarcation lines, it will be treated as if it corresponded to a situation of certainty.

This defense of the notion of certainty, related to general economic theory, may be the main reason why the misunderstanding of economic theories leads increasingly to suspicion and diminished credibility. Economists, especially when they have become journalists, tend to say too often that managers and entrepreneurs lack a broad vision of things and a scientific approach. At the same time, entrepreneurs and managers no longer accept the abstract way of thinking of economists and their lack of understanding with regard to practical problems.

This is highlighted in e.g. the definition of economists as people who look at something in practice and ask if it will work in theory [76].

At this point, the advantages of demarcation lines disappear. Every manager and entrepreneur who is confronted with real economic problems knows that the notion of certainty in economic theory is of no practical use. What they need is a better appreciation of a complex reality and a highly complex economic system in order to match uncertainties which are indicators not of shortcomings but of challenges, and of the irreducibility of the problem of risk in real economic life.

Will economics have to open up its boundaries and its demarcation lines and mix with other social types of analysis? Accepting the idea that every human action is plunged into a "global" environment, where reality is permanently and intimately linked with psychology, meteorology, sociology, politics and legal problems, does not mean to destroy the advantages of having specialized disciplines to more efficiently increase our knowledge and understanding in all directions.

It would be wrong to consider the opening-up of the present demarcation lines of economics as a dissipation of economics itself in the generality of an overall social science going back to the situation in which it was up to the 18th century [77].

The development of the new Service Economy clearly requires the definition of *new* demarcation lines in order to make economic science more efficient in coping with present conditions. The search for a new notion of value; the integration of non-monetarized activities which are significant for the real "production" process: these are the references for setting up the new demarcation lines of economics in parallel with defining the new goals. Having recognized the Service *Economy* as the new priority in the development of the wealth of nations, the new Service *Economics* will develop as the necessary tool to increase our knowledge and capacity to develop the economic potentials of our time.

Some readers will find it difficult to accept that the notion of demarcation lines for each discipline like economics has to adapt with time, and therefore implicitly admit that demarcation lines per se have no "universal" value. Nevertheless, each theory or each body of theory (each science or discipline) is just a tool to increase our knowledge in order to face ignorance. And each level of knowledge has, at some critical points in time, to be adapted and reintegrated into another, more advanced frame.

We need economics and we need some demarcation lines in economics, even if they will always contain some imprecision. The important thing is that the new emerging system of thought, the new body of theory enabling a better development of the wealth of nations in the present world, will function positively within an acceptable frame of uncertainty.

Among scientists and knowledgeable people it is very fashionable to speak about modesty; however there is no modesty in the pretension that our knowledge is absolute and definitive. These are rather connotations of arrogance, the remnants of the way of thinking which has dominated the civilization of the 19th century and had produced the terrible dream that humankind could be omniscient and could master a definitive reality. The age of uncertainty gives us more confidence in our future ability not to *know*, but to *know more*.

3.6.3. The Role Of The Market System. Opening boundaries, destroying demarcation lines and exploring new territories is thus a process in which we have to redefine and rediscover new boundaries in order to advance even further. For practical purposes, we absolutely need to develop our tools of knowledge along demarcation lines. But in doing this, we never should forget the following advice by the Danish poet Piet Hein:

> Our simple problems often grew
> to mysteries we fumbled over,
> because of lines we nimbly drew
> and later neatly stumbled over.

Restructuring demarcation lines at a higher level is especially crucial at moments when many disciplines are so detached one from another that they loose the benefits of mutual stimulation. One of the characteristics of the recent difficulties in organizing and stimulating economic life lies in the segregation of learning into many categories of isolated experts, particularly between engineers and economists, and between natural scientists and economists. If a minimum of understanding were possible between them, many difficulties could be overcome much faster, especially in understanding the assumptions on which the other profession or specialization is based. *Demarcation* lines have to be drawn at *points of encounter*, thus avoiding the creation of deep zones of *empty space between* disciplines and sciences.

The focal point in the re-demarcation of economic science in the modern Service Economy is the role of the market economy. Due to the complexity of the market functions, the quest for rationality and the search for certainty derived from the Western culture of the last century often led to the conclusion that market uncertainties, complexities and even situations of indetermination are "bad" and that only rationality, looking for definitive certainty, would lead to perfectly ("scientifically") known and predictable systems and functions. It is strange that a civilization which has developed private enterprise and the Industrial Revolution, both largely based on the market system, should in parallel have produced this type of background idea which succeeded in some cases in killing the dynamics (based on risk and uncertainty) of the market system, for the sake of rationality related to the mirage of certainty.

A free market system is neither completely perfect nor imperfect. But it is a *very* good system for *short*-term decisions, involving transactions based on *monetarized* goods and services.

In the modern economy, the market system and particularly the free market cannot be identified with the whole of the economic problem: the free market system is important, but is only a sub-system of the economy as a whole. Many pretensions to rationality and certainty have in the past been forms of irrationality, based on dogmatic ideology and resulting in negative results. The free market system has also been at the source of some of the great crises which were in most cases related to problems of long term adaptation: the crisis of 1929, when the economy was not yet organized enough to adapt to the quantum leap of the mass-production and mas-consumption which started to gain ground in those years and arrived at full expansion after World War Two; the crisis that began in 1973, when adaptation signals pointing towards the Service Economy started as the result of a long term evolution that might continue for many decades. On long term phenomena, short term mechanisms sometimes produce negative results: they have to be adapted, incentivated or regulated, which is normal practice in absolutely all "free market" countries.

Oscillating between abstract concepts of pure market mechanisms, i.e. without any control, and total control by a planning "rationality", is similar to oscillating between Carybde and Scylla: the sirens singing the songs of certainty that inevitably lead to shipwreck.

*Imperfect* and, inevitably, uncertain and risky market systems are an important pillar for an advancing economy that needs uncertainty to operate properly. The basic issue is thus not so much to be for or against uncertainty, but to be able to distinguish between the destructive parts (to be reduced) and the constructive parts (to be accepted as a challenge) of uncertainty.

Uncertainty is the only certainty. In an economy of growing complexity, the market sub-system has a key role to play in the new Service Economy and its role will be even more decisive than in the period of the maturing Industrial Revolution. In addition, the relevance of the "prosumer" and the increase of exchange and production activities outside the monetarized system will also give a broader connotation to the notion of market itself.

Notes Chapter 3

    (for notes nos. 1 to 40, see end of Chapters 1 and 2)

41.  see for a further reading on this point of planning strategies; Giarini, Orio (1978) The Diminishing Returns of Technology, Pergamon Press, Oxford.

42.  Kahn, Hermann and Wiener, Anthony (1967) The Year 2000, The Macmillan Co., New York, N.Y.

43.  see in particular Hailey, Arthur (1985) Strong Medicine, Pan Books, London.

44.  O'Connell, Jeffrey (1975) Ending Insult to Injury, University of Illinois Press; Rokes, Willis P. (1971) No Fault Insurance, Insurers Press, Santa Monica, CA; Jackson, Rupert (1982) Professional Negligence, Sweet & Maxwell, London.

45.  on the problem of uncertainty in medical decisions, see Weinstein, W. (1986) "Risky Choices In Medical Decisions", The Geneva Papers on Risk and Insurance, Geneva.

46. Toffler, Alvin (1981) The Third Wave, Bantam Ed., New York, N.Y.. See also on this notion, from a practical angle: Norman, Richard (1984) Service Management, J.Wiley & Sons, Chichester /UK.

47. Giarini, Orio (1984) Cycles, Values and Employment, Pergamon Press, Oxford.

48. Landes, David (1969) The Unbounded Prometheus, Cambridge University Press, Cambridge.

49. as 48.

50. as 48.

51. Marshall, Alfred, Principles of Economics.

52. Hicks, John R. (1939) Value and Capital, Oxford University Press, Oxford /UK.

53. Friedman, Milton (1980) Free to choose, Penguin Books, Middlesex /UK.

54. Clark, Ronald (1980) Einstein, sa vie et son epoque, Stock, Paris.

55. see among others: Arrow, Kenneth (1978) "New Developments in the Theory of Risk Allocation", The Geneva Papers on Risk and Insurance no 8, Geneva, and bibliography therein.

56. Popper, Karl (1977) Unended Quest, Fontana Collins, Glasgow /UK, p. 86.

57. quite interesting and accessible to non-specialists are: Kline, M. (1980) Mathematics the Loss of Certainty, Oxford University Press, Oxford; a short article giving a straightforward explanation of the relative truth of mathematics: Little, J. (1980) "The uncertain Craft of Mathematics", New Scientist, 88, p. 626-628; with regard to the field of physics: Bohm, D. (1980) Wholeness and the Implicate Order, Routledge & Keenan, London.

58. for a clear description and analysis of this point, see Clark, R.W. (1973) Einstein, the Life and Times, Hodder & Stoughton, London.

59. this is precisely the type of dialogue that Giarini's Dialogue on Wealth and Welfare has tried to initiate.

60. Weisskopf, Walter (1984) Reflections on Uncertainty in Economics, Seventh Annual Lecture of the Geneva Association, The Geneva Papers on Risk and Insurance, Geneva.

61. Rene Passet is one of the pioneers in building the bridge, among economists between the modern development in scientific thinking and economics. see for instance : Passet, Rene (1979) L'economiqe et le vivant, Payot, Paris.

62. his verification of the economic paradigms with the work of Ilya Prigogine is very promising.

63. excerpts taken from the Honda Lecture 1983 by Professor Ilya Prigogine , Nobel Prize in Chemistry in 1977, Professor at the Universities of Brussels and Austin, TX.

64. see among others: Capra, Frank (in preparation) Keppel: Uncertainty, the ground for life.
65. published by Hutchinson Group SA Ltd, London. 66. as 63. 67. on this issue, see the notion of "deducted values" in Giarini, Orio (1980) Dialogue on Wealth and Welfare, p. 121.
68. see Tevoedjre, Albert (1978) Pauvrete, Richesse des Peuples, Editions Sociales, Paris.
69. see Weisskopf, Walter (1972) The Psychology of Economics, University of Chicago Press, Ill., pp. 57 ff.
70. as 69., pp. 11 ff, 33 ff, 166 ff.
71. see "Assessing Wealth and Welfare", in Giarini, Orio (1980) Dialogue on Wealth and Welfare, pp. 200 ff.
72. Marshall, Alfred, Principles of Economics.
73. there is also of course an opposite form of inefficiency: when specialization leads to myopia on how a specialized part of activity fits into a greater whole.
74. Max Weber and many other sociologists have given in the description of the entrepreneur a much higher relevance to the notion of risk in the period of the Industrial Revolution than have economists themselves. Frank Knight wrote a first book on this subject in the 1920's.
75. the notion of complexity has become increasingly popular as a subject of research in many areas. Among others, the University of the United Nations has started a programme in this direction. See: UNU (1985) The Science and Praxis of Complexity, The United Nations University, Tokyo.
76. in an article published in 1985 in Business Week, economists were referred to as an "endangered species".
77. see Henderson, Hazel (1980) The End of Economics Creating an Alternative Future, Pergee Books, Putman's Sons, New York, N.Y.

(for notes nos. 78 to 85, see end of Chapter 4)

# Chapter 4: At The Roots Of Uncertainty

## 4.1. RISK, UNCERTAINTY AND THE INDIVIDUAL

4.1.1. <u>The Perception Of Risk</u>. People respond to the hazards they perceive and they can relate to. However, uncertainty also stems from unperceived risks, and this is where the trouble begins: every action undertaken by anybody contains risks unknown to and thus unperceived by the majority of other people until the day of the unexpected outcome. Risk perception is based essentially on personal experience, but also on psychological anxieties of a subjective nature.

Risk perception differs greatly according to the perception dimension, i.e. the group concerned: individuals, groups within society, companies, nations; and also according to historical and cultural contexts and geographical regions. The only certainty in the life of any individual is death! But there are risks that "kill" companies and nation-states. For the vast majority of companies, such a risk is represented by the discontinuity of activity: most companies that have their major plant destroyed by fire never recover and disappear! For nation-states, the ultimate security need is existence, in a mental or physical way: a nation can survive without a homeland for a long period of time, as the examples of Jews, Poles and Kurds have shown.

Differences in perception lead to many risk management decision that do not work: an individual who feels he is irreplaceable in his job may find that he can be sacked within a few minutes; a politician who ignores uncertainty takes the risk of upheavals under various forms from losing elections to terrorism.

But radical uncertainty is also routed in the irreversible flow of time. Living systems are non-equilibrium systems which renew their energies in their own logic. Whenever technology overtakes science for example, new forms of uncertainty result: a technician today can manipulate human or plant genes, but nobody can tell him if he should and what for. A computer operator can put the personal data of everybody on a computer, but he ignores who should have access under what conditions and for what purpose.

The level of perceived uncertainty drops when the risk has become "acceptable" in society. But this level of acceptance is not homogeneous throughout the population in a country. Scientists and engineers use the risk assessment process to identify and quantify potential harm. This process relies sometimes on inadequate scientific information, its tool is probability which, among other imperfections, gives no clue to the timing of a disaster, nor its actual frequency. An example: Mrs Evelyn Maria Adams beat odds of 17.3 trillion to one in winning New Jersey's Pick-6 lottery the second time in 6 months in February 1986, becoming the first two-time winner of a million-dollar-plus state lottery ever. Scientifically speaking, she should never have won a second time. Social implications of risks are considered in risk management, which, together with risk assessment, forms risk analysis. If, for instance, engineers qualify an electric hairdryer as safe to use, it may still kill the owner who drops it into a bath-tub full of water. For the engineer the product is safe, but it has been used in an unsafe way: again the logic of the Industrial Revolution that does not concern itself with use over a period of time. But the same problem also exists on a higher level:

> Studies done in the U.S. by Lichter and Rothman at Smith College showed that 89% of energy experts polled think that nuclear power is safe. A similar percentage of the leading lights in journalism and TV media think that nuclear power is unsafe, according to the same survey. [78]

Both groups are right in their own way. Similarly, engineers can marvel about new plants which are much safer than the ones built ten years ago, which were then regarded as "safe". To the laymen, this must mean the older plant is unsafe, to the engineer it means it needs different safety precautions. How risky is safe, then?

Furthermore, risk perception is linked to the appropriateness of a technical solution, and the thrill you get out of it: a child who jumps from a wall into the arms of his mother is thrilled by the possibility of missing but relies on a system of trust, i.e. that the mother is watching and catching him. An investor who puts up venture capital is thrilled by the potential gain, as against the anxiety of losing. Similarly, many preventable hazards are accepted in every day life for their thrill benefit, such as smoking, fast driving, certain sports.

In economics, a similar phenomenon of differences in risk perception exists between explorers and exploiters. All the famous explorers, such as Columbus, the builder of the Suez Canal, the founder of the Red Cross, or NASA for the Apollo Moon Programme had to under-cost their budget and under-estimate risks and time schedules in order to find the minimum support needed to start their project. Innovation had traditionally been created under very hard conditions, and in many cases, the project went bankrupt when it was 90% finished, or when the inventor and promoter died. At that moment in time, if the economic and technical feasibility had been proved, an exploiter picked up the ruins for nothing, finished the project and operated it successfully and profitably.

This interdependence of risk perception is vital for society. Explorers have a fundamental role of opening enormous alternatives in societal development, but are "wasting" resources as the natural selection process probably eliminates 99% of their ideas as irrelevant. Exploiters have the function of diffusing explorers' innovation and of making them socially significant, but as concentrators, they narrow the field of vision and knowledge in favour of deeper know-how in profitable areas of activity.

Explorers have to take unknown new risks; exploiters try to limit themselves to entrepreneurial "reasonable" risks.

But in parallel to the change in the accountability of hazards over the last decades, the notion of entrepreneurial risks has been enlarged. Hazards in the use of products lead to the recall of goods by the manufacturer; hazards linked to the use of "free goods" i.e. air and water, such as pollution that used to be considered an act of God, now lead to criminal proceedings. The same way that economic theory is abandoning the concept of free goods, i.e. the introduction of the notion of deducted values that have to be accounted for, free risks increasingly have to be accepted as man-made risks and accounted for by the producer, as witnessed by the asbestos and chemical industry (e.g. Seveso, Bhopal and Love Canal).

In the case of death by a real act of God, on the contrary, e.g. through floods or lightning, there is often a mental preparedness and a cultural instinct to the disaster and its aftermath in religion: God never promised us safety on earth but only in heaven!

Uncertainty may be described as the sum of all potential hazards around us, perceived or not. Each individual can ignore some of these potential hazards, take preventive action against others through physical or financial protection, or fall into a state of anxiety that takes him to hospital. However, it is difficult to get any thrill out of excessive uncertainty! A car speeding towards a pedestrian is an intolerable uncertainty (approaching certainty!), even if it gives the driver a thrill.

Cigarette smoke is a far more potent carcinogen than asbestos. Yet it is John Mansville who almost went bankrupt, not Philip Morris. It is not the comparative risk as perceived by the scientist but the risk/thrill analysis of the individual that makes risks acceptable to people: bed is the most dangerous place to be, as 75% of people die in bed. Yet no-one would dream of not going to bed for this reason!

The perception of some risks by the individual is intrinsically linked to periods of life. The responsibility and the risks involved to produce and rear the next generation lies with young adults, who have to be given the opportunity to earn a living in order to accept this responsibility. Absolute poverty is no base for risk taking! Yet the age group of 20-34 year old men, that includes 46% of the labour force in the USA (as a typical industrialized country), had an unemployment rate of 10.8% as compared to 5.8% of the group of 35-64 year old men (figures Dec 1983). Society should have an interest in its own survival and thus in the reduction of economic uncertainty for the key group of its population through the provision of e.g. a guaranteed basic income.

A further "irrational" factor influencing risk acceptance by individuals is the gravity and potential chain reaction in major man-made system, such as nuclear power stations. The more complex and the more vulnerable a system becomes, the more questions will be asked about the necessity of this single risk, its insurability and the alternatives of risk avoidance and risk diversification over a long period of time, including an overall optimization of the periods of production, distribution, utilization and final waste disposal.

In fact, every growing system's size and complexity, and thus vulnerability and risks, are at the roots of the increasing feeling by many people who see themselves as the victims rather than the beneficiaries, of technology. Most arguments in favour of bigger systems are of a financial nature which was acceptable in the times of scarcity at the beginning of the Industrial Revolution. Today, in the transition towards the Service Economy, non-monetarized factors may dominate in the risk perception of the individual.

Scientific risk assessment therefore needs to consider non-monetarized factors. i.e. risks should not only be measured in deaths per million dollar invested, the normal yardstick of the capital-intensive industries, but also in deaths per 1.000 jobs created, or in deaths per unit of wealth and welfare.

Risk avoidance, such as not to ski in areas exposed to avalanches, seems an obvious possibility, but often goes both against the profit maximization motive and the "thrill" of the skier. Yet not all risks can be avoided: the "certainty" of death is there! However, modern medicine and science has incurred tremendous costs of risk avoidance in this field, leading to a frequent prolongation of human agony in an anti-death approach. This has fueled the discussion about the "right to die" of each individual in many of the industrialized countries, and about the means of using money in a pro-life approach of risk avoidance, i.e. in systems of preventive medicine to enhance the quality of life: health creation as wealth creation! Up to the point that in some "advanced" countries, 50% of the overall health expenses are absorbed by people during the last three weeks of their life.

Risk diversification is another possibility to reduce the impacts of hazards, such as using mono-engine planes for transatlantic flights. However, the maxim of economy of scale in the Industrial Revolution is often incompatible with risk diversification, as shown in the case of the tanker (shipping) industry using modern ULCCs (ultra large crude carriers) of up to 500,000 tons (dwt) of size. The vulnerability and risk factors need to become key components in optimizing the scale and the dimensions of economic activities.

Culture also plays a crucial role in risk perception. When railways were first proposed, opponents forecast disasters killing dozens of people in a single accident, while the explorers strongly denied any such possibilities and pointed out all the security to prevent this kind of disaster. Reality has long surpassed those forecasts, but railway accidents as a whole have been overtaken by aircraft disasters as eye catchers: the concentration of up to 550 people dying simultaneously in a rare aircraft accident has a stronger mental power than the 150 deaths in U.S. automobile accidents that happen every day. Death in a railway accident has become a non-subject.

An important point to stress is that public perceptions of risk differ greater from the judgement of risk analysts (in both ways) as is put in evidence by *Figure 23* [79].

Figure 23: Judgments on frequency and probability of risk by the general public.

| MOST OVERESTIMATED | MOST UNDERESTIMATED |
|---|---|
| 1. All accidents | 1. Smallpox vaccination |
| 2. Motor vehicles accidents | 2. Diabetes |
| 3. Pregnancy, childbirth, abortion | 3. Stomach cancer |
| 4. Tornado | 4. Lightning |
| 5. Flood | 5. Stroke |
| 6. Botulism | 6. Tuberculosis |
| 7. All cancer | 7. Asthma |
| 8. Fire and Flames | 8. Emphysenia |
| 9. Venomous bite or sting | |
| 10. Homicide | |

Example:  Stroke kills 85% more people than do accidents. Yet people estimate that accidents take 25 times as many lives as does stroke.

Example:  Asthma causes about 20 times as many deaths as do tornadoes. People estimate that tornadoes kill about 3 times as many people as does asthma.

Source: Kahneman, Slovic and Tvesky (1983) Judgement under Uncertainty: Heuristics and Biases, Cambridge University Press.

Clearly, as Slovic notes, frequencies of dramatic, sensational causes of death which get heavy media coverage are over-estimated. Frequencies of silent, undramatic killers of one person at a time, or lethal events that are also common in non-fatal form, are under-estimated.

The risk situation is clearly related to the adequacy (or rather the inadequacy) of the information and the communication systems in our society as it appears in *Figure 24*.

Figure 24: Statistical Frequency and newspaper coverage, comparing the Eugene, Oregon Register-Guard (RG) and the New Bedford, Massachusetts Standard-Times (ST) for 41 causes of death.

| Cause of Death | Rate per $2.05 \times 10^8$ U.S. Residents | Subjects' Estimates | Reported Deaths R-G | S-T |
|---|---|---|---|---|
| 1. Smallpox | 0 | 57 | 0 | 0 |
| 2. Poisoning by vitamins | 1 | 102 | 0 | 0 |
| 3. Botulism | 2 | 183 | 0 | 0 |
| 4. Measles | 5 | 168 | 0 | 0 |
| 5. Fireworks | 6 | 160 | 0 | 0 |
| 6. Smallpox vaccination | 8 | 23 | 0 | 0 |
| 7. Whooping cough | 15 | 93 | 0 | 0 |
| 8. Polio | 17 | 97 | 0 | 0 |
| 9. Venomous bite or sting | 48 | 350 | 0 | 0 |
| 10. Tornado | 90 | 564 | 36 | 23 |
| 11. Lightning | 107 | 91 | 1 | 0 |
| 12. Non-venonous animal | 129 | 174 | 4 | 7 |
| 13. Flood | 205 | 736 | 4 | 30 |
| 14. Excess cold | 334 | 314 | 0 | 0 |
| 15. Syphilis | 420 | 492 | 0 | 0 |
| 16. Pregnancy, birth & abort. | 451 | 1.344 | 0 | 0 |
| 17. Infectious hepatitis | 677 | 545 | 0 | 0 |
| 18. Appendicitis | 902 | 605 | 0 | 0 |
| 19. Electrocution | 1.025 | 766 | 5 | 0 |
| 20. MV/train collision | 1.517 | 689 | 0 | 1 |
| 21. Asthma | 1.886 | 506 | 1 | 0 |
| 22. Firearm accident | 2.255 | 1.345 | 8 | 1 |
| 23. Poison by acid/liquid | 2.563 | 1.014 | 3 | 3 |
| 24. Tuberculosis | 3.690 | 658 | 0 | 0 |
| 25. Fire and flames | 7.380 | 3.336 | 94 | 46 |
| 26. Drowning | 7.380 | 1.684 | 47 | 60 |
| 27. Leukemia | 14.555 | 2.496 | 1 | 0 |
| 28. Accidental falls | 17.425 | 2.675 | 15 | 7 |
| 29. Homicide | 18.860 | 5.582 | 278 | 208 |
| 30. Emphysema | 21.730 | 2.848 | 1 | 0 |
| 31. Suicide | 24.600 | 4.679 | 29 | 19 |
| 32. Breast cancer | 31.160 | 2.964 | 0 | 0 |
| 33. Diabetes | 38.950 | 1.476 | 0 | 1 |
| 34. Motor vehicle accident | 55.350 | 41.161 | 296 | 83 |
| 35. Lung cancer | 73.850 | 9.764 | 3 | 2 |
| 36. Stomach cancer | 95.120 | 3.283 | 0 | 1 |
| 37. All accidents | 112.750 | 88.679 | 715 | 596 |
| 38. Stroke | 209.100 | 7.109 | 12 | 4 |
| 39. All cancer | 328.000 | 43.609 | 25 | 12 |
| 40. Heart disease | 738.000 | 23.599 | 49 | 30 |
| 41. All disease | 1.740.430 | 88.836 | 111 | 87 |
| Total number of reports (causes 29, 31, 37 & 41) | | | 1133 | 910 |
| Correlations (R-G vs. S-T) | | | .97 | |

Source: Combs, B. and Slovic, P. (1979) "Causes of death: Biased newspaper coverage and biased judgments", Journalism Quarterly, 56, pp. 837-843.

Comparisons between the perceived benefits and the perceived risks also show a very unbalanced situation (see *Figure 25*).

Figure 25: Psychometric studies of risk perception, perceived risk and need for risk adjustment for 30 activities and technologies.

| Perceived Risk and Need for Risk Adjustment for 30 Activities and Technologies[a] | | | |
|---|---|---|---|
| Activity or Technology | Perceived Benefit | Perceived Risk | Need for Risk Adjustment[b] |
| 1. Alcoholic beverages | 41 | 161 | 4.4 |
| 2. Bicycles | 82 | 65 | 1.5 |
| 3. Commercial aviation | 130 | 52 | 2.3 |
| 4. Contraceptives | 113 | 50 | 2.0 |
| 5. Electric power | 274 | 52 | 1.0 |
| 6. Fire fighting | 178 | 92 | 1.1 |
| 7. Food coloring | 16 | 31 | 3.0 |
| 8. Food preservatives | 44 | 36 | 2.7 |
| 9. General aviation | 53 | 114 | 2.1 |
| 10. Handguns | 14 | 220 | 17.3 |
| 11. H.S. & college football | 35 | 37 | 1.7 |
| 12. Home appliances | 133 | 25 | 1.1 |
| 13. Hunting | 30 | 82 | 2.5 |
| 14. Large construction | 142 | 91 | 1.7 |
| 15. Motorcycles | 29 | 176 | 5.3 |
| 16. Motor vehicles | 137 | 247 | 6.1 |
| 17. Mountain climbing | 28 | 68 | 1.0 |
| 18. Nuclear power | 52 | 250 | 29.0 |
| 19. Pesticides | 87 | 105 | 9.5 |
| 20. Power mowers | 30 | 29 | 1.5 |
| 21. Police work | 278 | 111 | 1.8 |
| 22. Prescription antibiotics | 209 | 30 | 1.3 |
| 23. Railroads | 185 | 37 | 1.2 |
| 24. Skiing | 38 | 45 | 1.0 |
| 25. Smoking | 20 | 189 | 15.2 |
| 26. Spray cans | 17 | 73 | 7.8 |
| 27. Surgery | 164 | 104 | 1.9 |
| 28. Swimming | 68 | 52 | 1.0 |
| 29. Vaccinations | 194 | 17 | .8 |
| 30. X rays | 156 | 45 | 1.7 |

[a] Data adapted from Fischhoff et al. (1978), by Paul Slovic.
[b] Values of 1.0 indicate that the activity is presently at an acceptable level of risk. Values greater than 1.0 mean the activity needs to be safer by the factor indicated in the column; values less than 1.0 mean the activity could be riskier and still be acceptable to society.

Source: Paul Slovic, Decision Center on Risk Perception and Risk Communication.

All these references clearly indicate that the central issue of our life and our behaviour - the risk component - is not yet sufficiently accepted as such in our societies at large.

Psychoanalysis has something to say in this matter:

> Human anxieties, building up our feelings of insecurity, lead to the self-deceptive search for certainty ... if an excessive uncertainty can lead to a pathological situation, we have - at the other extreme - excessive rigidities built up around a vision of reality fixed and "certain", blocking any possibility of finding alternatives and developing creativity. [80]

The game is then not to find alibis for an anxiety, but to identify life as essentially a strategy in risk management. And, as for any good manager, the first rule is to avoid the sorry plays of self-deception.

### 4.1.2. The Certainty Of Misery - The Misery Of Certainty (Nihilism). Misery is a situation of impotence, physical or material, moral or natural. It is a situation in which the capacity to fight for life, for development, is broken. It is a situation of negative certainty, of destitution.

The role of religions, philosophies, myths and even science as perceptions at the individual and social level is essentially to reduce at least moral or psychological impotence, so that the uncertainties of life can be faced or fought against.

Walter Weisskopf describes [81] several belief systems which have historically developed to reduce anxiety and the feeling of impotence.

> The medieval world outlook believed in a super-natural, but comprehensible order. The Newtonian model believed in an order routed in nature and comprehensible through reason. Having abandoned a belief in providence, grace and other worldly rewards for religious virtue as well as the deterministic belief in nature and reason, the Heisenbergian [82] paradigm seems to deprive us of all protection against the threat of the unknowable future and of the unknowable reality. (4)

(4) However, both belief systems are of a dualistic nature. Each of them represents man as simultaneously omnipotent and impotent. The Newtonian paradigm enthrones man as a potentially omniscient observer of an objective reality, able to understand with his reason the logos–structure of the world. At the same time, man is dethroned by being subjected to inexorable natural laws which unequivocally determine his fate. In micro-economic models the individual is allegedly able to know and to predict the future equilibrium price. In spite of this omniscience he is unable to influence this price or to deviate from it. This inner contradiction between an omniscient detached observer and an impotent economic actor both one and the same person is the essence of the competitive model. This contradiction is not restricted to the economic sphere; it is part of the Cartesian-Newtonian, deterministic world outlook; the individual is powerless in view of the laws of nature in spite of his potential omniscience. The Heisenbergian paradigm shows the same dualistic ambivalence; only the situation is reversed. The individual is bereft of his omniscience; events are not predetermined nor predictable. The impotence consists in un-knowledge and in the unpredictability of the future. However, the Heisenbergian paradigm was part of the revolution in physics which made the splitting of the atom and hydrogen bombs possible with nuclear power as a by-product. This has enhanced man's power over nature. In economics the new model is related to private and governmental market power and with managerial

administration of the economy. Thus, power and powerlessness are synthesized in the Heisenbergian as well as in the Newtonian model, only in a different way. Newtonian man is powerful in his knowledge and his predictions but powerless in his actions. Heisenbergian man is powerless in his knowledge and in his predictions but powerful in his role as a participant in the evolutionary process of creation and destruction.

Walter Weisskopf further observes:

> If one surveys Western History from the Middle Ages to the present, one sees a continuous disintegration of anxiety-reducing belief systems.

He means by that a disintegration of systems of beliefs (religions and the visions of science) which did provide feelings of certainty for a humanity coming out from a first period of childhood. The very indication that we can stand higher levels of uncertainties is a sign of growing maturity and of an increasing capability in accepting the dynamics of life as they really exist. It is a gradual sorting out of the tendentiously schizophrenic attitudes of the child, who, because of his impotence, needs stronger intermediates (its parents) to build on in order to survive psychologically and materially.

This does not mean that every sort of religion or myth will one day have to be abandoned: dreams, religions and utopias are hypotheses with different degrees of metaphysical contents, for which a long time will continue to be necessary in order to elaborate goals, define directions in our evolution, make trials, and even to face unsustainable levels of uncertainty. Becoming adult does not mean to overcome anxieties and uncertainties, but simply to cope better than a child in facing such situations.

In this sense, and referring to the above quotations from Walter Weisskopf, the reference to the feeling of omniscience and of power referred to in the 19th century in the Western philosophy based on determinism, is simply an abstract intellectual choice which tries not to face the normal stream of an uncertain reality.

The positivistic dream of achieving omniscience in an abstract static world is essentially a psychological fantasm. It is the indicator of a high remaining degree of schizophrenia in the childhood of mankind, the pretention to a total capability of prediction, rationalizing in the old positivistic and deterministic sense on the possibility by man to control everything sooner or later, is a clear indicator of a lesser development of civilization, of the need to project images of certainty and to make the present more tolerable, at least psychologically. But such a schizophrenic attitude is inevitably self-defeating: if the normal reality of life continuously contradicts the hope of building a future of uncertainties, the inevitable reaction is nihilism.

It is our contention that this form of rationalism, this aspect of Western culture diffused under the names of determinism, positivism and scientism particularly during the 19th century, is in fact not only the expression of a tendency to grow and to mature as a civilization, but has at the same time been at the root of various forms of nihilism. Once the promise of definitive, determined, future happiness and certainty has been declared an accessible state or goal, the *normal* contradictions, hazards and uncertainties of life are interpreted as a situation of failure, instead of being accepted as the reality, as the raw material for development, as an occasion for real maturation and growth.

Even Walter Weisskopf remains slightly attached to the old schemes when he writes that "there is a feeling of impotence in recognizing that there is no certain prediction in a reality where uncertainty is contemplated". If a feeling of impotence is still there in face of a future which is probable and indeterminate, this is an indication of how difficult it is to *reasonably* accept the *normal* path of life and to really integrate our attitudes, recognizing that "the trend towards an indeterminate paradigm" is in fact increasing the "openness for human action". This is evolution; this is progress!

At the same time we are living in a period of growing uncertainty in concrete terms, the possibility of a nuclear holocaust being a good example. But this dimension of uncertainty has been created by us as human beings. Thus it is a specific opportunity to demonstrate by positive action our capacity of maturation towards a real civilization, of *our* incapacity to deal with ourselves. Self-consciousness and higher levels of understanding and consciousness are obviously essential here. We need to behave in a more civilized way, we need to have new social, political and economic philosophies, capable of helping us to *face* such uncertainties. We are responsible for producing them and for making them work. The future is our business: the danger and the uncertainty of a nuclear holocaust give an impression of the quantum leap we have to make as human civilization. The outcome of this leap will be outside any predetermined scheme.

The problem of misery is not only a philosophical, psychological or nuclear one, but also a problem of everyday life, and therefore of economic nature. These problems may sometime seem less essential, but they constitute a key preoccupation of our life. Absolute misery and destitution are situations in which there is no space for dealing with risk and uncertainties. Misery is a world of certainty, a world in which the implicit uncertainties and risks of life cannot be faced nor the opportunities they offer be grasped: the possibility of a choice, of making change, of growing, of improving, of fighting for one's own human dignity.

The notions of destitution or misery and the notion of poverty should not be confused. As Walter Weisskopf pointed out: "The true dimensions of poverty are existential rather than economic". For a medieval monk, the poverty of his life was a way to become rich in heaven: poverty itself was an indicator of this type of riches. Albert Tevoedjre has written a book on "Poverty, the Wealth of Mankind" [83], its aim is not to preach poverty around the world, but to better identify what really makes people richer or poorer.

In "Porgy and Bess", an opera by George Gershwin, a very clear distinction between poverty and misery is made in a popular song:

> Oh, I got plenty o'nuttin
> An' nuttin's plenty for me
> I got no car, got no mule,
> *got no misery.*

This does not necessarily mean that a car or a mule are an element of misery, but that they are part of our riches only by the test of their utilization value. This brings us back to the Service Economy and to the problem of misery.

The revision of the notion of value in the Service Economy, taking into account real utilization and respecting cultural differences in the perception of value, is we hope a step forward in eradicating misery. This is not only because any product or service has to be of real positive utilization value for the user or the consumer, but also because our own level of wealth is defined in terms of our material and moral capabilities to face life, i.e. the risks and uncertainties of life. Our liberty can be measured in terms of the availability of different paths and strategies with relation to the conditions of life and therefore to situations of risks and uncertainties. We cannot sell security in any other form than as increases in the number of our choices to cope with all possible risks and uncertainties. No one can sell us, at least in economic terms, a security product, but only the means to face accidents or to take challenges.

The true pact with the Dr Faustus of our times is to immobilize time, to sell our soul and our identity for a piece of certainty. Our anxiety, which goes back to the anxiety of our individual death as the only certainty in life, does not incite us to use it as an energy for life, but to surrender to anxiety itself, which is equal to preferring death to life. A situation with no anxiety is one of absolute certainty, which does not exist.

The limits to certainty are precisely the indicators of those frontiers ahead of us to develop our moral and material possibilities. On earth, only total misery, spiritual and material death is a situation of unlimited certainty.

## 4.2. A DIALOGUE : FOUNDING THE SECRETARIAT FOR UNCERTAINTY

Did you say Ulrich, Ulrich Tuzzi?

Having left my office, it took me a quarter of an hour to walk to the Grangettes Clinic in Chene-Bougeries, a suburb of Geneva. Near the parking area of the Clinic, on the West side of the building, I found an old two-storey house surrounded by trees. Perhaps they still include some survivors of the four pine trees, already old at the time, or of the two birch trees that Musil had described in the notes recounting the final years of his life. Unless, of course, they were among the trees that had been sacrificed to make room for the parking lot. I was in the process of looking to see whether the semi-circular pond was still there when I noticed a friend of mine who is a research fellow at CERN (European Nuclear Research Centre). He is a physicist, and was accompanied by another person of around 40 years of age, with bold features, balding head, and black hair combed straight back. Both of them seemed to be searching for something around the old house.

We shook hands and my friend introduced his companion: 'This is one of my colleagues from CERN, Ulrich Tuzzi [84]. And he explained that they had come to see if it would be possible to rent the ground floor of the house which has a veranda, and set up there the secretariat of a new Centre for Reflection on Uncertainty.

'The thing is', Ulrich Tuzzi explained to me, 'a few years before the outbreak of the First World War which was to destroy the Austro-Hungarian Empire (I am of Viennese origin), my grandfather was thinking of setting up a General Secretariat for Precision and the Soul'.

'I seem to remember reading somewhere...'.

'.. but he didn't succeed. He hoped to be able to reconcile culture and the European scientific tradition which, from Descartes through Newton to the present day, has increasingly widened the breach between the soul and the body, between knowledge resulting from the natural sciences and that - far more difficult to define - engendered by artistic perception, between the certain and the uncertain. He often said that, in his universe, until then all truth appeared to be divided into two half-truths'.

'You - working as you do in a highly prestigious basic research centre - are not going to tell me that the discoveries of modern physics are no more than half-truths!'

'In some way, that is true. Something that was not clearly apparent in my grandfather's time - subject as it was to the old positivist and determinist traditions - is that science is not like a warehouse in which packages of definitive and universal knowledge are constantly being accumulated. As Popper has said, science progresses as the result of a process of "falsification"; it studies the laws of Newton until it finds that, in part and under certain conditions, these laws are false. Up until the time when Einstein arrived on the scene and revealed their inadequacies. And after Einstein, Heisenberg; and then, Prigogine. Research is a dynamic process and not the definitive acquisition of details which accumulate with eternal validity; any synthesis, the addition of any single detail, will change the meaning of its component parts'.

'But a chair will always be a chair, a tree - a tree, an atom - an atom'.

'Up to a point, and under certain conditions. Heisenberg's principle of uncertainty leads us to recognize that, at the level of the infinitely small, the equivalent of a chair may, at a given point in time, appear to be something totally different'.

'But is it not nonetheless true that technology is becoming increasingly efficient and powerful and that I can see - so to speak - the infinitely small more and more clearly?'.

'There comes a point when the simple fact of observing the infinitely small changes it, because the energy released by the observer interacts with what is being observed'.

'Dear Mr Tuzzi, in that case, what you are telling me is that there is no longer any difference between human or social sciences (in which we ourselves are immersed) and the natural sciences which, by definition, are subject to objective and certain observation'.

'This definition has limits of its own. The "exact" sciences and the "social" sciences are more and more frequently found to be in the same situation: they both deal with varying degrees of uncertainty. But thanks to this uncertainty, we have the possibility of closing the gap which so worried my grandfather. As a result, it is now possible to consider setting up a Centre for Reflection on Uncertainty to achieve something that a General-Secretariat of Precision and the Soul could never have achieved at a time when it was considered that these two poles were inevitably and permanently separated. This is the reason the Secretariat was never set up and why my grandfather lived all through his life as if in an endless novel split by the contradictions between the nature of man and that of science of certainty, and in pursuit of an unseasonable synthesis. However, today, his novel can now be brought to its conclusion, to the word "End", in readiness for a continuing renaissance and research'.

'What you are therefore telling me then is that *your* grandfather's life or rather his "novel" is coming to an end precisely because it has the possibility of continuing ...'.

'This is not just a paradox. Musil wrote on this point that, "men of that ilk certainly occur today, but they are still few in number and this, in itself, is not sufficient to reunite what had been put asunder". Nowadays, a new culture is developing and spreading throughout the world: a culture in which it is less and less common to encounter isolated elements. A culture in which a New Alliance is being formed, as had said the Nobel Prigogine: a culture in the process of integration and construction'.

'It seems somewhat problematic to me that all this can, in fact, develop on the basis of uncertainty; if you take from under our feet the little certainty that remains in the world, such as the scientific certainties, I would think that you would just increase the chaos and the feeling of emptiness amongst the upcoming generations'.

'Just the opposite is the case. All the dogmas and those pseudo-religions, that have become certain political ideologies, have fully exploited the concept of an exact, certain and ineluctable science: they have deduced from it all sorts of foundationless legitimacies. In the Middle Ages, wars and massacres were permitted and organized in the name of God. In our contemporary "Middle Ages", even worse massacres have been organized in the name of the "scientific" laws of society. Never before has chaos been organized so effectively'.

'But how can one live and give life proclaiming the value of uncertainty?'

'It is not a question of spreading uncertainty. It is a matter of recognizing that life is uncertain. Humanity must decide sooner or later to create a world which is really civilized, made up of people capable of being mature. It is a matter of recognizing reality. It is an act of in-depth cultural awareness which is essential if we are to avoid the gerrymandering of the purveyors of definitive certainties. It is a matter of learning to live better, assuming one's responsibilities, confronting uncertainty, accepting it. It will be the best of psychotherapies ...'.

'I can see ... you are Viennese ...'.

'A Viennese who accepts reality and one who even demands an urgent study to find out what is false in Freud'.

'I must say, my dear Mr Tuzzi, that I am somewhat perplexed, even extremely perplexed. I can understand that you have considerable affection for your grandfather. But, could it not be said the his attitude was to a large extent due to a world in crisis, to a world undergoing decomposition? If my reckoning is correct, grandfather lived in Vienna mainly during the years immediately preceding the fall of the Austro-Hungarian Empire. His wish to set up the General-Secretariat of Precision and the Soul - I hope you will excuse me if I speak frankly - was this not basically a way of fleeing from reality and, in this way, of taking part in the political dis-aggregation of his country, and of even being to some extent responsible for it?'.

'Obviously, the Austro-Hungarian Empire was immersed in a major crisis and unable to face up to the historical developments of the time'.

'A period which lasted for several decades and which might been seen as covering the whole Industrial Revolution'.

'Just so. The logic of Descartes and Newton was also that of industrial specialization, manufacturing productivity, population "specialization" and, consequently, of nationalism and class specialization; the drama occurred when the dividing line between dialectic and conflict was breached and the breach became irreversible. The incompatibility between these two poles is, once again, one which exists between precision and the soul; it is a Cartesian way of subdividing the world and life, an approach which is intrinsically unable to stimulate diversities in a positive way. Here, in Switzerland, it has been accepted that the Federal State guarantees and protects the sovereignty and the individuality of the cantons. This system substitutes a state of legality for the law of the international jungle. And our modern world is no longer capable of accepting conflicts and irreparable breaches without the survival of humanity as a whole being endangered'.

'But, at least an independent State can defend its freedom'.

'That depends on its strength. Independence between unequals places the weak at the mercy of the strong. Only the strongest State, in absolute terms, has perhaps an interest in being really completely independent. Yet there are currently in the world over 150 "independent" states. All of them are in one part of "half-truth", with the other part of this "half-truth" being the strength of the superpowers. It is for this reason that the world currently follows with baited breath the nomination or election of the leaders of the superpowers, without being able, in the name of the independence of all countries, to participate directly'.

'Then, for you, the fall of the Habsburg Empire was a historic disaster. Do you not think that this is, in fact, merely pure nostalgia on your part? You wouldn't, by any chance, be setting up your Centre for Uncertainty so as to celebrate the forthcoming anniversary of the birth of Franz-Josef?'

'I have to admit that you are right on one point. On the other hand, it should clearly be stated that there are numerous reasons why the old Habsburg Empire had to disappear: its inability to give rise to a valid plan for modern federalism, its blundering management of the splintering effects caused by the Industrial Revolution, the inadequate renovation of social structures... However, on the other hand, it is necessary to highlight the positive aspects of the co-existence of different nations and also not forget that the disintegration of this Empire opened the way to the rise of Nazism. The main point is to find in the new culture, which is spreading throughout the world, a new possibility of advancing beyond the current situation, of progressing, of recreating an image of the future and opportunities that the ancient culture and the old ideologies (which nowadays are no longer those of Austro-Hungarian Empire, but those which destroyed it) have increasing difficulty in putting forward'.

'Your Centre for Uncertainty certainly has global ambitions. I fear you are looking for a type of humanity which just does not exist'.

'True enough, there is a challenge here. But if no one takes up this challenge, our planet will perish. It is a challenge for the evolutionary ability of mankind and, in addition, more than ever today, for developing a minimum of intelligence, common sense and human quality'.

'That depends on what you mean by quality. My grandfather used to say that he was a man without qualities, since he did not have the one that his era required: "quality" meant the ability to limit one-self to a specialization, a clearly defined activity, without integrating one's specific universe into a general scheme, without uniting the two poles of the two half-truths'.

'From this point of view, I too would be inclined to define myself as a man without qualities'.

"Then, join our Centre for Reflection on Uncertainty!'.

And we began to discuss the amount of the registration fee. Night had fallen and someone had switched on the lights on the veranda of the house in Chemin des Grangettes (No. 29 to be precise).

Before we parted, Ulrich Tuzzi handed me a document which bore the title, "Centre for Reflection on Uncertainty - Draft Declaration". And here it is:

## CENTRE FOR REFLECTION ON UNCERTAINTY - DRAFT DECLARATION

It is only by trying to resolve his moral uncertainties that man can, *by creating,* discover what he is.

In the same way, it is only by attempting to resolve their moral uncertainties that an institution or a group can, *creatingly,* discover what they are. [85]

It is not just "objective facts" - those which exist outside of man - which count. Facts become history when a human culture, a certain attitude, has revealed or even created them. There is only one fact which imposes itself intrinsically, only one single future certainty: death both of the individual and of our universe. All the rest is life, uncertainty, the thread of history, the birth of new universes.

Europe, today, is full of facts which allow a picture to be seen of the true attitude of its people and governments. Dozens of opportunities present themselves at every instant and it is for each individual to define and reflect in the mirror of these facts by selecting, refusing, accepting and, above all, creating them. Basically, freedom is above all a way of shaping our personality by the construction, selection and use of facts: this is why it is so difficult to agree with other people about the facts.

Yet, a civilization is a certain way of living and of creating facts: it is a specific "attitude" to living and to the acceptance of uncertainty. It is a constant battle to ensure that the mirage of certainty does not progress to the stage at which it affects what is living, by shattering the mind with the false hope of the definitive, which would stealthily introduce into man the attraction of dogma, i.e. abdication.

It is this very uncertainty, the source of life and responsibility, which allows us to believe in the possibility of a strategy of progress: thanks to this, no totalitarian concept or regime can resist indefinitely. Thanks to this, we know that conditions are always renewing themselves, that hope can remain eternal, even under the worst circumstances. Yet, the combat is far from easy when one realizes the extent to which in the course of human history, it has proved possible to petrify any affirmation of life, by the certainties of a Holy Inquisition, no matter whether it be red, white or black.

For this reason, when speaking of Europe and its crisis of civilization, it is important not to confuse its lack of concepts with its uncertainties.

Europe is in a crisis because it is set in outdated and frustrating certitudes. The crisis is, above all, in attitudes by a choice of images from the past or the future which makes it possible to exorcise the present. On the other hand, if the uncertainties of the present are accepted, the future becomes a raw material for action, the probability of active creation, the possibility of life.

The world in which we live has seldom been so complex, so "reactive" in all its components, so fully evolutive in all fields: there have seldom been so many opportunities

- for both Europeans and other people - to create, and consequently to live at a planetary scale. The major uncertainties and even the dramas of our era, contain, and offer to Europeans, a vast opportunity for action, self-discovery, creation and self-creation as a part of and together with the rest of the world. If they are suffering from a feeling of specific crisis, this is not because of the extent of the challenge but of the extent of their willingness to face up to it. The feeling of crisis stems from our own attitudes, from the lack of ability or - quite simply - from the desire to exist.

Admittedly, on the surface, Europe understands the facts of the world: there is a surfeit of experts on all questions. An extensive and in-depth report can be obtained on any question, minor or major, in any field. However, only too often, all these reports do is to fill up the archives of alibi. In the same way as a government which proclaims European union but continues to practice nationalism. In the same way as any intellectual who proclaims justice and liberty but loses them by developing bureaucratic attitudes of mind and thought.

For a number of years now, numerous experts have been labouring to propose projects for Europe: nevertheless, the value of an expert's work is not in the fact that the work has been carried out but rather in the action of the person making use of it. A person who, in the face of uncertainty, in the face of life, discovers a new opportunity.

It is time for Europe to be reborn, to recreate itself in the new world, to find itself again in research and projects for the future, or more simply: to really create itself.

An united Europe, capable of guaranteeing the plurality of its people and their diversities, will open the way to a united world an ambitious step towards a more elevated level of civilization, a fact which needs to be started for the new millennium.

Notes Chapter 4

(for notes nos. 1 to 77, see end of Chapters 1, 2 and 3)
78. Ritter, Don (1985) Risk Management Reports, XII/2, page 13.
79. Decision Research Center on Risk Perception and Risk Communication; see in particular: Kahneman, Slovic and Tvesky (1983), Judgement under Uncertainty: Heuristics and Biases, Cambridge, University Press.
80. from Haynal, Andre (1985), Anxiety Security and Certainty, contribution to the Rencontres Internationales de Geneve.
81. Weisskopf, Walter (1984) Reflections on Uncertainty in Economics.
82. see comments on Heisenberg and Indetermination and Uncertainty in the notes from Walter Weisskopf in chapter 3.4.
83. published by Pergamon Press (1978), Oxford. It is also significant to read in this book, at page 57, a clear reference to the Service Economy in the sense that it is argued that "the exchange economy, whether regulated by the market or by planning, is necessary at all levels if it is accepted that specialization is required for certain activities in order to increase their productivity. However, it should not be allowed to eliminate the production of goods for direct use by the producers themselves. Moreover, there must be room for what might be called a true service economy, not, as has hitherto been thought, the result but the actual source of development. An economy of this kind, which furnishes direct services, promotes use value and at the same time its activities benefit the greatest number of people. It is not, therefore, a matter of the systematic "tertiarization" of society, (which is) ... deplored in many industrialized countries".
84. Author's note: Ulrich is the name of the hero of a novel by Musil entitled The Man Without Qualities. The house in Chemin des Grangettes was Musil's last abode.
85. Szasz, Tomas S., Ideology and Madness.

# Bibliography

Arrow, Kenneth (1978) "Risk Allocation and Information", The Geneva Papers on Risk and Insurance no 8, Geneva.

Arrow, Kenneth (1978) "New Developments in the Theory of Risk Allocation", The Geneva Papers on Risk and Insurance no 12, Geneva.

Baglini, Norman (1976) Risk Management in International Corporations, Risk Studies Foundation, New York, N.Y.

Basic Income Research Group in London, regular publications.

Bell, Daniel (1973) The Coming of the Post-Industrial Society, Basil Books, New York, N.Y.

Berliner, Baruch (1982) Limits of Insurability of Risks, Prentice Hall, Inc., Eaglewood Cliffs, N.J.

Bohm, D. (1980) Wholeness and the Implicate Order, Routledge & Keenan, London.

Borlin, Max (1986) "Hidden costs : The Use of Natural Resources and the Pollution of the Environment", Science and Public Policy no 4, London.

Bressand, Albert and Distler, Catherine (1985) Le Prochain Monde (Resopolis), Paris.

Brooks, Chris (1986) "The Role of Local Employment Initiatives", Science and Public Policy no 4, London.

Campbell, R.H. and Skinner, A.G. (1982) Adam Smith, Croom Helm, London.

Capra, Frank (in preparation) Keppel: Uncertainty, the Ground for Life.

Clark, Ronald (1980) Einstein, sa Vie et son Epoque, Stock, Paris.

Clark, Colin (1960) Les Conditions du Progres Economique (The Conditions of Economic Progress), PUF, Paris.

Clark, R.W. (1973) Einstein, the Life and Times, Hodder & Stoughton, London.

Ekins, Paul (1986) "Health as Wealth", and "Indicators of Economic Progress", Science and Public Policy no 4, London.

Enthoven, Alain (Stanford University) "The HMOs", lecture presented in Paris, April 23, 1985, at the Institut la Boetie.

Forrester, Jay (1975) Counter-Intuitive Behaviour in Social Sciences (collected papers), Wright-Allen Press, Cambridge, Mass.

Fourastier, Jean (1958) Le Grand Espoir du XXe siecle, Gallimard, Paris.

Friedman, Milton (1980) Free to Choose, Penguin Books, Middlesex /UK.

Furstenberg, George von (ed.) (1979) Social Security versus Private Savings, Ballinger Publishing Company, Cambridge, Mass.

George, A. (1979) "Les Pertes Informatiques", The Geneva Papers on Risk and Insurance no 13, Geneva.

Giarini, Orio and Louberge, Henri (1978) The Diminishing Returns of Technology, Pergamon Press, Oxford.

Giarini, Orio (ed.) (1980) Dialogue on Wealth and Welfare, an Alternative View of World Capital Formation; a Report to the Club of Rome, Pergamon Press, Oxford.

Giarini, Orio (ed.) (1984) Cycles, Value and Employment, Pergamon Press, Oxford.

Giarini, Orio (1986) "Coming of Age of the Service Economy", and "Developing Productive Activities for the Wealth of Nations in the Service Economy", Science and Public Policy no 4, London.

Hailey, Arthur (1985) Strong Medicine, Pan Books, London.

Haynal, Andre (1985), Anxiety, Security and Certainty, Contribution to the Rencontres Internationales de Geneve.

Heilbronner, R. (1971) Les Grands Economists, Editions du Seuil, Paris.

Henderson, Hazel (1980) The End of Economics - Creating an Alternative Future, Pergee Books, Putman's Sons, New York, N.Y.

Hicks, John R. (1939) Value and Capital, Oxford University Press, Oxford.

Hugues, Thomas P. (1983) Network of Power, John Hopkins University Press, Baltimore, Maryland, and London.

Huxley, Aldous () Brave New World, Triad/Panther Paperbacks, London.

Jackson, Rupert (1982) Professional Negligence, Sweet & Maxwell, London.

Jordan, Bill (1986) "Basic Incomes and Hidden Economic Potential", Science and Public Policy no 4, London.

Kahane, Ernest (1979) Parmentier ou la Dignite de la Pomme - Essais sur la Faim, A.Blanchard, Paris.

Kahn, Hermann and Wiener, Anthony (1967) The Year 2000, The Macmillan Co., New York, N.Y.

Kahneman, Slovic and Tvesky (1983) Judgement under Uncertainty: Heuristics and Biases, Cambridge, University Press.

Kline, M. (1980) Mathematics - the Loss of Certainty, Oxford University Press, Oxford.

Knight, Frank (1921, 1971) Risk, Uncertainty and Profit, University of Chicago Press, Chicago, Ill.

Kunreuther, H. (ed.) (1986) Transportation, Storage and Disposal of Hazardous Materials, papers from a conference at IIASA, Laxenburg /Vienna, Wharton School, University of Pennsylvania, Philadelphia, Penn.

Landes, David S. (1972) The Unbound Prometheus, Cambridge University Press, Cambridge.

Laslett, Peter (1987) The World we have lost, Methuen on the Domesday Book.

Leveson, Irvin (1985) The Networking Economy, Hudson Institute Papers, New York, N.Y.

Leveson, Irving (1985) Hudson Institute Strategy Group, New York "The Service Economy in Economic Development", paper presented at the Graduate Institute of European Studies, University of Geneva, April 16.

Little, J. (1980) "The uncertain Craft of Mathematics", in New Scientist, no 88, p. 626-628.

144

Marchetti, C. (1980) "Society as a Learning System: Discovery, and Innovation Cycles Revisited", Technological Forecasting and Social Change, no 1812.

Malaska, Pentti (1985) "The Outline of a Policy for the Future", in UNU United Nations University (ed.), The Science of Complexity, Tokyo.

Malthus, Thomas Robert (1797) Essais on the Population Principle

Marshall, Alfred (1890, reprinted 1977), Principles of Economics, Macmillan Press, London.

Meadows, D. (1972) The Limits to Growth, a Report to the Club of Rome, Universe Books, New York, N.Y.

Mensch, G. (1977) Das Technologische Patt, Fischer Verlag, Frankfurt.

Mill, John Stuart (reprinted 1968) Principles of Political Economy, Routledge and Kegan, London.

Miller, Arthur (1946) Death of a Salesman, Cresset Press / Penguin Books, Great-Britain.

Musil, Robert (1969) l'Homme sans Qualites (The Man without Qualities), translated from German by Ph. Jacottet, Editions du Seuil, 2 volumes.

Norman, Richard (1984) Service Management, J.Wiley & Sons, Chichester /UK.

Nussbaumer, Jacques (1984) Les Services, Economica, Paris.

O'Connell, Jeffrey (1975) Ending Insult to Injury, University of Illinois Press.

OECD (periodical) Newsletter of the Co-operative Action Programme on Local Initiatives for Employment Creation, OECD, Paris.

Passet, Rene (1979) L'Economiqe et le Vivant, Payot, Paris.

Passet, Rene (1984) "The Paradigms of Uncertainty", The Geneva Papers on Risk and Insurance no 33, Geneva.

Perutz, Peter and Stahel, Walter R. (1980) Arbeitslosigkeit - Beschaftigung - Beruf, Neue Berufe und Innovationen, Beitrage des Institutes fur Zukunftsforschung, no 11, Berlin, Minerva Publikationen, Munchen.

Popper, Karl (1977) Unended Quest, Fontana Collins, Glasgow /UK.

Popper, Karl (1983) Realism and the Game of Science, Hutchinson Group SA Ltd, London.

Popper, Karl (1983) The Logic of Scientific Discovery, Hutchinson Group SA Ltd, London.

Popper, Karl (1983) The Open Universe: an Argument for Indeterminism, Hutchinson Group SA Ltd, London.

Popper, Karl (1983) Quantum Theory and the Schism in Physics, Hutchinson Group SA Ltd, London.

Prigogine, Ilya and Stengers, I (1979) La Nouvelle Alliance (The New Alliance), Paris.

Prigogine, Ilya (1983) "The Honda Lecture".

Prigogine, Ilya (1984) papers circulated at the seminar on Complexity, IDATE /UNU, Montpellier, France.

Ritter, Don (1985) Risk Management Reports, XII/2, page 13.

Robertson, James (1985) Future Work; Jobs, Self-employment and Leisure after the industrial Age, Gower Publishing Co., London.

Rokes, Willis P. (1971) No Fault Insurance, Insurers Press, Santa Monica, CA.

Rose, Richard (1985) Public Employment in Western Nations, Cambridge University Press.

Rougemont, Denis de (1972) Penser avec les Mains, Gallimard, Paris.

SIGMA Bulletin (periodical) Swiss Reinsurance Company, Zurich.

Smith, Adam (1776, reprinted 1977) The Wealth of Nations, Penguin Books, London.

Stahel, Walter R. and Reday-Mulvey, Genevieve (1981) Jobs for Tomorrow, the Potential for Substituting Manpower for Energy, Vantage Press, New York, N.Y.

Stahel, Walter (1984) "The Product-Life Factor", in Orr, Susan Grinton (ed.) An Inquiry into the Nature of Sustainable Societies: The Role of the Private Sector, HARC, The Woodlands, Texas.

Stahel, Walter (1986) "Product-Life as a Variable: The Notion of Utilization", and "R & D in a Sustainable Society", Science and Public Policy no 4, London.

Stiglitz, Joseph (1983) "The Pure Theory of Moral Hazard", Sixth Annual Lecture of the Geneva Association, The Geneva Papers on Risk and Insurance, no 26, Geneva.

Swan, Simone and Walsh, Michaela (1986) "Local Capital Generation - Rethinking Employment Initiatives", Science and Public Policy no 4, London.

Tevoedjre, Albert (1978) Pauvrete, Richesse des Peuples, Editions Sociales, Paris.

The Geneva Association (1985) Energy Outlook, Etudes et Dossiers no 93, Geneva.

The European Communities (1985) Directive on Product Liability, Brussels.

The Product-Life Institute /Institut de la Duree, Geneva, periodic publications.

Tobias, Andrew (1982) The Invisible Bankers, Pocket Books, New York, N.Y.

Toffler, Alvin (1981) The Third Wave, Bantam Ed., New York, N.Y.

UNU (ed.) (1985) The Science and Praxis of Complexity, The United Nations University, Tokyo.

Weinstein, W. (1986) "Risky Choices In Medical Decisions", The Geneva Papers on Risk and Insurance no 40, Geneva.

Weisskopf, Walter (1984) "Reflections on Uncertainty in Economics", Seventh Annual Lecture of the Geneva Association, The Geneva Papers on Risk and Insurance no 33, Geneva.

Weisskopf, Walter (1972) The Psychology of Economics, University of Chicago Press, Ill.

Women's World Banking (yearly) Annual Report, WWB, New York, N.Y.

Zigler, Martin (1985) "The Changing Face of Health Care Delivery", Emphasis, Tillighast Actuaries, Atlanta, Georgia.

Zimmermann, Erich (1933, 1951) World Resources and Industry, Harper & Broth, New York, N.Y.

# Index

150

158